FLY NAVY

FLY NAVY

The View from the Cockpit, 1945–2000

Published on behalf of the
Fleet Air Arm Officers' Association

Edited by
**LIEUTENANT COMMANDER CHARLES K. MANNING
AFC, ROYAL NAVY**

'Lightheartedness is essential if you would take your work seriously.'
GENERAL THE LORD ISMAY
Memoirs

LEO COOPER

First published in Great Britain 2000 by
LEO COOPER
an imprint of Pen & Sword Books Ltd,
47 Church Street, Barnsley,
South Yorkshire S70 2AS

Copyright © 2000 The Fleet Air Arm Officers' Association

ISBN 085052 732 5

CONTENTS

CHAPTER THREE - **The 1960s**

CHAPTER FOUR - **The 1970s**

CHAPTER FIVE - **The 1980s**

CHAPTER SIX - **The 1990s**

BUCKINGHAM PALACE

Between the wars, a lecturer at the Royal Naval College, Greenwich, wrote: "It can be assumed that if there is one requirement which has remained constant throughout the whole of British naval history it is the ability to handle ships, guns, machines and all kinds of sea gear under the realistic influence of sea conditions." Adding an air dimension to Brian Tunstall's elegant definition of seamanship produces Naval Aviation, to the challenging nature of which, as to the enduring 'can-do' spirit of the Royal Navy's Fleet Air Arm, this collection of stories bears eloquent witness.

The View from the Cockpit. HMS *Hermes* 1969.

Introduction

By Admiral Sir Raymond Lygo KCB

It has been said that history begins where the events described are no longer comprehensible in contemporary terms. If that is true, then much of this book is history: those brought up in our modern caring society will be at a loss to understand why young men should choose to live so dangerously – and appear to enjoy it.

This book presents the post-war Fleet Air Arm, warts and all, in a way that graphically illustrates its metamorphosis from the hectic days of 1939-45 towards the more clinical professionalism of modern times. And, as soon becomes evident, there were warts a-plenty. Many of these are traceable to the odd history of British naval air power, in particular the ill-considered Keyes-Trenchard Agreement of 1919, a Navy-Air Force pact, implacably enforced by the RAF, which denied the Navy any control of its own 'air' until May 1939, the very eve of the Second World War. Thus seriously deficient in air personnel and material, and further disadvantaged by lack of air awareness and expertise among the Navy's senior officers, the FAA fought the war on the back foot. The contrast with the United States Navy, which entered the war with a whole generation of aviation-qualified senior commanders, is stark: it says much that the USN, whose aircraft were integral with its fleet, felt no more need for an 'Fleet Air Arm' than a 'Fleet Gunnery Arm'. Nevertheless, to the immense credit of those concerned, the FAA, equipped for the most part with excellent American Lend-Lease aircraft, emerged six years later as the strongest element of British maritime power.

Lend-Lease Martlets, Avengers, Hellcats and Corsairs having been returned to the U.S. or dumped in the ocean after VJ-Day, the Keyes-Trenchard legacy is again evident in some of the early contributions to this book: the inadequacies of some of the Navy's indigenous post-war aircraft called for exceptional skills from 'maintainers' and aircrew alike, a superb blend of engineering, seamanship and airmanship in the best naval tradition.

The end of the Second World War coincided with the climax of piston aero-engine technology and the rise of the jet, and it fell to the next two generations of naval aviators to carry through the all-embracing transition from wartime pistons to the computerized omni-capable jets and helicopters of the 1980s and 90s, and one of the major problems of the immediate post-war period was the need to reconcile all this with the need for a far more professional and cost-conscious approach to aviation. Almost all the Fleet Air Arm's aircrew in the immediate post-war period had voluntarily transferred from Hostilities-Only engagements, bringing with them their operational experience, their great enthusiasm and independence of mind, and a brand of personal initiative that not infrequently clashed with the style of the conventional naval officer, an attitude of *joie de vivre*. But accident rates alone indicated that much needed to be done. The transition was for some a fairly painful experience, but the results were clearly to be seen in the years that followed. Thanks to the invention of the angled deck and the mirror sight, which when transferred to the U.S. Navy at least partly recompensed their wartime contribution to the FAA, the jet age at sea was embraced with a safety record that was far ahead of anything that had been achieved before – the one big advantage of the jet being that the pilot could actually see the deck!

The single thread of continuity through all the years of change – the 'can do' professionalism of the navy's aviators – shines through this book. In the rapid evolution of techniques and equipment, driven by the relentless imperatives of the Cold War, mistakes and failures were inevitable, and the line between those who died and their contemporaries who survived to tell 'how it was', was often invisibly thin. The book speaks for the 915 young men who have lost their lives in naval aviation since the War and are not here to tell their own tales. At the turn of the millennium, it seems worth remembering that it was entirely thanks to them, and those like them throughout what was once called 'The Free World', that Nelson's statue never looked down on Soviet tanks in Trafalgar Square.

Preface

The exploits of The Royal Navy's Fleet Air Arm up to the end of the Second World War in 1945, and to some extent since then, are well recorded in many excellent books. With the approach of the Millennium, the Fleet Air Arm Officers' Association commissioned this work with the aim of preserving something of the ethos of British naval aviation since then, while the memories remain.

The Association's 2800 members were asked to contribute recollections and photographs telling 'what it was like' flying in the post-war Navy. Their stories, some touchingly frank and most from members long retired, clearly relate the outstandingly memorable – although the business of naval aviation is never dull, and safety margins are necessarily tight, it must be emphasized that most of the events described here are exceptional. Whilst the highest contextual accuracy has been aimed at, the stories have been faithfully edited for the general reader, and little elaboration is offered on technicalities that are adequately dealt with elsewhere.

The Association is indebted to the 133 members who took the trouble to search their memories and commit to paper their small pieces of history, some regrettably excluded by exigencies of space. The editor's contribution is included to underline the universality of these experiences. Carrier flying being among the most visually entertaining of military activities, many photographs were received; those from official sources are used by permission of MoD Crown Copyright Office and acknowledged accordingly. Acknowledgement is also due to John Winton's *Air Power at Sea* (Sidgwick & Jackson, 1987), Ray Sturtivant's *British Naval Aviation* (Arms & Armour Press Ltd, 1990), and to Captain F.D. Stanley Royal Navy and Captain Alan Brooks MBE Royal Navy, as sources of data for the chapter intoductions; to Lieutenant Des Cracknell Royal Navy Rtd. for his generous help with costs; to Lt Cdr Jack Waterman VRD Royal Navy for valuable help with proof-reading; and finally to the Navy's Helicopter Aircrewmen, without whose often heroic efforts many of these stories would never have been written – the reader will judge whether, as they would say, they were 'only doing their job'.

The Fleet Air Arm's Roll of Honour contains the names of 915 men who lost their lives in flying operations from 1946 to the present day and it is the earnest hope of the Association that this book tells their story, and in a manner of which they would approve. It should be read as a somewhat patchy communal diary of the Fleet Air Arm, 1945-1995, containing only what would have been worth writing home about.

Glossary

ATC	Air Traffic Control. Hence ATCO: ATC Officer.
Batsman.	Stood on the Flight Deck aft, port side, guiding pilots into position for landing with large coloured 'bats' (wands at night).
Bolter	Aircraft misses all the wires and goes round again (angled deck only).
Cab-rank	Airborne loitering Ground-Attack aircraft.
CAP	Combat Air Patrol: airborne loitering fighter-interceptors.
CASEVAC	Casualty Evacuation.
Catwalk	Narrow platform below flight deck level both sides.
Charlie	Land-on. Charlie Time: scheduled land-on time.
D/F	Radio Direction-Finding (HF, VHF or UHF).
FDO	Flight Deck Officer. In charge of all Flight Deck operations.
FLYCO	Flying Control. Controls launching/land-on. Run by Lt Cdr (Flying).
g	Acceleration. Apparent increase in weight.
Goofers	Spectators. G. Platform: Upper island deck e.g. funnel deck.
HF	High Frequency (long-range) radio.
IFF	Identification Friend or Foe (radio transponder).
LSO	Landing Safety Officer: radio-equipped latter-day 'Batsman'.
Mae West	Life-jacket.
Mayday	The most urgent Distress Call.
Mother	An aircraft's home carrier.
PAN	Emergency Call. Less urgent than 'Mayday'.
RNAS	Royal Naval Air Station
RPM	Revolutions Per Minute (engine or rotor speed).
SAR	Search And Rescue.
UHF	Ultra High Frequency radio. Exclusively military in this period.
u/s	Unserviceable
VHF	Very High Frequency radio. Used by civilian aircaft and ATC.
Wave-off	Mandatory order to pilot to discontinue his landing approach.
W/T	Wireless Telegraphy, usually Morse code.

CHAPTER ONE

1945-49

Introduction

At the end of hostilities in 1945 the Royal Navy's Fleet Air Arm had 59 assorted aircraft carriers, 47 front-line squadrons, 56 Naval Air Stations and 72,000 men and women operating 3700 aircraft. Most of the aircraft, being Lend-Lease, were promptly returned to the U.S. or destroyed, and 39 escort carriers were either laid up or sold into merchant service. In December 1945 Cdr E.M. Brown made the first jet carrier landing in a Vampire jet aboard the new light carrier *Ocean*. Naval helicopter flying was also at the developmental stage with the Sikorsky Hoverfly.

By 1947, six wartime 23,000-ton Fleet Carriers had been joined by four new 22,000-ton Light Fleet Carriers (CVLs), *Glory*, *Ocean*, *Theseus* and *Triumph*, flying Seafire fighters, Firefly fighter-reconnaissance, ground-attack, and night-fighter variants, Firebrand (aka 'Firebrick') torpedo-bombers, and new Sea Fury fighter-bombers. The latter was one of the very few world-class purpose built carrier-borne aircraft ever provided by the nation for its Navy, but offered little advance on the American Corsair which had been in service since early 1943. The Fleet Air Arm had operated 2000 Lend-Lease Corsairs during the War, the last squadrons disbanding in August 1946 – the year the Navy's first helicopter squadron formed with Hoverfly IIs. Rising international tension at the start of the Cold War led to the reactivation of the Royal Naval Volunteer Reserve (RNVR) Air Branch in 1947.

In the absence of major technical developments during this decade, operating techniques remained largely unchanged from those perfected during the late war. Aircraft normally made unassisted 'free' take-offs along the whole length of the deck, occasionally with rocket boosters. Hydraulic catapults were used in light winds. The landing was made at the rear end of the deck under the control of the 'Batsman' or Landing Safety Officer, an experienced pilot who guided the aircraft in a continuous turn to a point just short of the stern where he signalled the pilot to 'cut' his engine, whereupon the aircraft descended rapidly among the arrester-wires. During landings, the forward parking area was protected by a barrier of steel cables stretched across the deck: an aircraft whose tailhook failed to engage a wire would 'take the barrier', with variable amounts of damage.

The Fleet Air Arm's Roll of Honour, inaugurated in January 1946, contains the names of those who lost their lives in flying operations during the remainder of the 1940s. The numbers are:

Pilots	141
Observers	15
Aircrewmen	9
Others	25

Temporary Acting Sub Lieutenant (A) G.E. Dunning, RNVR
Pilot, Barracuda, RNAS EASTHAVEN, 1944

[A testimony to engineering standards on the threshold of our period]

The traditional way of working up deck-landing skills, before going to sea, was by doing ADDLs, or Aerodrome Dummy Deck Landings, on a 'deck' marked out on a runway. On this particular April night at the Deck Landing Training School at Easthaven, a Naval Air Station perched on the Scottish cliffs between Carnoustie and Arbroath, six of us were scheduled for ADDLs, using three Barracudas. As the Barracuda had plenty of fuel for a couple of hours of ADDLs, to save time pilots would change over with engines running.

Flying the second detail in 'DR 149', when the time came I hauled myself up the wing against the slipstream, climbed into the cockpit and immediately noticed that one of the two fuel tanks was registering full, the other nearly empty. This was not too unusual, as the fuel tanks in the Barracuda often drained unevenly, and we were told not to worry about it.

It was pitch dark as the three of us took off in the second wave and went straight into the routine of circuits and landings. After three successful landings I was coming in for the fourth when I got a bit close to the one in front and the Batsman signalled me to go round again. I opened the throttle, raised the undercarriage, turned slightly to fly parallel with the runway lights and was climbing away when there was what seemed like a blinding flash as the red fuel warning light came on, followed by a deathly silence as the engine cut out.

Being much too low to bale out, I instinctively pushed the nose down to maintain flying speed; this must have shot a little more petrol into the carburettor, for the engine gave a brief roar of power, then died again. I was low and slow and could see absolutely nothing outside the cockpit. Was this IT?

All I could do was put the aircraft down straight ahead and hope. By guess and by God in total darkness I came down on the airfield, slithered to a halt on the grass alongside the runway and was thankful to be able to climb out, shaken but unscratched, in time to greet the fire wagon and ambulance.

Visiting the scene next morning I found I had stopped about fifty feet short of the boundary hedge, on the other side of which was a very large hangar. The aircraft was virtually undamaged except for a smashed propeller, and the engineers soon got to work to find out what had happened.

DR 149 was a new aircraft and they found that the factory had fitted a non-return valve the wrong way round, effectively trapping the fuel in the starboard tank. And it was my misfortune that, having never flown for more than about an hour and a half, it had never needed its starboard fuel before that night.

If the engine had stopped downwind in the ADDLs circuit I would have 'gone in', as we say, among the rocks on the coastline, and the accident would undoubtedly have been attributed to pilot error. As it was I received an official pat on the back in the form a 'Green Endorsement' in my Logbook which, on reflection, I think I deserved.

Lieutenant H. Hunt
Pilot, Firefly, HMS *Ocean*, Mediterranean, 1946

On 19 September 1946, HMS *Ocean* was preparing for a major exercise south of the Dodecanese. Detached from the main body of the Fleet, her brief was to find the Fleet during the dark hours, shadow it until dawn and then launch a strike against it. I was in charge of 816 Squadron's 'Black Flight' of four night-fighter Firefly NF1s, and it was going to be a busy night. The usual 'Night-Flying Tests' were scheduled during the afternoon to check radars, homing equipment and other night aids, and all was going well until Eddie Ward took off in Firefly 'Z'. Minutes later, at 300 feet in the circuit, his engine stopped without warning.

He ditched in copybook fashion and he and his observer were soon back aboard the ship, damp but unharmed; but 'Z' went straight to the bottom, taking with it the secret of the sudden failure of its Rolls Royce Griffin engine.

Immediate investigations of the limited facts yielding no clue, and none of the other aircraft having had any problems during the whole of the day's flying, it was decided not to jeopardize the forthcoming exercise because of this single event: the programme would continue with the first NF Firefly taking off half an hour after sunset, flown by me with observer John Keddie.

Launching in 'W' in the gathering gloom, we headed north towards the Dodecanese and climbed to 6000 feet, safely above local high ground. The aircraft behaved impeccably and we were looking forward to an interesting two to three hours' flying.

After about 35 minutes airborne, the engine died.

John made a Mayday call and gave me a course to steer back to 'mother'. In the whistling silence we discussed baling out, but neither of us was keen on parachuting into the water at night. The alternative, however, was to ditch with

1792 Squadron Night Fighters, HMS *Ocean*, c. 1946. Hunt

no engine and only the radio altimeter and landing lamp to help me see the sea before we hit it - a dicey business. Either way I did not fancy our chances. Could I sort out the engine trouble? I asked John to monitor altitude whilst I wrestled with the problem in the front office. I should explain here that before becoming a Fleet Arm Air pilot I had spent many years building and testing engines from Austin 7s to Rolls-Royce Merlins, Bristol radials and several American types. If I do say it myself, few pilots knew more about engines than yours truly, and I was convinced the problem was neither mechanical nor electrical. I considered a well-known Griffon weakness, rocker arm flaking, but this usually caused a progressive loss of power, whereas our engine had simply died – although rather slowly. Was this a clue?

The Firefly was no glider and we were losing height fast.

If it was neither mechanical nor electrical, I decided it must be a fuel problem. And if the pumps were delivering fuel to the engine, which they seemed to be because the fuel pressure warning lights were out, then there had to be something wrong with the fuel itself. That left fuel contamination. It really is amazing how a positive conclusion can steady the nerves. Convinced I knew what was wrong, I felt rather pleased with myself and announced my findings to John.

'Well make it quick, old boy,' he replied, 'or we're shark bait. We're passing 4000 feet.'

I couldn't see the propeller, but the RPM gauge indicated it was windmilling slowly. I turned off main fuel and both magnetos and opened the throttle up to the gate, rocked the aircraft laterally for fifteen seconds or so to stir up the fuel, then operated the priming pump (normally used to squirt fuel into the cylinders for starting), closed the throttle, turned the fuel back on, crossed my fingers and switched on one magneto. The engine gave a few hearty coughs and burst into life, so I switched the second magneto on and gingerly opened the throttle. All seemed well. I asked John how we were doing.

'About 15 minutes to the ship,' he replied. 'Can't you get any more out of her?'

'She' answered with a great cough and gave up the ghost again. I repeated my routine several times as the altimeter unwound, ever faster it seemed, through 2500 feet. No matter what I did the Griffon refused to run for more than a few seconds.

I had one trick left. Up to now I had been using fuel from the main fuselage tank, but there were forty gallons in the wing tanks. At 900 feet I switched to wing-tank fuel, went through my well-practised routine again, and at last managed to keep the Griffon running. This was getting a bit nerve-wracking.

I set the absolute minimum power I thought we needed to make it to the ship in a long powered glide, and we were down to 500 feet with the engine coughing and banging when John picked up *Ocean* on his radar five miles ahead, just to port. Feeling that any harsh movement might disturb our precious equilibrium, I changed course exceedingly carefully, already below circuit height and very near the invisible water, and a couple of minutes later saw the ship.

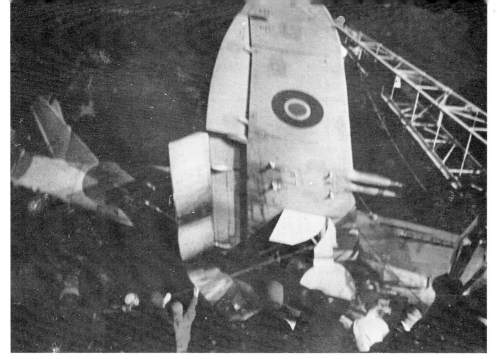

Lt Hunt's first attempt at night deck landing HMS *Ocean*, 1946. Hunt

She was a wonderful sight, lit up like a Christmas tree, but a peremptory cough from the Griffon up front reminded us we weren't there yet. I told Flyco I was coming straight in, and having identified which end was the stern, charged straight aboard. 'Bats' was ready, and the Firefly with its sick Griffon (unlike my first attempt at night deck-landing) thumped safely aboard in one piece. Now we would find out what the problem was.

John and I told our story to the engineers and went below to restore our spirits. *Ocean* pulled out of the exercise pending investigation of the Firefly

Night Fighter lands on. HMS *Ocean* 1946. Planeguard HMS *Meynell*. Hunt

engine problem, for it seemed likely that the afternoon ditching had resulted from the same kind of failure.

And it had indeed. 'W's fuel was found to contain water. All four Black Flight aircraft, and only those four, had been refuelled that afternoon from a fuel line in which the filtration system had failed, so my other two Fireflies would have had the same problem, had they flown.

I was naturally pleased at the outcome, especially as it proved that 'finger trouble', a supposedly common pilot's complaint, had played no part. I was happier still when the Squadron C.O. Lt Cdr Crabbe returned my log book at the end of the month with a commendation signed by Captain Caspar John.

Lt Hunt (third from left, front row) 790 Squadron Mosquito, 1948. Hunt

Lieutenant R.C. Ashworth,
Observer, Beechcraft Expeditor, Trincomalee to Lee-on-Solent, 1947

On 14 November 1947, three 772 Squadron Beechcraft Expeditors departed RNAS Trincomalee in Ceylon for RNAS Lee-on-Solent, Hants, England. Expeditors were small twin-engined general-purpose aircraft, always underpowered, and on this occasion overladen with passengers, baggage, and the exotic presents expected by tradition of homecoming sailors. Like so many flights in those days, in retrospect it looks like a diary of potential disaster; at the time it was fun, mostly.

First, across the water to Madras, then Bangalore for a first night-stop, buying more presents at every opportunity. Our pilot Ben Rice (who in 1940 sank a U-Boat in a Norwegian fjord) warned we were getting a bit nose-heavy, but we got off from there successfully and spent the next night in Bombay.

Ben sweated in the co-pilot seat for the next day as Squadron Boss, Lt Cdr H.J. Mortimore RNVR, flew us to Karachi (RAF Mauripur). After a night there, we lunched off Indian beer and corned beef sandwiches at RAF Jiwani in Baluchistan. The stoical C.O. of this outpost of empire, a Flight Lieutenant, told us his nearest entertainment was in Karachi (400 miles). That afternoon we crossed the Hormuz Straits to RAF Sharjah, now an international airport, then an oiled sand strip marked out with forty-gallon drums.

After a night on a rope charpoy in a broiling Nissen hut I was glad to be up early and get on to Bahrein, a second breakfast of good old RAF bacon-and-eggs, a swim in the pool – first bath for days – then off again for RAF Shaibah in the Shatt-al-Arab, then up the Tigris to RAF Habbaniyah near Baghdad. Next morning we set out for 'LGH3', a landing ground alongside the oil pipeline to Haifa, but the weather was not good, my navigation was a matter of a few pencil lines on a blank chart, and in the end we had to turn back to Habbaniyah.

After refuelling, to avoid another RAF bacon-and-egg breakfast we overflew LGH3 and made straight for a night stop at Agir, near Tel Aviv. There was gunfire in the night but we got out of there unscathed next day, heavily laden with oranges and lemons, to Cyprus and a splendid weekend at RAF Nicosia, most of it in the Chanticleer nightclub.

From there, via Calato in Rhodes with its burnt-out German Junkers alongside the runway, we hopped over the water to RAF El Adem near Tobruk and RAF Benghazi for fuel and thence to Malta and two nights at RNAS Hal Far. This permitted a memorable visit to the 'ghut', a steep street of bars that becomes narrower and more noisome the lower you get - ironically called Straight Street.

Nearly home, after calling at Cagliari in Sardinia for fuel, we stopped a night in Marseilles where the evening's entertainment was funded by selling unspeakably awful cigarettes bought cheap in Bahrein. The French were delighted with them.

Take-off next morning was delayed waiting for the C.O., who slept soundly throughout the flight to Bordeaux – and the refuelling there – to wake at last when we ran into low cloud and turbulence over the Channel. Finding he had not shaved, he contrived to remedy this using soap and brush and the only liquid available, cheap red wine, and was presentable enough when we got to Lee-on-Solent to make his official call on the Captain while we unloaded an unbelievable amount of junk from the three aircraft. Our nose compartment was crammed full of luggage labelled 'Mr Rice' - he who had complained all the way about being nose-heavy. It was 29 November.

Some weeks later, the Boyd Trophy for outstanding contribution to Naval Aviation was awarded to - Lt. Cdr. H. J. Mortimore, RNVR. I often think about that Flight Lieutenant in Baluchistan. Where is he now?

Lieutenant 'Spiv' Leahy,
Pilot, 801 Squadron, Airspeed Oxford, RNAS, Arbroath 1948

On a surreal calm day at Arbroath one morning after a Mess Dinner in 1948, alone down at the Squadron dispersal, as junior pilot and Squadron Staff Officer my job was to make sure all was in good order before the C.O. turned up. Outside the office, trying to get some fresh air into my system, I was accosted by two of our dinner guests - Cdr 'Peg-Leg' Lamb of Taranto fame, and Lt 'Smokey' Cowling.

'What ho, Spiv! What are you doing?' 'Smokey' greeted me.

'Just taking the air.'

'Fancy a trip in the Oxford to clear the head?'

He knew as well as I did that 801's Squadron Orders restricted flying the morning after a mess dinner. But, thinking I would only be a passenger, in short order I was airborne sharing the back seat of the Station Flight Oxford with a Wren Officer, the two dinner guests up front doing the piloting. Before I had time to get acquainted with the Wren Officer, the wheels came down for landing.

I was bright enough to see that this was not Arbroath, but RNAS Donibristle, about forty miles south-west near Dunfermline. To drop off the Wren? I hoped they would be quick because I was supposed to be in the Squadron office; but when we parked, the dinner guests stopped the engines and disembarked, taking their parachutes, helmets, and Wren-O with them.

'Take it back, Spiv, would you? Oh, and by the way the radio doesn't work.'

Panic! Before I could go anywhere, the radio had to be fixed. And to use the radio I needed a helmet. And to reach the controls and see out I needed a parachute to put in the bucket-seat and sit on. I borrowed an old helmet from Hoagy Carmichael of 807 Squadron but nobody was going to part with an expensive parachute; we found a bit of old rubber carpet and rolled it up to make a cushion. I rang the office at Arbroath where I should have been and was relieved to hear from the Air Engineer Officer, Mike Nicholas, that nobody of importance had yet turned up. I told him where I was and to make excuses for me, and made my way back to the Oxford with my carpet. A pair of bell-bottom trousers were protruding from the radio bay, and as I climbed the wing their owner, a Wren, looked up and said she'd fixed it. I nearly fell off the wing - not because she'd fixed the radio, but at the sight of her neat little goatee beard. A famous lady at Donisbristle, I learned later, she played the bugle in the station band.

A worried man, I took off carefully for the short return trip. The undemanding navigation let my imagination get to work. From where I sat on my rolled-up carpet, the order prohibiting flying after a mess dinner seemed eminently sensible and I could be court-martialled on that count alone. Much worse, my flight had not even been authorized: every flight in a military aircraft has to be officially approved in writing in advance, on the Squadron Authorization Sheet, by an Authorizing Officer, and this had not been done – another court-martial offence. And finally it was illegal to fly an aircraft without inspecting and signing the Form A700 Technical Log, of which I had seen no sign throughout. Court-martial on three counts awaited me at Arbroath – was this my last flight as a Royal Navy pilot?

Anxious to avoid adding a broken aeroplane to the list of charges, I put the Oxford down gently on the runway and taxied round to Station Flight dispersal, to be met by – nobody. No prisoner's escort, no marshaller, no chockman, and after the Cheetah engines rattled to a stop, nothing to mar the surreal calm. In a trice I was out of the aircraft with my awkward bundle of carpet, across the hardstanding and into the nearest hangar before looking back. The Oxford, bless her, alone out on the sunlit concrete, looked as if she hadn't moved all morning.

The flight never appeared in my logbook or in any other official record. And according to a book called *Squadrons of the Fleet Air Arm* which I was reading recently, there never was an Airspeed Oxford at Arbroath anyway.

Lieutenant Commander G. McC. Rutherford DSC,
C.O. 1832 Squadron Seafires, HMS *Implacable*, English Channel, 1949

When the Admiralty first decided to embark Royal Naval Volunteer Reserve squadrons in carriers for their annual fortnight's training, few could foresee how it would work. Reserve pilots flying at sea was a departure from convention. Some had never deck-landed before, the rest not for many years, and unlike the intensive airfield deck-landing training enjoyed by regular squadrons before embarkation, all their flying had to be fitted into weekends.

I was the Commanding Officer of 1832 RNVR Squadron, and on 13 July 1949 led twenty Seafire Mk.15s and 17s, flown by a mixed group of salesmen, students, journalists, lawyers and engineers, most of whom had never landed on a carrier before, from our base at RNAS Culham near Abingdon to RNAS Lee-on-Solent. 1832 was the first squadron to embark, and the C-in-C Home Fleet, Admiral Rhoderick McGrigor, wanted us aboard his flagship, the 30,000-ton fleet carrier *Implacable* in the Channel, to see what sort of performance could be expected of the RNVR. Our forty RNVR ground crew were already in the carrier.

'...salesmen, students, journalists, lawyers and engineers...' RNVR aircrew at Culham, Coronation Flypast, 1953. Official Crown copyright/MoD via Rutherford

At Lee I divided the squadron into four-plane flights and led the first two of these off towards *Implacable*, about twenty miles south of the Isle of Wight. Unfortunately she chose that moment to steam into a fog-bank and I had to take my eager weekend warriors back to Lee, and I blame the delay for our rather shaky start late next day when the sea fog finally cleared and the ship signalled us to come aboard: three pilots missed all ten arrester

Shaky start. Rutherford

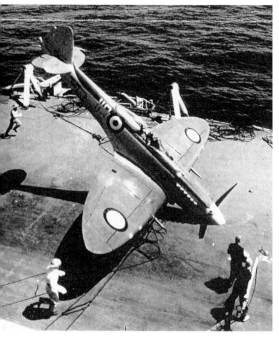

10

wires and engaged the safety barriers, causing the only injury of the whole fortnight - a slight cut on one forehead from a gyro gunsight. Deck-landing training started immediately, one aircraft at a time, each pilot doing four landings under the control of Lt. D. G. McQueen RN, one of the Navy's most experienced batsmen (who batted on his 8000th aircraft during our fortnight), and by the second day enough pilots had been 'passed deck-qualified' to make up a team to practise interceptions under the ship's radar control. By the end of the week all twenty pilots were deck-qualified.

After a break in Torbay, the ship laid on an ambitious programme of interceptions and cannon-firing which went on throughout the second week with great success, the towed splash-target astern of the carrier frequently disappearing in a flurry of shell-foam. Everything was going extremely well until Lt P. J. Robins, trying to land-on late one afternoon, drifted sideways and caught a wire just as he reached the port-deck edge. The aircraft nosed over the edge and toppled into the sea, leaving the whole tail unit on one of the weather-decks.

The tailless Seafire sank like a stone but somehow Robins got out and bobbed up in the wake 200 yards astern, to be rescued by the plane-guard destroyer HMS *Aisne*. They were very kind to him and eventually delivered him back to the carrier 'full of sea-water and brandy', to quote the signal.

We had now settled down to carrier drill, practice interceptions and cannon firing. 1832's own batsman, Lt Burman RN, who had overseen our shore training at Culham, shared the batting with Lt McQueen and, despite the handicap of our troublesome 'sting' hooks, we got landing intervals down to a very respectable 30 seconds. Few pilots had fired rockets before, but we were soon 'straddling' the splash-target and doing better, we were told, than the ship's own squadrons on their work-up. RNAS Culham's Commanding Officer, Captain J.W. Grant DSO Royal Navy, who had always taken a great personal interest in the squadron, flew aboard in an Avenger and spent a day watching us at work, expressing himself well pleased.

'...unfortunately Robins went over the side...' Rutherford

Signal from HMS *Implacable*, 18.7.49. Rutherford

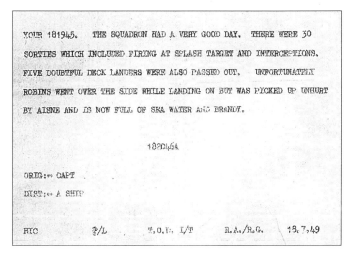

YOUR 181945.   THE SQUADRON HAD A VERY GOOD DAY.   THERE WERE 30 SORTIES WHICH INCLUDED FIRING AT SPLASH TARGET AND INTERCEPTIONS. FIVE DOUBTFUL DECK LANDERS WERE ALSO PASSED OUT.   UNFORTUNATELY ROBINS WENT OVER THE SIDE WHILE LANDING ON BUT WAS PICKED UP UNHURT BY AISNE AND IS NOW FULL OF SEA WATER AND BRANDY.

182046A

ORIG:- CAPT

DIST:- A SHIP

RTC   P/L   T.O.R. I/T   R.A./R.G.   18.7.49

The grand climax on the last day was an attack on the carrier by its own Sea Hornets and Firebrands flying from Lee-on-Solent, 1832 defending.

With the help of *Implacable's* fighter-directors, eight 1832 Seafires tackled the escorting Hornets and others prevented the Firebrands getting through to the splash target with their rockets. Thirteen serviceable aircraft then flew off to Culham, the squadron having been congratulated by the C-in-C.

On our side we had every reason to be grateful for the support we got from the ship, and particularly for the quick reactions of the crash-barrier operators whose fine judgement saved more than one Seafire: a Seafire pulling out No.10 arrester-wire would destroy its propeller on the barrier if it were not lowered a split-second after the hook engaged the wire. As one of 1832's instructors, Lt I. G. W Robertson DSC RN, summed up at the end: '...a happy trip, but let's face it, a bit of a strain!'

Coronation Flypast, RNAS Ford, 1953. Rutherford

Lieutenant H.J. Abraham,
Pilot, Seafire Mk.17, 800 Squadron, H.M.S. *Triumph*, Mediterranean, 1949

*T*riumph's 17th Carrier Air Group was well worked-up and proud of her slick 20-second landing intervals. Thus one day when a visiting Seafire Mk.47 came across from H.M.S. *Ocean* and got ahead of me in the landing pattern, I was close behind him. For reasons best known to himself, probably to ease the parking problem, Lt Cdr (Flying) decided to put the visitor down into the hangar via the for'd lift.

Sadly, neither I nor the after-deck crews were made aware of this plan, so after landing in my Mk.17, '172', I opened up to full throttle as usual to clear the wires and taxy forward. Too late I noticed the large square hole in the deck and executed a half-roll down the lift-well onto the 47's wing which, fortunately for all concerned, had power folding.

'...saw the hole in the deck a bit too late...' BCC/MOD via Abraham

'...and executed a half-roll down the lift well...' BCC/MOD via Abraham

The only casualty was the visiting pilot who tried to get out of his cockpit in a hurry when he saw the dark shape of my aircraft looming overhead. He caught his foot on the cockpit hood and fell flat on his face on the lift.

Aftermath. BCC/MOD via Abraham

Lieutenant Commander L.R.Tivy,
Pilot, Firefly, Dartmouth, Nova Scotia, 1949

On loan service with the Royal Canadian Navy in 1949, I was C.O. of a training group flying Harvards and Fireflies at Dartmouth, Nova Scotia. One September day we got a request to take a Firefly 'Trainer' to Moncton in New Brunswick, about 200 miles away, for an Air Day display, and I decided to go myself, taking with me an Air Mechanic named Dunne to service the aircraft.

I flew a short display at Moncton and took off for the return flight in the early evening, the weather fine with little wind, as I recall. About fifteen minutes later, unable to raise Moncton on the radio, I asked Dunne in the back to check the radio switches, telling him where they were – immediately to his left, at about seat level.

In 'Trainer' Fireflies the pupil pilot occupied the front cockpit with the instructor in the rear where he had duplicated flying controls, plus some other vital controls like engine ignition switches. On this occasion I was naturally sitting in the front, where you had a better view, the only disadvantage being that

Firefly - front cockpit.

Rear cockpit. RCN Copyright via Tivy

some of the radio switches could only be operated by the occupant of the rear seat.

Moments after I asked Dunne to check the radio switches the healthy roar of the Griffon in front of me was suddenly replaced by a ringing silence when he put both his ignition switches, also on his left, down to OFF.

Such was the shock that it never entered my mind to tell him to put them up again. We were 5-6,000ft above dense forest stretching in all directions as far as the eye could see, except for a single tiny clearing, so I made for that. We lost altitude very quickly, sliced through and decapitated a number of trees, hit the ground with a monumental thump and slid across the clearing, the Firefly disintegrating around us. Amazingly there was no fire and neither Dunne nor I was hurt beyond minor cuts and bruises. Equally amazingly, a farmer appeared out of the trees and took us to a small hospital some way off.

Anonymous Rating Pilot,
Seafire Mk.17, RN Ferry Flight, Scotland, 1949.

After pilot training and eight uneventful deck landings on HMS *Illustrious*, I was drafted to the Ferry Flight at RNAS Anthorn, in the marshes west of Carlisle. Officers were *appointed*; I, as one of the first products of the short-lived Rating Pilots Scheme, was *drafted*. In my plain black trousers and jacket, but for the gold pilot's wings on my left sleeve I might have been a steward. I was made most welcome by the officers of Anthorn's Ferry Flight and their boss, but a rating doing an officer's job often collided with the niceties of the Navy's age-old disciplinary system. At flight-line offices trying to sign out aircraft from Air Stations and Repair Yards at home and abroad, I got used to raised eyebrows. And a rating pilot, invariably without a 'Draft Chit' (naval Movement Order), wanting a bed for a night at one of HM Shore Establishments, guaranteed chaos. To the Navy, an itinerant rating without an official Draft Chit is a non-person; but usually I was found a non-bed and non-meal, and got on very well.

In fact I enjoyed it so much I very nearly killed myself. The Grim Reaper had me in his sights: I heard the swish of his scythe.

The main runway at RNAS Lossiemouth was being extended, their Fireflies and Seafires had to be moved to RNAS Eglinton on the shores of Lough Foyle in Northern Ireland, and Anthorn Ferry Flight got the task. Six of us duly piled into the Flight's de Havilland Dominie twin-engined runabout, as usual with our own personal parachutes and flying gear, plus overnight bags. It was fairly obvious the old 'cloth bomber' was overloaded, though not unusually so.

The Dominie being ill-equipped for instrument flying and ferry pilots not noted for their love of this black art, and the weather being a bit dire up the east side of Scotland, we took the western scenic route up to Oban, planning to hop from there across to Lossiemouth on the Moray Firth. But a few miles south of Oban the starboard engine started leaking oil seriously, its oil pressure dropped and the temperature soared until it had to be shut down. Our overladen old Dominie started losing height fairly rapidly.

The sudden prospect of the flight terminating untidily on a rock-strewn braeside stirred memories of an Air Training Corps camp I had spent on a primitive airstrip called Connel Ferry a few miles east of Oban and, knowing that the west of Scotland boasts very few airfields, I wasted no time yelling this information from the back of the crowded cabin. Shortly thereafter, ignoring the big white 'Disused. Do Not Land' crosses, our pilot was braking to a halt on Connel Ferry's grassy strip, scattering sheep who hadn't seen such excitement in years.

We dossed down in a small local hotel and continued next day to Lossiemouth by coach, arriving too late to start ferrying that day - another 'Where's your Draft Chit?' saga for me.

Next morning the forecast for the 200-mile trip to Northern Ireland was far from good. A warm front over the highlands was giving low cloud and drizzle all the way to Eglinton and beyond and thick layers of cloud up to a considerable height. However, the delivery was already late, so, despite our healthy aversion to cloud flying, we ferry pilots were just going to have to get on with it.

Light rain fell out of the overcast on to my battered old Seafire Mk17 on the tarmac. She had been ridden hard in Lossie's Operational Flying School and looked worn out. I checked her bits and pieces, climbed aboard, shut the hood and fired her up.

Without a drop-tank, my destination was only just in range. I was last to take off and, rather than waste fuel catching up with the others, turned southwest on my own and started a slow cruise-climb. The Seafire was never meant for serious cloud-flying so I had to lower the seat to see the instruments properly, and thus, lost in my own little world, I hummed along quietly with throttle and propeller fine-tuned to give me maximum miles from every gallon of fuel.

It wasn't long before I heard on the radio that the Fireflies, who had taken off first, were in a spot of bother. Still in cloud, they had flown past Eglinton who gave them an erroneous radio bearing which took them even further away. But Fireflies had plenty of fuel so I wasn't too concerned for them. The bad news for me was that the weather ahead was living up to the forecast. I purred on.

A few minutes later, among all the Firefly chatter, a Seafire called running short of fuel and contemplating a forced landing somewhere in Donegal, over beyond Eglinton in the Irish Free State. Shortly afterwards, he said he was down OK in a potato field, unhurt.

Rather than add to the growing confusion by calling for the bearing I so badly needed, after carefully checking my map I throttled back and started a slow descent that I calculated would take me safely down below cloud, out over the sea well clear of Scotland. I could then do the rest of the flight across to Northern Ireland under the cloud - and with less of a headwind. The base of the cloud was reported as 400-600 feet, but that would be no problem over the sea.

The engine ticked over quietly. All outside was grey mist. Slowly the altimeter unwound. The needle passed 1000ft and I began to sneak the occasional quick glance up from the instruments. At 500ft it momentarily grew darker and an instant later I was in the clear below cloud.

Looking back over many years, my memories of the next few terrible seconds are crystal clear. It was every pilot's nightmare. I was descending in a narrow valley, dark brown rain-sodden hills climbing steeply into the cloud left and right, a small loch dead ahead with what looked like a wall of solid rock just beyond that. This was it. I froze.

I clearly remember yelling at my own stupidity. At last an ice-cold burst of adrenalin galvanized my survival instinct and I jammed the throttle and propeller levers fully forward and hauled the stick back. The Seafire shot back into the clouds.

At 3000ft, trembling with shock, I checked the map. I guessed that the headwind was stronger than forecast and that I had come down over Islay. If that were so, safety was only a mile or two further on, so I let down again and this time broke cloud at 400ft over the sea with no land in sight. At this point the big red 'Fuel Low' warning light came on.

Well, it was nip and tuck, as they say, but that Seafire got me to Eglinton. Tired she might have been, but she performed like a thoroughbred. I never told anybody what had happened. It has taken all these years to be able to reveal the folly that so nearly terminated my young life.

Lieutenant Commander Bill Holdridge,
Observer, 1942-1959

Some photographs of Fleet Air Arm flying in the 40s and 50s: A Seafire Mk. 47, VP 436 of 804 Squadron, is shown going overboard landing on HMS *Ocean* in the Mediterranean in early 1949. In the first photograph the aircraft is passing the lowered W/T aerial, hook visible just behind the tail engaged to an arrester-wire, the position of the controls showing the pilot's instincts at work trying to avert the inevitable - elevators hard up, full right aileron. In the next shot moments later he has passed the mast and is over the side, elevators still full up, the black and yellow arrester hook now clearly visible half way along the rear fuselage. In the third shot - the photographer had to scramble down from his perch above the bridge and across to the port side of the deck - the aircraft is suspended from the fully extended arrester-wire, nose in the water and the pilot coming up on the end of a rope. The

1. '...the pilot's instincts at work...' BCC MOD (Holdridge)

2. '...over the side...' BCC MOD (Holdridge)

4. '...the pilot was unhurt...' BCC MOD (Holdridge)

3. '...up on a rope...' BCC MOD (Holdridge)

Sea Hornet NF21, 809 Squadron, HMS *Eagle* 1953 'about to enter No.1 Barrier...'
BCC/MOD via Holdridge

foam around the Seafire's nose shows the ship still at speed, and the angle of the wake under the W/T aerial suggests she is under port helm and beginning to turn; the helm order would have been given at about the instant of the first photograph with the aim of swinging the ship's propellers away from the ditched aircraft. The pilot was unhurt, and the aircraft was lightered off for repair in Malta.

Incidently, a few weeks before this, I saw the same pilot (who was actually a Firefly driver in 812 Squadron) bale out of a Firefly off Malta after it shed a propeller blade on a dive-bombing run. He hit the water with his chute still streaming, was rescued quite quickly and was back in action after a few days in hospital over Christmas.

The barrier crash in the second sequence has a number of interesting features. The aircraft is a Sea Hornet NF21 of 809 Squadron, VW 960, landing on board HMS *Eagle* in 1953. The only clue I have to the identity of this crew is the small white ensign on the tail: in my time in the squadron the previous year, this was the C.O.'s aircraft. And as to the cause of the accident, after all this time I can only suggest either the hook failed to lower fully or the pilot failed to catch a wire: he looks a little fast.

In the first shot the aircraft looks normal and intact, about to enter the No.1 barrier with both engines running; its arrester hook is obscured but may be visible passing over the penultimate arrester cable. Although the sea looks calm

'...undercarriage legs ripped off...' BCC/MOD

'...the pilot strides purposefully away...' BCC/MOD via Holdridge

and there would be little deck movement, it is well left of centre line. The 'batsman', having done his part, peers round his screen, right aft port side, to watch the next act.

In the second photograph the undercarriage legs have been ripped off by the lower barrier cable and the aircraft is on its nacelles, props bent back and engines abruptly stopped, sliding over the lowered cables of the second barrier. The part-lowered hook, under the fuselage just aft of the figure '4', has plainly not engaged an arrester wire and is also passing over the barrier cables lying flat on the deck. The cockpit canopies are closed as protection from the upper cable, which appears to be wrapped around the tail. The pole in the background is the port barrier stanchion, from which the contraption shown in the first photograph was suspended.

Finally the Sea Hornet is at rest on top of the third set of barrier cables, engine covered with fire-suppressant foam (several hoses have been run out from deck-edge fire-points and two foam drums are on the extreme right). The left undercarriage leg and wheel lie on the deck by the second barrier cables; the latter being undisturbed suggests the hook was not fully lowered. The pilot strides purposefully away from his open cockpit just this side of the nose radome; the rear canopy is gone and the observer, complete with helmet and navigation bag, having retired to a safe distance, is taking his gloves off, bottom left.

Deck markings put the No.1 barrier 450 feet from the bow and the aircraft at rest on the 300-foot mark. Thus in fifty yards and a couple of seconds did an elegant and potent, if obsolete, flying machine became a sorry wreck. I do not think either crew member was hurt.

CHAPTER TWO
THE 1950s

Introduction

Communist North Korea invaded the south in June 1950. On 3 July HMS *Triumph* launched her first strike of Fireflies and Seafires against the invaders, to be joined in the ensuing thirty-seven months of the Korean War by carriers *Theseus, Glory* and *Ocean,* whose Fireflies, Seafires and Sea Furies provided the sole British air effort apart from some RAF flying-boat reconnaisance at the outset. 23,000 sorties were flown, pilots getting so much practice that deck-landing accident rates plunged dramatically. Twenty-two aircrew were lost on operations and eleven in accidents.

Although in most respects Korean War operations differed little from those of the Second World War, this was the decade that changed the face of naval aviation. The Navy's first jet, the short-lived Supermarine Attacker, entered service in August 1951, to be superseded in 1953 by the Seahawk ground-attack fighter and this in turn by the twin-jet supersonic nuclear-capable Scimitar in 1958. The anti-submarine piston Avenger was replaced by the twin-turbo-prop Gannet in 1955. Piston Sea Hornet all-weather fighters gave way to jet Sea Venoms in 1954, and these to twin-jet missile-armed Sea Vixens in 1958.

In these few years, aircraft weights more than tripled: Seafire 10,000lb, Sea Vixen 40,000lb. And landing speeds rose by 50 per cent: Seafire 90 knots, Scimitar 135. Without the steam catapult, angled deck and mirror landing-sight, all developed within the Royal Navy, such increases in the weight and speed of combat aircraft would have rendered fixed-wing carriers extinct worldwide.

Heavy swept-wing jets, launched by the immense power of the steam catapult, landed on an angled landing area – the 'angled deck' – which allowed not only a longer pull-out for the arrester wires but also an unobstructed overshoot – a 'bolter' – if the tailhook failed to catch a wire. The mirror landing sight requires some explanation. A gyro-stabilized curved mirror reflected a beam of yellow light up the approach path astern of the ship at a fixed angle of about 4°, unaffected by deck movement. To the pilot this appeared as a yellow blob – the 'meatball' – between two horizontal bars of green lights – the 'datums' – the geometry being so arranged that if he kept the meatball exactly in line with the datums all the way down to the deck, then his hook would engage the target wire. Most jets had excellent forward visibility and were ideally driven straight into the deck off a 4° approach at a steady speed without reducing power. Failure to catch a wire – 'bolting' – was a simple matter of applying full power and accelerating off the end of the angled deck for another circuit, a big advance on the steel-wire barrier that awaited the errant pilot on a straight deck. If the ship's arrester gear failed, or the aircraft's hook would not lower, and there was nowhere else to land, an emergency nylon barrier could be rigged across the angled deck to stop the aircraft, usually with considerable damage.

Regrettably the British aircraft industry did not match these achievements in ship design, and all the aircraft introduced in this decade were inferior to low-cost lightweight USN equivalents: too big for our small carriers because of the insistence upon twin engines for reliability over water; too expensive and therefore always too few, and, as many of these stories show, still of questionable quality.

Dragonfly helicopters came into use for Search and Rescue and Planeguard during the Korean War. More powerful helicopters, the Sikorsky S55 and subsequent British-engined Whirlwind variants, extended the scope of naval rotary-wing operation into routine anti-submarine work as well as troop-lifting, supply and casualty evacuation as in the Malayan Emergency and Suez invasion.

In 1951 the new 46,000-ton Fleet Carrier *Eagle* commissioned; in 1954-55 the last working wartime carriers were laid up and three new Light Carriers, *Centaur, Albion* and *Bulwark*, and Fleet Carrier *Ark Royal* commissioned, the latter with the first steam catapults. *Victorious*, whose keel was laid in 1941, joined the fleet in 1958 after an eight-year rebuild as a thoroughly modern carrier of 23,000 tons.

World-wide commitments, intensifying Cold War pressures, six new carriers, jets, turbo-props, steam cats, angled deck, mirrors and 'bolters', 'bone-domes', swept wings, ejection seats, airbrakes, dunking sonar, jungle flying, commando assaults, casevac etc. etc...the Navy's air and ground crews had to learn new tricks quickly and adjust rapidly. The mirror and the angled deck made deck operation easier and safer, but in the rapidly accelerating pace of innovation and constant striving to exploit new capabilities, many mistakes were made and boundaries sometimes overstepped. One costly error was to dispense with the Landing Safety Officer ('Bats') on the assumption that the mirror solved all deck landing problems.

In terms of challenge and excitement, this decade was the best of all times. In terms of peacetime casualty rates, it was the worst.

The Fleet Air Arm Roll of Honour contains the names of those who lost their lives in flying operations in the 1950s. The numbers are:

Pilots	335
Observers	49
Aircrewmen	21
Others	38

Lieutenant Maurice Tibby,
Pilot, Firebrand, 813 Squadron, HMS *Implacable*, Moray Firth, 1950.

In the immediate post-war years the Fleet Air Arm endured a number of very *ordinary* aircraft. Some evoked a stronger description, and none more so than the Blackburn Firebrand.

Affectionately known as the 'Firebrick', it was designed with an in-line Merlin engine, re-hashed to incorporate the Centaurus radial, and entered service as an underpowered monster in which the pilot sat eighteen feet behind the propeller with a forward visibility, on the approach to landing when you most needed it, of absolutely nil. Equally unnerving for deck-landing at 85 knots was the CAUTION in Pilot's Notes: 'Below 90 knots aileron control is somewhat ineffective...'

Not a popular aircraft at sea, in an attempt to make it easier to handle on the approach, Blackburn added an external Air Speed Indicator so the pilot wouldn't have to keep looking in the cockpit to check his speed - a brilliant idea which caught on years later, but this primitive early version proved hopelessly inaccurate and therefore useless.

To be fair to the old Firebrick, it could perform a wide variety of tasks with its guns and rockets, bombs, torpedoes or mines, but all at a gentle lumbering pace that made it extremely vulnerable. The only squadron to operate it with any degree of success was 813, embarked in the carriers *Implacable* and *Indomitable* in the Home Fleet. Noting that there were problems, however, the authorities

Firebrand aka Firebrick. Tibby

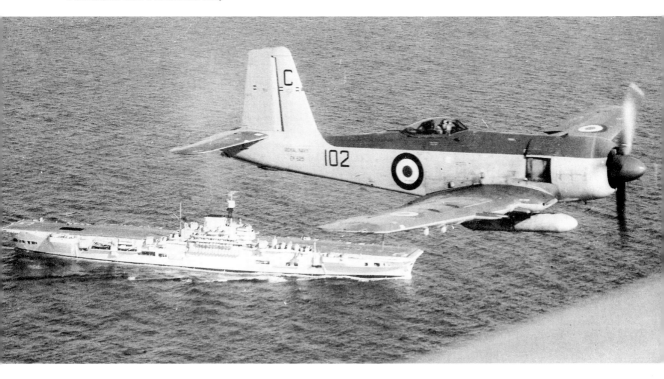

drafted in a number of very experienced pilots: in 1950 813 boasted no fewer than four Qualified Flying Instructors, at the time a very rare species indeed.

On 6 July 1950 we joined *Implacable* in the Moray Firth for Home Fleet exercises prior to a visit to Scandinavia. I was No. 2 in a flight of four Firebricks approaching the ship in the late evening, following the usual drill – up the 'slot' past the carrier as she turned into wind, peel off left across the bow at thirty-second intervals, close the throttle, lower undercarriage and hook, feed power back on as the speed came down towards 100 knots and set up for the final approach. That was the script.

However, among its refinements, the Firebrand sported a wonderfully complex throttle-box which, instead of the customary neat arrangement of throttle and propeller levers, mixture, cowl gills and oil-cooler shutter, sprouted fifteen different levers and knobs and switches, many related to operational equipment, and when I tried to push the throttle lever forward I found it jammed immovably shut. 100 feet above the sea, throttle closed, undercarriage flaps and hook down, there was soon nothing on the Airspeed Indicator but the maker's name and seconds later I hit the sea in a cloud of spray.

Whatever qualities the Firebrand lacked, this one at least had the decency to stay afloat just long enough for me to get out, and the planeguard HMS *Crossbow* picked me up within minutes.

All Firebrands were immediately grounded. An examination of the infamous throttle-boxes produced a remarkable collection of washers, nuts and bolts and bits of wire, any of which could jam the works. If I had not lived to tell the tale, others would undoubtedly have suffered a similar fate.

Firebrand? Not the Fleet Air Arm's favourite aeroplane.

Lieutenant Stan Leonard,
Pilot, Sea Fury, 807 Squadron, HMS *Theseus*, Korea, 10 October, 1950.

On HMS *Theseus*'s first patrol of the Korean War, Lieutenant Leonard was flying as No.2 to the Air Group Commander, Lt. Cdr. Stovin-Bradford, briefed to attack targets of opportunity. After rocket and cannon attacks on military vehicles south of Chinampo, during an attack on a camouflaged store near Chang Yon, an intense burst of light flak from a nearby hilltop hit Leonard's aircraft, forcing him to crash-land in paddy fields some five miles from the target. The aircraft broke up, trapping Leonard in the wreckage with a broken spine, 70 miles behind enemy lines.

Stovin-Bradford ordered two other Sea Furies to prevent anyone approaching the crashed aircraft and climbed to 14,000ft to report the circumstances; the American airfield at Kimpo immediately despatched a helicopter of the US 3rd Air Rescue Squadron.

Aircrew had been warned they would probably be tortured if captured, so when Leonard, who, though in great pain, remained conscious, sighted enemy soldiers approaching he resolved to put up a fight and fired his pistol. The shock of this caused him to pass out for a few moments and he came round to see his would-be captors being driven off by cannon fire from his Sea Fury colleagues.

Due to the extreme range from its base, the helicopter, escorted by US Tigercat fighters, arrived with only a pilot and doctor on board. When the doctor (Captain Shumate), experiencing great difficulty in getting Leonard free of the wreckage, came under fire from a nearby farmhouse, the pilot (Lt. McDaniel) got out and returned fire with his sub-machine gun before helping to get Leonard out of the Sea Fury and into the helicopter. He then took off for the return flight, escorted by Tigercats and additional Sea Furies from *Theseus*. The doctor gave Leonard morphia and a blood transfusion in flight, and they landed on the beach at Inchon from where he was transferred to the US Marine Corps hospital ship *Consolation*. For their outstanding bravery, Lieutenant McDaniel and Captain Shumate were awarded the Military Cross, presented by the British Ambassador in Washington DC.

After months in hospitals in Japan and England Leonard was still partially paralysed in his lower body and the medical prognosis was gloomy: he would never walk again, would be in a wheelchair for life, be invalided from the Navy, and would never be able to have children – this for a talented all-round athlete who was married two weeks before he sailed for Korea. He immediately embarked upon a long and successful campaign to prove the doctors wrong.

First he rejected the wheelchair sentence and acquired a cumbersome iron frame for his totally paralysed left leg which he wore for the rest of his life. With this and a stick he could walk, after a fashion. Through sheer strength of personality he persuaded the Admiralty Board to allow him to stay in the Navy, albeit in a limited non-flying capacity. His answer to this limitation was to devise a strap to attach his good leg to an aircraft rudder bar, so that he could both push and pull with one leg, effectively overcoming his handicap, and with the connivance of a friendly instructor he regained such proficiency in flying as to persuade the Flag Officer Air (Home) to reinstate his pilot category provided he did not fly over water, as it was thought the leg iron would take him to the bottom. Already a Qualified Flying Instructor, he was appointed for flying instructional duties to RNAS Stretton where his work earned him the MBE for his remarkable self-rehabilitation from his crippling injury.

Leonard's unique naval career continued for another twenty-three years, in a wide range of appointments making no concessions to his disability. Having persuaded the authorities that he could cope with vertical ladders and emergency escape at sea, he served in HMS *Hermes* as Lieutenant Commander (Flying) and later as Commander (Air). He was awarded the OBE for his outstanding contribution to British Forces, Hong Kong, 1962-64, and was promoted to Captain in 1970. His last appointment was as Commanding Officer of RNAS Culdrose, the largest helicopter airfield in Europe, a duty accomplished with distinction and typical commitment.

In 1978, after a complication of the leg injuries requiring continuous pain-killing medication and then hospitalization, he was advised that it would be unwise to place further strain upon his physical condition, and he decided to

Year 1950 Month / Date	DURATION TIME AIRBORNE	TIME LANDED	PILOT	Pilot, Passenger or Duty Performed	DUTY (Including Results and Remarks)	AIRCRAFT Type	No.	SINGLE-ENGINE AIRCRAFT DAY Dual (1)	Pilot (2)	NIGHT Dual (3)	Pilot (4)	MULTI-ENGINE AIRCRAFT DAY Dual (5)	Pilot (6)	NIGHT Dual (7)	Pilot (8)	PASS-ENGER (9)	INSTR/CLOUD FLYING Dual (10)	Pilot (11)
	—	—			Totals Brought Forward			—	—	—	—	—	—	—	—	—	—	—
Oct. 5			SELF	SOLO	Interceptions. R/P dives	Sea Fury XI			1.00							1 DL		
9			SELF	SOLO.	Strike and armed recco behind enemy lines in KOREA. 1st operational sortie by Sea Furies. Hit hangars, train, goods store and barracks. R/P and Cannon				2.05							1 DL		
Oct. 10			SELF	SOLO	Armed recco behind enemy lines in Korea. Shot down.	Sea Fury XI			1.05									

By Lieut., Cdr.(F) F. STOVIN-BRADFORD. A.G.C., 17TH C.A.G.

Lieut. Leonard was flying No.2. to me on an armed recco in the area 15 miles south of CHINAMPO, KOREA. After Strafing various targets along a road, a camouflaged store was found. Two attacks were made using R/P and cannon from the opposite hill and two haystacks below, which was seen. During the second attack an intense burst of light flak came up fields but his a/c was badly damaged and he was trapped, badly to hit Lieut. Leonards a/c. He made a good forced landing in paddy wounded in the cockpit. Lts Bevans and Austin were ordered to strafe anyone approaching whilst I climbed to 14,000 ft & reported the "down" to Theseus, Kimpo airfield & an American a/c. The position was established & passed to Kimpo by Theseus. The American 3rd Air Rescue Sqdn sent off a Helicopter, escorted by an USMC Tiger Cat. Theseus sent off a relief CAP to the crash. In the meantime Lt Austin kept 4 N. Koreans at bay who attempted to reach the crash. The Helicopter arrived piloted by 1st Lieut. McDANIEL with a doctor, Capt. SHUMATE. The doctor got out of the helicopter to get Lt Leonard out of the Fury. He was fired upon by the Koreans from a farmhouse. The pilot also got out to assist and used his "grease gun" on the Koreans. Between them, and under fire, they got Lieut. Leonard free & to the Helicopter. On the return flight the pilot radio'd the U.S.M.C. Hospital ship CONSOLATION, whilst the doctor gave Lt Leonard a blood

P.T.O.

* AIRBORNE TIME ONLY, NOT TAXYING, TO BE SHOWN.

GRAND TOTAL [Cols. (1) to (9)] Hrs. Mins.

Totals Carried Forward

Year Month / Date	DURATION TIME AIRBORNE	TIME LANDED	PILOT	Pilot, Passenger or Duty Performed	DUTY (Including Results and Remarks)	AIRCRAFT Type	No.	SINGLE-ENGINE AIRCRAFT DAY Dual (1)	Pilot (2)	NIGHT Dual (3)	Pilot (4)	MULTI-ENGINE AIRCRAFT DAY Dual (5)	Pilot (6)	NIGHT Dual (7)	Pilot (8)	PASS-ENGER (9)	INSTR/CLOUD FLYING Dual (10)	Pilot (11)
	—	—			Totals Brought Forward			—	—	—	—	—	—	—	—	—	—	—

transfusion & morphia. The Helicopter landed on the beach at INCHON where another doctor and an ambulance were waiting, and transferred Lt Leonard to the "Consolation". I flew to Kimpo with some clothes for Lt. Leonard & a bottle of whisky for McDaniel and Shumate. I obtained the whole story from the C.O. 3rd Air Rescue Sqdn and McDaniel and Shumate. The courage and efficiency shown by the Helicopter crew was beyond praise and the necessary signals have been made by F.O.2 i/c F.E. to the C in C and Admiralty.

I wish to record the courage and endurance shown by Lieut. Leonard over the period of 2 hours whilst he was trapped in his a/c, seriously wounded, 70 miles behind the enemy lines. His conduct during the rescue when he helped the doctor free himself was very highly praised by the American Helicopter crew.

I also accept responsibility, for leading the flight into attack a second time, thereby giving the gunners time to man their weapons and shoot back. WE LEARNT THE HARD WAY. The enemy positions were destroyed on 12th October by 8 Sea Furies.

F. Stovin Bradford.
COMMANDING OFFICER Lieut. Cdr.
12th October 1950.
17th C.A.G.

COMMANDER (AIR) 13 OCT 1950 H.M.S. THESEUS

COMMANDING OFFICER 17 OCT 1950 A.1300 H.M.S. THESEUS

Confirmed that Lieutenant Leonard's conduct during this episode was most courageous. Lt Cdr Stovin-Bradford was in no way to blame for the fact that one of his aircraft was shot down. He was carrying out his orders and was attempting to destroy an important target.
G.H. Hopkins Cdr.(Air)

Commander Leonard d.b. Dec 1971

Log-book extract, Lieutenant Leonard. Tim Leonard

Captain Stanley Leonard, OBE, Royal Navy. BCC/MOD via Tim Leonard

retire. Surgeon Rear Admiral F. J. O'Kelly wrote from the Royal Naval Hospital Haslar: 'To battle against the disability and pain, and to continue his duties for so long, were examples of his extraordinary courage and devotion to duty, which enabled him to overcome his physical disability in the highest tradition of the Royal Navy, and are already a legend in the Service.'

Captain Stanley Leonard OBE Royal Navy died on 1 August 1995, aged 70. At his funeral, Captain Keith Leppard CBE Royal Navy, a contemporary, colleague and close friend for over fifty years, concluded his tribute thus: 'Few men in our lives can have commanded such universal respect and affection, for his strength of character and leadership by example. Thank God that we have been honoured and inspired by knowing Stanley Leonard, a legend in the Fleet Air Arm, and a very gallant officer and gentleman.'

One of Captain Leonard's four children, Tim, won the first Sir Douglas Bader Flying Scholarship for disabled people, having suffered a tragic accident to his spine as a schoolboy. He has been admitted to Associate Membership of the the Fleet Air Arm Officers' Association.

Lieutenant Commander Don Moore-Searson RN,
Pilot, Attacker, RAF West Raynham, RNAS Ford, HMS *Eagle*, 1950-53

After the 'long jet course' at RNAS Culdrose in 1950, I went to the Naval Air Fighting Development Unit, NAFDU, based at RAF West Raynham in Norfolk. This was tasked with developing methods for operating jets from carriers and was to involve intensive trials with the Supermarine Attacker, the Royal Navy's first jet.

Because of their high fuel consumption, the Navy was concerned about how to achieve satisfactory operating cycles with jets at sea. Few of the tried and tested piston techniques were of any use. To exploit their full potential, jets had to stay at high altitude as long as possible at the end of a sortie and then descend and land quickly with about ten minutes fuel remaining. Instead of joining up and loitering at low level near the carrier – the old piston 'wall of death' – jets would have to wait above twenty thousand feet, often above cloud and out of sight of the carrier. This presented a new problem for ships' Fighter-Directors, and West Raynham soon taught us the importance of a mutual confidence between Director and pilot. NAFDU had its own Fighter Direction Officer, and whilst awaiting the arrival of our Attackers we used Vampire Mk.5s to try out the new techniques.

The first Attacker came in April 1951. At Martin Baker's at Denham, Bernard Leach had explained its new ejection seat, the Navy's first, and fired us up the test ramp to experience the tremendous 'g' forces of ejection. We learned that these Mk 1 seats required several thousand feet for safe operation, because after ejection the pilot had to separate himself from the seat and deploy his parachute manually. Also, during ejection the clearance between the pilot's knees and the Attacker's windscreen arch was 'marginal', which for long-legged pilots might present the prospect of saving one's life at the expense of one's kneecaps.

I liked the cockpit; everything was in the right place, and the control column had an American-style moulded handgrip instead of the old spade-grip. But unlike other jets the Attacker retained the old tail-wheel, which one had to remember to lock for take-off and landing. Also, unlike any jet before or since, the stick had to be pushed forward during the take-off run to raise the tail.

Simulated combat trials soon exposed stability problems, including a tendency to flick-roll in high-speed turns. Supermarine fitted an elongated dorsal fin, but poor directional stability could still result in disturbed airflow to the engine intakes with catastrophic effect: when this happened to Lieutenant McDermot he became the first person to eject from a service aircraft. Supermarine redesigned the intakes.

Fuel consumption rate was quite astonishing to pilots brought up on pistons and we had to get used to operating down to the last few gallons. 293 gallons from six tanks fed into a central main tank containing 82 gallons. When the other tanks had emptied and the 'main' was down to about 70 gallons, ten minutes' worth, a Fuel Low warning light told the pilot it was time to return to base.

On 26 April 1951, a cold damp morning with a low overcast of dark grey cloud and barely enough wind to stir the trees, I was one of a pair scheduled for 'trials', taking off at eight o'clock. The Met Office forecast varying amounts of cloud from eight hundred feet up to twenty-eight thousand with broken stratus below. Our particular trials were to be carried out above thirty thousand, and West Raynham had a VHF Direction-Finder with which ATC would home us back down to the airfield using a well-tried procedure known as Controlled Descent Through Cloud, or 'QGH'. In Attacker WA482 I took off ten seconds behind my colleague on the main runway heading west, away from the sea. With the wind from the west there was no risk of *haar*, a thick and persistent sea-fog that rolled in over the coast on an east wind, but it did strike me, just before I penetrated the bottom layer of low stratus, that there was no other activity on the airfield. The Attacker was, however, a good aircraft on instruments, so I concentrated on the flying and in a few minutes the gloomy turbulence of the cloud gave way to brilliant sunshine as we cleared the tops at about thirty thousand feet and got on with the trials.

Seconds after the other Attacker broke off to return to base, my fuel warning light came on and I also called for a QGH Controlled Descent. Raynham's controller homed us overhead on radio bearings at thirty thousand feet and turned us east for a high-speed descent. At fifteen thousand he turned me back inbound onto the runway heading and I reduced speed, following his instructions towards the airfield. I levelled off at four hundred feet, the lowest permitted height for this type of approach if you could not see the ground.

When my colleague called 'runway in sight' I informed the controller I was still in solid cloud at four hundred feet and was told to 'nudge down'. At three hundred feet, still in cloud, I requested a 'GCA' (Ground Controlled Approach), a precision radar procedure that would guide me down to a hundred feet above the runway. I had thirty-five gallons of fuel left, about five minutes' worth.

But my call for assistance came at exactly the wrong moment. In those days GCA equipment was contained in big mobile caravans parked near the runway, and the wind now having gone round to the east (whence the sea-fog), the glide-slope van was facing the wrong way and would take far too long to turn round. Two more unsuccessful blind attempts to find the runway left me without enough fuel to climb high enough for a safe ejection, leaving me no choice but to make a third and final attempt before the engine stopped. I said a very quick prayer, and at that moment the officer in charge of the GCA installation, who had been in the control tower, arrived hot-foot at the GCA site and took charge. His steady voice on the radio helped me to concentrate on the best bit of instrument flying I have ever done. Using only the GCA's search radar, he talked me round onto a 'step-down' approach, telling me my precise range from touchdown every half-mile, and what height I should be at, and it was up to me to fly these heights as if my life depended on it, which it did. I increased speed to 105 knots for manoeuvrability.

At 100 feet I was still in cloud. The talkdown continued steadily, a few minor heading corrections. I was keenly aware that after a high-altitude cold soak the altimeter could over-read by up to sixty feet, but when it read fifty feet I could still see nothing. A flare flashed passed the port wingtip. Seconds later the wheels hit the runway. I was on the ground doing 100 knots with no idea where I was, so I stop-cocked the engine, raised the undercarriage lever, slid off the end of the runway through the boundary fence, and came to rest in a field.

'...and came to a rest in a field...' Moore-Searson

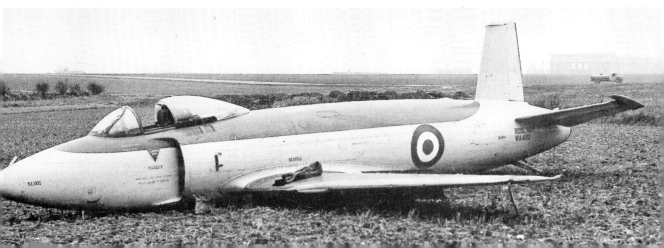

'...arranged a supply of rags in a cigarette tin mounted on the left-hand side of the cockpit...' HMS *Eagle*. Moore-Searson

Shortly after this, in August 1951, I joined 800 Attacker Squadron at RNAS Ford, preparing to embark in HMS *Eagle*.

Squadron pilots enjoyed the Attacker; it would just out-turn neighbouring RAF Tangmere's Meteor 8s when we met them in mock air combat. On the debit side, the pressurization system was barely adequate and cockpit heating virtually useless; in the Arctic during Exercise Mainbrace, four pairs of gloves failed to prevent my fingers going numb. Descending from high altitude, the inside of the canopy iced up badly with condensation, a serious problem solved only by wiping the perspex with a glycol-soaked rag before starting down. The Squadron Engineer Officer arranged a supply of rags in a cigarette tin mounted on the left-hand side of the cockpit.

Internal icing caused other problems: the vital fuel-transfer lever sometimes froze solid, making it impossible to transfer fuel from the internal wing tanks. Once at Ford I had to make an emergency descent through 30,000 feet of cloud to sea level to melt the ice before I could free the lever. And suspended water in drop-tank fuel would sometimes form ice crystals which blocked the main fuel filter, and in this case the ice would not thaw until some time after landing. After a number of 'fuel-starvation' forced-landings, the fault was revealed when one of these was jacked up after landing wheels-up: the engine started normally, and behold there was plenty of fuel in the tanks! The simple cure was to add methanol anti-freeze to drop-tank fuel.

The next problem, filters blocked not by ice but a sticky mess from dissolving drop-tank seals, caused a major hold-up to our programme and we flew aboard

Eagle with empty drops. Cleaning the tanks out revealed not only the offending sludge but also handfuls of rivet-heads and machine swarf from the factory.

'...100 feet to just abaft the round-down...' Moore-Searson

The Attacker deck-landed well, but required a change from the British 300-ft circuit to an American-style 100-ft approach, maintaining that height to a critical point just astern of the ship where the batsman gave the 'CUT' signal. You then closed the throttle, pushed the stick forward and dived towards the deck, rotating into a three-point attitude just before touchdown. The 'cut' technique was designed for piston-engined aircraft; the Attacker, whose jet engine took longer to wind down, was given the cut well out over the wake, and the landing was not always easy to judge.

Without an engine in front to protect the pilot, the old steel-cable crash-barrier would bave been lethal, so a nylon barrier was devised to stop Attackers that failed to catch an arrester wire. Our CO, George Baldwin, was the first to make use of this contraption; when his hook tore out on a ring-bolt, his hookless Attacker pulled out the barrier side supports, which causing the whole thing to form a 'vee' which pulled his wings off and brought the fuselage to a halt on its side a few feet short of the bow. The barrier attachments were strengthened, and from then on every flight-deck ring-bolt was countersunk into the deck.

On 11 March 1953 in the Mediterranean the Squadron was briefed for a

800 Squadron. Moore-Searson back row, bearded. Moore-Searson

formation flypast over the yacht taking Marshal Tito of Yugoslavia on a state visit to the UK. Up on deck, I found my aircraft in the wrong place, and as the launch sequence was important I was obliged to take the Attacker that was parked where mine should have been. Returning in close formation after the fly-past, we put out our dive-brakes for descent, at which point the aircraft I should have been flying, a few feet ahead of me, billowed white smoke out of its jet-pipe. The next instant flames engulfed the rear end of its fuselage and it dropped out of formation in a steepening dive. I followed it down, desperately trying to attract the attention of the pilot, but sadly he was still in the aircraft when it dived vertically into the sea.

My last Attacker flight was on 15 May 1953 at Ford. On my last day there, waiting for an aircraft to ferry me to Culdrose and my next job, I took a nostalgic stroll through a hangar full of brand new Mk.2 Attackers and came across my old friend from West Raynham, WA482, rebuilt as a Mk.2 and looking much happier than when I last saw her on her belly in a field in Norfolk. I spent some time with her in that quiet hangar before walking out of the Attacker world for ever.

Lieutenant Alan Hensher,
Pilot, Sea Fury, 738 Squadron, RNAS Culdrose, 1951

On Friday, 19 September 1969 Mr William R.J. Jewell of Porthleven, owner and skipper of the *Galilean*, caught something heavy in his trawl about twelve miles off Penzance. Unable to lift it, he dragged it into shallow water off Newlyn where skin-divers found an aircraft engine complete with propeller. It was lifted and delivered by way of the Harbourmaster to RNAS Culdrose nearby.

The engine was quickly identified from its nameplate, and enquiries through the British Aircraft Corporation, Rolls Royce and the Ministry of Defence identified it as the Bristol Centaurus fitted to Sea Fury VR 934, an aircraft of 738 Squadron which ditched on 5 October 1951. On that morning I was flying VR 934 about twenty miles from the coast of Cornwall, enjoying some aerobatics as part of my operational flying training with the Royal Naval Fighter School at RNAS Culdrose, when there was an sudden change in the beat of the engine and a loss of power. I turned north for the coast, called for an emergency

The rogue engine identified.

homing to Culdrose, but continued to lose power, and when the oil pressure fell below the in-flight minimum of 40psi I knew I was not going to make it.

I ditched near a group of fishing boats about twelve miles south of Penzance, making my approach at 110 knots with take-off flap and touching down at about 95 knots in a cloud of spray, the Sea Fury coming to rest about forty degrees nose-down in the water. I undid my safety harness, but the parachute quick-release box would not open and I had to scramble out with my chute on, losing a shoe in the process (never did claim for a new pair). A few seconds later the aircraft disappeared below the waves.

Once in the water, the parachute release worked perfectly and I took the opportunity to practise the drill so patiently taught by Second Officer Mary Ingledew, Culdrose's Safety Equipment Officer, inflating my dinghy and climbing aboard just before Skipper Joe Carr arrived and hauled me aboard his boat.

A little later 'Lofty' Wreford in the Culdrose Sea Otter amphibian landed nearby. I declined his offer to take me home and enjoyed a late breakfast of fresh fish with Joe Carr on the way in to Newlyn.

That was the last I saw of VR 934 until Skipper Jewell of the *Galilean* dredged up the engine that let me down. By a twist of fate I was then back at Culdrose, this time as Commander (Air), and so ensued the unusual reunion with the rogue engine shown in the photograph.

The reader may judge which of us has worn the best in the intervening eighteen years.

'...which of us has worn the best...' Hensher

Lieutenant Harold R. Gordinier USN,
Pilot, Sikorsky S.51, HMS *Theseus* and *Glory*, Korea, 1951

When my ship, USS *Valley Forge*, returned to the States for overhaul in April 1951 my crew and I transferred to HMS *Theseus* to act as their Helicopter Rescue Group. Helicopters were quite new at that time and the Royal Navy did not yet have them aboard their carriers.

I recall rescuing Warrant Officer Bailey two miles off the west coast of Korea on 12 April, and Lt Hamilton on 18 April. Lt Hamilton was further away from the carrier and it took me about an hour to get to him at my best speed of 60 knots; the Yellow Sea being very cold, by the time I got there he was unable to use his hands to get into the rescue sling, so I lowered my crewman, who had on

'Lieutenant Hamilton was very cold...' Gordinier

'...but recovered rapidly.' (Gordinier on right) Gordinier

his cold-weather 'Poopie Suit', down into the water to help him into the sling, and brought them both up together. By the time we got him back aboard Lt Hamilton was extremely cold, but recovered rapidly to fly another day.

We transferred to HMS *Glory* on 25 April and stayed with her until June, spending ten days at a time in the combat zone, alternating with one of the US carriers. My most memorable rescue on the *Glory* was an impromptu affair: I was airborne with a photographer taking pictures of the carrier and task force refuelling at sea when one of the tanker's hoses parted, knocking a crewman overboard. I tried to explain to the photographer how to operate the hoist, but this was too difficult and when we were in position over the man in the water I

'...a hose parted...' BCC/MOD via Gordinier

had to take control of it myself. I got the sling down near the casualty, but never having seen a rescue sling he just grabbed it and held on. I got him almost to the door when he lost his grip and plunged back into the water from a height of about 100 feet. As soon as he surfaced I lowered the sling again and he got into it backwards. This time I got him up to the door, but being the wrong way round he couldn't get onto the step, so the photographer and I grabbed an arm each and held him like that while I chased after the carrier and got him back aboard.

I was told afterwards that this man was listed on the records as a 'non-swimmer'. I recommended that they change their records.

Lieutenant 'Spiv' Leahy,
Pilot, Sea Fury, 801 Squadron, H.M.S. *Glory*, Korea 1952

Preparation for sea survival featured strongly in my flying training with the United States Navy in the Second World War. To practise 'ditching', they strapped you into the cockpit section of an old aircraft, hoisted you up a steep ramp and sent you hurtling down the slope at high speed into fairly deep water. The whole contraption then turned upside down and you had to extract yourself from the inverted cockpit and get to the surface. It was the unanimous view of trainee pilots that once was enough for that particularly grisly exercise. It was eight years before it paid off for me.

In 1952 801 Squadron was working up with Sea Fury FB11s aboard HMS *Glory* in the Mediterranean before deploying to Korea. Fully-loaded Furies were normally catapulted, but there was an alternative method; Rocket Assisted Take-

RATOG: 'spectacular, unsafe and unpopular...' (S/Lt Sheppard, HMS *Ocean*, Sasebo harbour, 1953). Sheppard

off Gear (RATOG) consisted of twin booster-rockets fired by the pilot at a certain stage of his 'free take-off' run along the deck. RATOG was spectacular, unsafe and unpopular: all was well if both rockets fired simultaneously and burned correctly, but one or both could fail – with unpredictable results.

The briefing for a RATOG launch went along the lines of:

'Do not forget your Master Switch when lined up.'

'When you are at full power and the man with the Green Flag drops the flag, release your brakes and start the take-off. When you reach the man with the Red Flag, fire your rockets.' The firing-button was hidden under the cockpit coaming.

'If the rockets do not fire, throttle back immediately and apply the brakes. It has been calculated that there will be enough deck left for you to stop before reaching the end.'

On a RATOG launch in Sea Fury VW659 at 0730 on 10 September 1952 everything went as advertised up to the man with the Red Flag, but when I pressed the button I got no rockets.

OK. 'Throttle back....apply the brakes.' But as the end of the deck came closer and closer it occurred to me that perhaps whoever calculated I would have room to stop might have made an error.

He had – though I must concede that we had slowed to walking pace by the time my Sea Fury skidded over the front of the ship. Having discovered that at that speed, no matter how hard you pull back on the stick, a Fury will not fly, I closed my eyes. After what seemed a long time with nothing much happening I opened them just in time to see my thrashing propeller hit the water with the nose pointing straight down. I closed my eyes again.

I was attached to the Sea Fury by various means. The dinghy I was sitting on was fastened by a lanyard to my Mae West, over which was fastened my parachute harness, and over all this went the four-point safety harness to hold me in the aircraft. Then there was the oxygen tube and the radio lead to my helmet. To get out of the aircraft normally at the end of a sortie, all these had to be disconnected, in reverse order.

The next time I opened my eyes the whole aircraft was under water and, the hood being open as usual for take-off, the cockpit was full of bubbles. I quickly undid safety harness, oxygen tube and radio lead and tried to stand up, parachute and dinghy still attached because I knew that if I got rid of the parachute the dinghy might snag in the cockpit; it always did when you tried getting out without undoing the lanyard. Not that this mattered because, as I tried to get out of the fast-sinking aircraft, the flow of water forced me back against the canopy arch and pinned me there, caught by its two little locking spigots which snagged my clothes. I had to pull myself back down into the cockpit and turn around and get out facing aft, avoiding the spigots. I got clear and saw my Sea Fury sink away down into the depths, by now almost upside down, just like that dummy cockpit all those years ago.

My next concern was the carrier. I counted myself incredibly lucky it had not hit the Fury with me inside it, and I had no wish to be caught by the propellers when they came along, so I decided to wait where I was until the ship had passed. I was composing my soul to patience when a little voice said to me 'Don't be a bloody fool, Leahy - you're drowning! Get up to the surface!'

A short period of indecision as to which way to go was ended by inflating my Mae West, at which point I started going up fast, endeavouring to swim away from where I thought the ship was.

I popped up about ten feet from the ship's side abreast the starboard propeller and took a huge breath which, with my oxygen mask still clamped to my face and the end of the tube submerged, resulted in a massive intake of salt water. Choking and gasping, I ripped off the mask. A sailor scrubbing the quarterdeck looked down as I drifted past. As the carrier sailed on he went back to his chores.

My parachute had gone, but I had my dinghy, so I inflated it, climbed in and waited to see what happened next. The 'Planeguard' destroyer, always in attendance upon the carrier during flying operations, promptly launched her lifeboat and soon had me alongside; the sea was not particularly rough, but the bumping and scraping and crashing of oars so frightened me that I had to be restrained from jumping back into the sea with my dinghy.

Once safely on board, I was offered a large medicinal tot of rum, which I felt I had to turn down because I was programmed to fly again that afternoon. I must have been suffering from shock.

Sub Lieutenant D.G.L. Swanson,
Pilot, Sea Fury, HMS *Glory* and HMS *Ocean*, Korea, 1952

Midwinter 1948/49. On father's farm in Cornwall, after a cold wet morning sorting potatoes it was good to get in for mother's hot dinner. Idly scanning the ads in the Western Morning News, 'Be a Naval Officer and Fly' caught my eye. I had never thought of doing either, but it sounded better than sorting rotten spuds and milking cows twice a day..

On 8 July 1949 I joined the training carrier HMS *Victorious* in Portland harbour as an Aviation Cadet. The pay, for hard manual labour and learning seamanship, was fifteen shillings a week. By our second pay day I was able to buy my first legal pint of beer.

On 23 October 1951 I was strapped into a Sea Fury waiting to start my first carrier take-off from HMS *Triumph*. I could see fellow trainee Andy Powell flying downwind and about to turn in for his very first deck landing. Exactly fifteen minutes later we had both completed four successful landings. In a few days we had all made some two dozen landings and been trained in basic carrier operations, including catapult launching.

In November 1951 I joined 804 Squadron aboard HMS *Glory* in Sydney, where her air group was relaxing after a tour of active service in the Korean War. On 7 February 1952, in the Yellow Sea, I climbed into a Fury for my first operational sortie.

It was Eskimo weather. To ensure any chance of survival should one go down over enemy territory, or in the water, many layers of warm clothing had to be worn under an immersion suit. But the last time I adjusted the straps on my personal parachute was in the tropics, and now, with all the extra underwear, they just would not do up! The ship was already turning into wind, the launch minutes away, and even being No. 4 in line for take-off was not going to give me time to lengthen my straps. But I was not going to delay the show, so I made my first combat flight over Korea effectively chute-less We fired our rockets at a target near Onjin, saw plenty of flak, and all landed back on board unscathed.

I see from my log-book that on 17 March 1952 I flew three rocket missions totalling seven hours, two against coastal gun positions, directed by the UN Fleet, and another to the Han River area. On 17 May, now with 802 Squadron in HMS *Ocean*, I flew four sorties totalling six hours forty-five minutes; two with 500lb bombs against a rail bridge and supply dumps, a Combat Air Patrol over the Fleet, and a spotting assignment for HMS *Belfast's* guns. The next day my Wing Leader on a coastal bombing and strafing mission, 'Penny' Penniston-Bird, baled out. I thought at first the smoke was a runaway cannon. When I told him he was on fire, he was over the side before my thumb left the transmit button.

By way of irony, on my *last* operational sortie in Korea, 4 July 1952, I was forced to take to my parachute when my aircraft

'...old enough to vote.' Swanson

was set alight by enemy gunfire. I was rescued by an American helicopter.

On 23 July 1952, homeward bound in the troopship *Devonshire* in the Indian Ocean, I became old enough to vote.

Sub Lieutenant (A) Brian Randall RNVR,
Pilot, Sea Fury, 802 Squadron, HMS *Ocean*, Korea 1952

In the Channel off Brixham in the course of a deck-landing training session with No 22 Pilot Training Course aboard HMS *Triumph*, when the CO called for two volunteers to join 802 Squadron in Korea to replace casualties, Lt Johnny Jones and I raised our hands. Turned down because I was near the end of my two years' National Service, I volunteered on the spot to extend my service to cover an operational tour. My offer was accepted with almost indecent alacrity, which suited me fine, operational flying being after all the whole point of my two years' training.

Triumph braked to a halt in mid-channel, the Captain's boat was lowered and Johnny and I with our bags sped into Brixham where the Torquay-London express was puffing impatiently, held up by request of the ship. The train set off and soon we were in the Admiralty Medical Centre in London where medics were waiting with the first series of Far East inoculations; we would get the rest when we got there, they said. A few hours at home and we were checking in at Heathrow. A whole book could be written about our adventures in finding and joining the ship: a four-day journey by BOAC Argonaut to Tokyo (during which, prophetically, I read Paul Brickhill's *Dam Busters*); finding and ferrying our own replacement Sea Furies across the Sea of Japan from Iwakuni to be met by Chris Jenne at 'K16', the squadron's shore-base near Seoul, in time to fly aboard *Ocean* for her Second Patrol.

British carrier patrols lasted ten days with one day's replenishment at sea from a Fleet Auxiliary. Johnny and I joined Bob Hallam's flight with Chris as section leader, and were soon being briefed by the Air Warfare Officer for an attack on a 'dam' east of Haeju.

It seemed he had been reading *Dam Busters* too; but this was no great hydro-electric affair, merely an agricultural dyke keeping sea water out of North Korean paddy fields. And in lieu of Barnes Wallis's spherical bombs we had 1,000lb HE which we were to drop against the foot of the wall, which meant approaching along the line of the dyke at low level, fairly slow speed, straight and level, giving the defending AA gunners the best possible chance of hitting us. To improve our chances we would attack in pairs. The bombs had 30-second delay fuses to allow us to get clear. The theory was that breaching the dykes at high tide would contaminate the irrigation water and ruin the enemy's rice.

We made a long approach at 500 feet, 250 knots, with me on Chris's starboard wing. He positioned us beautifully and gave the countdown, 5...4...3...2...1... DROP!

I squeezed the bomb-release and opened the throttle wide to get away from the flak and the coming explosions.

As I began to pick up speed a large rotating object rose lazily above my port wing – my bomb! When it reached its apogee I watched fascinated as it tumbled slowly, close enough for me to read the stencilled 1000HE on its scruffy green carcass, until I remembered its time-fuse was ticking off the last few seconds of its life – and mine! I rolled and pulled hard away, turning back a few seconds later to see Chris's bomb raise a water-spout alongside the dyke and mine blow a huge crater in a nearby road. After the next pair attacked, the flimsy dam burst and seawater poured through the gap.

The effect on the Korean War? – small. What has always bothered me is that if my bomb *had* taken me with it, would anybody ever have known what happened?

Lieutenant Roy Graham,
Pilot, Sea Fury, 802 Squadron, HMS *Ocean*, Korea 1952

Dam-busting brought out 802's specialist Air Warfare Officer Bill Illingworth's talents to especially good effect. I remember his first briefing very well.

When the usual preliminaries about weather and so on were over, Bill stood up with a sheaf of diagrams. The wicked North Koreans, he told us, were producing sufficient quantities of rice here (Diagram) – *right near the front line!* – to supply their troops without recourse to their Main Supply Route (which in any case was off-limits for us, being in regular use by delegates attending the everlasting 'peace negotiations' that were a feature of this war; it was known as Delegate's Road). *Ocean* was tasked to 'destroy the southern rice-fields'.

Intrigued by the notion of destroying a rice-paddy with a Sea Fury, I settled back for Bill's well-prepared brief, which went something like this:

INFORMATION

Rice is grown in fresh water. The rice-fields we are to attack are on the coast and separated from the sea by dams. (Diagram). The dams keep out the sea water. Breaching the dams means an influx of salt water, which ruins the rice crop for up to three years.

ARMAMENT

Mixed 500 and 1000lb bombs (Diagram). These bombs follow this path when dropped from height 'X' at speed 'Y' and dive-angle 'Z'. They must not actually hit the dam; they must fall short or near, like *this*, but only by just so much. Timing is critical. A fuse delay of 'T' seconds will cause all sorts of havoc to the dam foundations if they all go off at the same time (Diagram). This is the sight-picture you must have on your gyro gun-sight at the moment of release - the aiming diamond just...*here*. Any questions?

No. Bill was the expert and had done all the work. By this time we were all fairly competent at bopping things, usually bridges up to now, and sallied forth with high hopes of success – though I confess that climbing into my Sea Fury, WJ237, the butterflies were fluttering as usual. It was 17 September 1952.

Our confidence was justified. Huge gaps opened in the dams and salt water flowed unhindered over the communist paddy-fields with every incoming tide –

all very satisfactory. And we had the photographs to prove it.

But the operation left two questions in my mind: who instigated this operation, and did it do any good? The North Koreans always repaired the bridges we kept knocking down, but I don't recall them ever bothering to mend our dams.

Lieutenant A.W. (Hap) Chandler USN,
Pilot, Attacker, 803 Squadron, HMS *Eagle*, English Channel, 1952

I can't count the times I have told people how enjoyable my exchange duty with the Royal Navy was.

Having said that, I want you to know it taught me humility in that I never mastered the technique of taxying a tailwheel jet (Supermarine Attacker F1) with bicycle brakes. Believe me, going round in circles on the active runway is downright embarrassing.

And my education continued when I made my first jet sea-water landing on 10 July 1952. During a catapult shot off the starboard cat of HMS *Eagle*, for a flight home after a successful cruise, I heard an explosion. Airborne off the bow, I got control problems, more muffled explosions, and a call from Flyco: 'Attacker 522 - you're on fire!' Unable to climb high enough to eject (1000ft in those days), and afraid that old '522' was going to blow up, I shut off the engine and landed in the water. Planeguard HMS *Ulysses*' whaler – manned by their Boys' Division – fished me out, and I had a hot bath and a generous over-abundance of the Queen's whisky.

Having failed to get home by air I had to take the train and arrived still full of whisky, to be greeted by my father (a US Navy Rear Admiral) on a surprise visit. He took a dim view of my bedraggled condition, which he regarded as unbecoming a representative of the United States Navy in foreign parts..

I salute the Fleet Air Arm for the wonderful contributions they made to improve the safety, efficiency and potency of Naval Aviation, contributions which have allowed the Carrier to remain a major player in the strategic planning of both Britain and the United States.

Commander C.H.A. Harper,
Supply Officer, HMS *Ocean*, Korea, 1953. Pages from a Private Journal

Saturday 13 June: *At Sea*

Not a lucky morning for the Fireflies, who went off to beat up a village reported by intelligence as full of communist troops (one of my targets as part of the briefing team) and came back well-peppered. I am most thankful that they all got back - one with a hole in the engine, another with a hole half-an-inch from the fuel feed, another with holes in the rear cockpit, wings and tail. I gather 'Pants' Bloomer, the Firefly C.O., shot off his rockets and then took the Flight in for a second straffing run, when they got almost as good as they gave. It would be very stupid for any of them to go and get themselves killed at this stage of the war, with a truce expected any day. Personally I think it criminal that Fireflies are employed on this sort of work at all. They are too slow, they carry utterly unsuitable armament for the work in hand, and are altogether an expensive and unjustifiable risk.

P. Earl painted the name 'THE BITZA' on his helicopter, as it is 'bitza' three helicopters – the front and engine of one, the tail of another, and the rotor blades of a third. But Commander (Air) has made him remove the inscription. Shame!

Sunday 14 - Wednesday 17 June: *At Sea*

Just four more days on patrol. I have done a fair amount of work in the A.I.R. (Air Intelligence Room), and have been interested by detailed reports of the results of some of our operations obtained from 'sources' in an enemy boatyard, e.g. 'Boatyard at YC105212 was attacked on...at...by four single-engined U.N. aircraft. Two fishing boats used for catching fish for the side-dishes of NKA (North Korean Army) sunk, 17 NKA men killed, 14 NKA wounded, 21 para-military personnel killed, 1 (one) ox killed.' I wonder whether 'para-military personnel' means women and children. Probably just innocent civilians. It's a bloody business, this war, and very wasteful. The Chinese are going hammer and tongs to try and dent the U.N. lines – and meanwhile rumours of a truce are always in the air.

Thursday 16 - Saturday 18 July: *At Sea*

Up anchor and away for our fourth Patrol, with prospects of an armistice somewhat brighter. Wednesday, the first day of operations, was, however, a very black day. We were in very patchy foggy weather all the forenoon, and were lucky to retrieve Sub. Lieut. Sheppard who ran short of fuel and had to make an emergency landing. Owing to fog, he couldn't see the ship and had to be 'talked down'. I was on the signal bridge taking a breath of air with Venour (with whom I now 'brief' and 'de-brief') when Sheppard's Sea-Fury suddenly appeared out of the fog coming straight for us. He veered off, missing the bridge by not many feet, and landed on a few moments later.

Then the catapult broke down, and the Captain decided to send the next detail off by RATOG (Rocket-Assisted Take-Off Gear). I was watching from the Communications Officer's sea-cabin, just below and for'ard of the bridge. The first Fury went off all right but the second (Lieutenant Mulder of the Royal Netherlands Navy) fired his rockets far too soon, and I was horrified to see him go straight over the bows into the sea, where his aircraft disintegrated. His bombs did not go off, thank God, and miraculously he came to the surface. He twice had to kick himself off the ship's side and was picked up very neatly by Lieutenant Earl in the helicopter as he drifted astern. The following Furies got off all right, but tragedy came with the first Firefly. Some say two of his rockets did not fire; certainly it seemed to me that the rockets were giving insufficient boost as he left the deck. For he got lower and lower, and though he got his front wheels up, his tail wheel eventually dragged in the water and suddenly he crashed and went down, his tail sticking up in the air for about two seconds only. The observer, Lieutenant Thomas, went down with the aircraft. The pilot, Lieutenant Paddy Evans, eventually came to the surface and was picked up by an American destroyer, but four hours of artificial respiration failed to bring him round. He came back aboard over the jack-stay at sunset, with the sun lighting up a great 'V' in the clouds above the horizon; and we buried him over the stern soon afterwards in the dusk, a very moving ceremony. He was a very nice little man, unmarried, looked like a little monkey and had many friends on board. Thomas was a very quiet, gentle man, and leaves a widow, poor thing. It all seems so wasteful and unnecessary to me. Certainly let the men take any necessary risks over the front line, but when their contribution can make so little difference to the battle owing to weather conditions, the distance from the ship and other factors, it seems to me not only an unjustifiable risk but against commonsense and prudent utilization of one's resources to risk valuable pilots in foul weather, fog and rocket-assisted take-off operations. But one mustn't say so, whatever one feels, as that strikes at the roots of discipline. The great majority of our Close Air Support missions were a pure waste of time and energy, as so many American aircraft were milling over the battlefield that the American directing personnel couldn't find targets for our aircraft in the short time available to them. So for the most part they just threw their bombs away over the bomb-line. I only 'de-briefed' one really successful attack, which knocked out two bunkers, two caves, and 25 yards of trench, and obtained some satisfying secondary explosions. Some, but little, consolation for the loss of Evans and Thomas. I have been thinking more and more about their loss, and less and less can I accept the theory that two of their rockets did not fire. My impression at the time was most strongly that he had fired a moment too soon. I felt alarm about the aircraft even before it came in sight, going up the deck, just as I had about Mulder; and I felt no anxiety over the three Furies which took off perfectly. They say that Evans did not fire his rockets until he had passed the firing flag, in which case I think it more than probable that the flag was too far for'ard. I cannot honestly remember any difference in the state of the rockets between Mulder and Evans, and the theory that two of Evans' rockets failed seems just too pat for me. Too easy to throw that blame at the Electrical Department. If anything, Evans' rockets had a little more boost than Mulder's, and certainly he went further before crashing.

The nub of the matter was this. There was almost no wind. The weather over the bomb-line was foggy. The catapult was out of action. Was it worth risking aircrew in fully-armed aircraft to use RATOG, which requires split-second timing and absolute faith in rockets (which are, to my mind, always a bit unpredictable)? I should hate to have had the responsibility of ordering the operation – and particularly of persevering with it after Mulder had crashed.

Thursday 16th was a somewhat better day, though one stupid accident wrote off four aircraft. The brakes failed in a Fury landing from CAP (Combat Air Patrol), and he ran straight into another Fury and two Fireflies when taxying into the park. The pilot was, of course, the inevitable Hick. Poor young chap, he sounds certain to get into trouble. But I believe the hydraulic failure is established, and I hope he is relatively exonerated. I was entrusted with the briefing as well as de-briefing (under the eye of Captain Venour, our Army Intelligence expert), and much damage was done by some of our Sea Fury divisions in Close Air Support of the Commonwealth and ROK (Republic of Korea) Divisions. We had fine weather today - perfect flying weather and bombing conditions. Thank God, moreover, no casualties to our pilots or observers.

* * *

A Timeless Story of the Korean War.

It was Squadron policy for pilots to fly their 'own' aircraft whenever possible. One day a pilot pilot flew three strike missions, all in the same aircraft. When he landed-on at 1000 after the morning sortie the Squadron's Chief Radio Artificer, an efficient young man, jumped up on the wing.

'Radio serviceable, sir?'

'No, Chief,' replied the pilot.

The Chief checked the radio out, but after the second sortie, the reply to the same question was,

'No, chief. Still u/s.'

After the third landing of the day at 1815, the Chief tried again.

'Radio OK, sir?'

'Bloody thing's still u/s, Chief,' answered the pilot crossly.

Without hesitation the Chief suggested, 'I think, sir, the trouble is probably between the headphones...'.

(Paraphrased from *With the Carriers in Korea, 1950-53* by kind permission of John. R. P. Lansdown)

* * *

Lieutenant Roy Hawkes,
Pilot, Sikorsky S.55, 848 Squadron, Malaya, 1953

The Malayan 'Emergency', which began in 1948 when three European estate managers of rubber plantations in different parts of Malaya were gunned down in their offices and rapidly escalated into a full-scale communist insurrection, lasted eight years and saw much bitter guerrilla fighting in jungle and swamp between the British Army and Communist Terrorists (CTs) intent upon taking over what was then the Federated Malay States. 848 Naval Air Squadron with its twelve US-built Sikorsky S55 helicopters entered the fray in 1952 and brought a new flexibility to the army in Malaya whose only way of reaching the CTs up to then was footslogging through the jungle.

In 1953 I was at 848 Squadron's advance base in Kuala Lumpur where the flying task was a mixture of troop-lifting, supply drops and intelligence work, and 'Casevac' or Casualty Evacuation. On 13 February the well-rehearsed Casevac procedure swung into action when an emergency call was received from a Special Police Force patrol in the jungle, just to the east of Malaya's central mountain spine; they had encountered a party of CTs, killed two of them, but unfortunately injured a number of innocent aborigines in the crossfire. The late Geoff Luff and I were soon airborne in WV 192 heading for an army airstrip near Tapah where the 1st Manchesters had organized a refuelling bowser – a 45-gallon drum of Aviation Gasoline on the back of a truck. The supply of fuel was by an orally activated syphon through a flexible hose, and the regiment's fiery colonel was there in person to urge his soldiery to greater efforts of suck:

'This is an EMERGENCY! Don't waste time spitting it out, man! SWALLOW it!'

But despite all his best efforts, and theirs, to speed us on our way, our first attempt to cross the ridge had to be abandoned. The morning mists over the central mountain ridge were slow to clear. Eventually, accompanied by an army AOP Auster, we threaded our way up a river valley and succeeded in getting over the ridge into better weather beyond. The Auster pilot guided us to a well-prepared clearing in a bamboo forest where Geoff disembarked with our passengers, an RAMC Medical Officer and an army intelligence officer, to size

'...a well-prepared clearing in a bamboo forest...' – In front of the Sikorsky's tail: the late Lt Cdr Jeff Luff, Lt Hawkes, and the Police Lieutenant killed shortly afterwards. Hawkes

up the situation.

The doctor needed time to prepare his patients, so we shut down our engine – not a thing we often did in such remote locations. When everything had stopped I leant out of the cockpit to find myself gazing down the barrel of a 'friendly' rifle that someone had propped against the side of the aircraft. One had to get used to that sort of thing.

Taking care not to split families, we flew out the wounded with their close relatives – four men, two women and a baby. Then there was the amorous deaf mute who had become a sort of camp-follower and was making a nuisance of herself, able to wreck the best-laid ambush. The unfortunate girl must have been utterly confused by the trauma of the past forty-eight hours, but still managed to hoist her sarong a couple of contours higher than necessary while boarding the aircraft for her flight into 're-settlement'. Oddly though, the poor girl did elect to cover her normally exposed breasts.

The Police Lieutenant and his Malay patrol were left behind, a motley band who, despite appearances, were steadily getting their section of the jungle under control, establishing order out of insurrection. I was saddened to learn that the lieutenant was killed in a skirmish with terrorists soon afterwards.

Just before nightfall we were ready for our final departure. The weather was closing in. The way home, down the west side of the mountains, became a tunnel down a valley between tree-lined slopes and a low roof of swirling, lowering cloud and the tumbling river below. Once again we had to place our whole faith in the army Auster pilot who led the way. At that stage we had no radio contact with either him or the forces on the ground, but he knew what he was doing and in the last vestiges of the brief tropical twilight we punched out of a hole at the end of the valley, just before it self-sealed.

From there it was all downhill to Tapah, where the 1st Manchesters in their tented camp on the edge of the jungle provided shelter for the night and generous hospitality. At a formal dinner, the tables groaning with all the regiment's priceless silver, our immaculately dressed hosts seemed to take genuine pleasure in the presence of two naval officers in scruffy jungle-green.

Apart from the routine work, there was always something new for helicopters to do, like Target Marking.

To the uninitiated, terrorist camps and aboriginal settlements were easily confused, but with experience it became apparent that, in deep jungle, the average terrorist clearing would be neater: unlike the Chinese terrorists, aborigines never planted their vegetables in neat rows. The rule could break down, as when the terrorists employed aboriginal gardeners, and sometimes, if they had access to 'protection' food from a Malay village, their camp might not have a cultivation at all, in which case the only thing that gave it away was a glimpse of bared ground underneath the continuous canopy of foliage. Closer inspection might then reveal the huts of a permanent camp.

Flying a representative from HQ Malaya over a known trouble area one day, we located such a camp. Normally an army patrol would have been inserted by air to deal with it, but on this occasion, for reasons best known to itself, the

'...normally an Army patrol would be inserted by air.'
Iban tracker in the Sikorsky. Hawkes

Royal Air Force Command insisted it be annihilated by high-level saturation bombing. And furthermore, since I had found it and knew where it was, I was to be their Pathfinder and mark the target for them. As I said, there was always something new, but for me this was a bigger than usual step into the unknown.

Come the appointed day, 29 April, I had a very difficult job to do in a noisy helicopter. First I had to relocate the target, and then loiter far enough away not to arouse suspicion: CTs had a reputation for fighting only where they held the initiative, and any terrorists with normal faculties would leg it at the first sign of unusual air activity. But at the same time I had to be close enough to pinpoint and mark the camp when ordered in by the bombers at, literally, sixty seconds' notice, this being the minimum time for the bomb-aimers to make their final adjustments.

I relocated the camp without difficulty and flew past in what I hoped was a nonchalant fashion until I guessed I was out of earshot. Then, desperately hoping I was keeping station on the correct group of trees, in an area where look-alike trees grow by the million, I circled slowly in the steamy air until, high overhead, a formation of Lincoln heavy bombers came into view, running in on their map reference – a sight so awe-inspiring that the numbers have probably grown over the years and I will not try to say how many. At the last possible moment for them to make their final aiming correction, actually less than one minute, came the radio call:

'Mark!'

Now it was all up to me. I sped forward just above the forest canopy and, to my intense relief, found the terrorist camp right on cue and slowed up to allow Naval Airman Watters, a non-aircrew Ordnance Mechanic who had volunteered for the trip, to ignite and heave out a smoke canister. I think we avoided being shot at by the terrorists, but in any case the prospect of being peppered with bandit buckshot was considerably overshadowed by the imminent arrival of a rain of bombs from above, so I exited the scene in double quick time and took cover behind the nearest rise.

The bombing was commendably accurate and utterly devastating, but, in my humble opinion, of questionable value as a method of terrorist control. Perhaps others agreed: as far as I know, Helicopter Target Marking did not catch on.

Commandeur H.J.E. van der Kop,
Royal Netherlands Navy, Pilot, Sea Fury, HMS *Illustrious*, 1953.

Wwhen our Navy acquired HMS *Venerable* and renamed her *Karel Doorman*, the deal allowed us to fly from Royal Navy carriers when she was in dock, which explains why, after gunnery and deck-landing training at RNAS Culdrose, Dutch squadrons of Sea Furies and Fireflies embarked in HMS *Illustrious* in 1953 to take part in the big annual NATO Exercise MAINBRACE. Cornish weather being what it is, we were some time at Culdrose and greatly enjoyed the hospitality of the wardroom there; when everyone was fully qualified we flew aboard *Illustrious* in the Irish Sea for work-up exercises.

The Sea Fury force grew with the addition of some well-known FAA aviators including Anson, Leahy and Mitchell. When 815 Avenger Squadron flew aboard the C.O. extracted a mini-scooter from his bomb-bay, kicked it into life, secured his cap with the strap, and made a stately pass down the deck, saluting the captain on the bridge. We Dutch newcomers, with hardly any decklanding experience, were given more practice, with some cracking results. On 3 September a Dutch Fury landed fast and off-centre, hit a barrier-pole, ripped off its port wing and caught fire. In jumping out of the cockpit the pilot sprained his ankle badly and was out of flying for the rest of the trip. To the disgust of our mechanics, the wreck was dumped overboard before they could salvage any parts, especially the much coveted cockpit clock.

We were told that officers generally went ashore over the rear gangway in plain clothes, on condition that they wore a hat. In the windy Clyde we Dutch had much difficulty with our newly-acquired Christie foldin' hats, which kept having to be

'...and sprained his ankle badly...' Van der Kop

fished out of the water by the ship's boats, driven by midshipmen, one of whom had great trouble with the tidal current. The ship's Commander was waiting with us to go ashore, and having watched this poor lad make three unsuccessful attempts to get alongside, used a megaphone: 'My dear fellow, why don't you stay there and we'll bring *Illustrious* across to you!' The boat came neatly alongside at the next try.

In Exercise MAINBRACE the Sea Fury proved superior to the Air Force jets which jumped on us at various times, and much valuable experience had been gained by the time the Dutch squadrons flew off near Edinburgh and went home to Valkenburg.

In 1954 at Gibraltar, when *Karel Doorman* hosted a party of aviators from HMS *Eagle*, an ugly incident took place which might have sparked the latest in the long list of Anglo-Dutch Naval Wars – our unsightly wooden goldfish mascot was stolen. A thorough search of the British carrier, carried out surreptitiously next day during their return party, failed to find it. *Eagle's* magnificent silver eagle trophy, presented to the earlier *Eagle* by General Franco for saving his brother's life after a flying boat accident, left the British carrier late that night under a Dutch raincoat.

Next morning *Doorman* received a curt signal from *Eagle* demanding their trophy be returned immediately, or there would be 'consequences'; the Captain was informed, all officers assembled in the wardroom, the culprits owned up and were ordered to march off immediately to *Eagle* with the trophy and a letter of apology, which they did. Strangely, *Eagle's* Commander knew nothing about the 'signal', which had been a ruse cooked up by their 'fly-boys'. And what is worse, we never saw our goldfish again.

Sub Lieutenant Pete Sheppard,
Pilot, Firefly Delivery Flight, RNAS Anthorn to RNAS Hal Far, 1953

Shortly after Christmas 1953, home from Korea, I was at a loose end at RNAS Anthorn, a Maintenance Unit on the Solway Firth, when a call came to deliver a Sea Fury and two Fireflies back to a Carrier Air Group in the sunny Mediterranean after extensive repair.

To my intense chagrin, I was elbowed out of the gleaming Sea Fury fighter,

'...deliver two Fireflies...' Sheppard

'...determined to get some winter sunshine...' (Sheppard and Firefly). Sheppard

on which I was in current practice, by someone more senior. However, determined to get some winter sunshine, I settled for one of the Firefly 'bombers', which I had never flown, found a copy of Pilot's Notes and got myself a 'First Fam' trip. 'Familiarization' on a new aircraft required four 'Fams', after which you were signed up as 'Qualified on Type'. My 'Fam 2' in Firefly VX 430 next morning was Anthorn to Lee-on-Solent, led by a slightly more experienced pilot in the other bomber, and 'Fam 3' that afternoon was from there to Istres, a French Aeronavale base near Toulon, where we stayed overnight.

Next day, notwithstanding the ominous route forecast, Leader led us off after lunch, destination Hal Far, Malta, distance some 650 track miles south-east.

As usual in the 50s, when Air Traffic Control was seen as an infringement of civil liberty, we were already on a private frequency when our two Fireflies entered the base of some very black cloud at 1,000ft on my Fam 4. 'We'll go above it,' Leader called, and I tucked into close formation. At 14,000ft, still in thick cloud, he pointed down and called, 'We'll have to go below it.' His non-aircrew passenger, a Petty Officer returning from compassionate leave, had no oxygen. We descended.

Our planned track was west of Corsica over the sea, but at around 4000ft in the descent I caught a fleeting glimpse of rocks and trees just the other side of

Leader's Firefly. I yelled something frightening enough to put him into a max-rate climb. Expecting to die any instant, I managed to stay with him in the turbulent cloud until we levelled off at a safe height and droned on blind towards the straits of Bonifacio.

After three hours of this, my neck stiff as an angle-iron from staring fixedly at the other Firefly a few feet beyond my wingtip, I heard Malta ATC tell Leader: 'Be advised, all Malta airfields are zero-zero in fog.'

We circled, the cloud getting darker. What were we going to do? I suddenly had an overwhelming urge for a drink.

'El Aouina's open,' somebody called. 'Divert to El Aouina!'

'Where's that?'

'Tunis!'

'Ah!'

Leader rolled his wings level and transmitted the first of several MAYDAYs. Stiff as a joist I stared grimly sideways at his horrible Firefly, steeling myself for what had to be the last leg of this awful trip. Fuel was low and I knew neither how much the Griffon was using nor how far Tunis was. What I did know was what I had thought all along: we should have spent another night at Istres.

I was having trouble seeing and thought my sight was failing until it dawned on me it was getting dark. Eyes fastened on the fading shape of the other Firefly, I groped around the unfamiliar cockpit trying switches until I got some lights on. Leader apparently felt no need of lights, so I had to reposition myself so that my nav-light lit up enough of him to formate on. We had been airborne four and a half hours and the aircraft was beginning to sound empty.

When Leader called Tunis ATC an American voice answered with bearings and instructions to descend. To my intense relief we broke cloud at 300ft with lights all around us. I stole a quick look ahead and saw what looked like the runway, two tapering rows of red lights, and was easing away from Leader in preparation for landing when I sensed something wrong. The 'runway', now that I'd got my eyes in focus, turned out to be a gigantic radio mast with red lights all the way up its supporting wires, dead ahead, and CLOSE! JEEPERS!

'LEADER BREAK PORT BREAK PORT GO!!'

I rolled hard right and pulled, missed the mast and recovered to find myself on my own above a sea of lights, fuel gauge on zero, and no idea where the airfield was.

'Tunis this is Firefly Two, can you give me a flare for ident?' I bleated.

They obliged immediately. I picked up the pyrotechnics, crossed the city, lined up on what looked like a runway and put the Firefly down – downwind as I discovered when my landing-lamp flitted across the windsock. I was safe, but where was Leader?

I had an idea. I had come to rest at the touchdown end of the runway, facing the wrong way. Why not use my landing lamp to guide him in? Then he could land over my head. Plenty of room. He sounded keen so I started flashing.

'Got you!' Leader called. 'Keep flashing...keep flashing..OK you can stop now!'

I turned off my landing-lamp.

'Stop flashing!'

'I have!' I yelled back, aggrieved at the ungrateful tone.

There was a fairly long pause, then, 'Two, start flashing again. I just nearly landed on a b....y train!'

I resumed lighthouse duty, occulting into the dark. After a few minutes of this my engine died. The tanks were dry. I kept flashing with the fading battery but of Leader there was neither sight nor sound. After a while, fearing the worst, I tried calling him.

'I'm down!' I could just hear the peevish reply. 'Where the hell are you?'

At that point my battery expired, the radio faded and the lights went out. I climbed out stiffly and stood in the warm African air beside VX 430, unlit on the touchdown end of El Aouina's duty runway. The only sound was the tinkle of contracting metal from the exhausted Griffon. So much for Fam 4, I reflected. I was now 'Qualified to Fly' the Firefly.

The white-helmeted American MPs who roared up in a jeep were plainly at a loss to know what to make of this ancient nocturnal aeroplane and its wry-necked young pilot. What happened next is another story. There was this gorgeous female who had been hanging around North Africa ever since Humphrey Bogart left, waiting for the right man to come into the right bar on the right night and...

Commander Mike Crosley DSC★,
Test Pilot, Commanding Officer 813 Squadron, HMS *Albion* and *Eagle,* 1954
Commanding Officer Naval Test Squadron, Boscombe Down, 1960-63

I thought the Wyvern was a beautfully built aircraft, but engine and airframe were both new and this is usually a drawback. Taking over 813 Squadron in December 1954, and wishing to arrive in style, I got a Wyvern from Lee-on-Solent to fly out to Malta to join the ship. This particular one had the very latest

'I thought the Wyvern was a beautifully built aircraft...' Starting Up. Lt Des Cracknell, West Raynham 1955. Cracknell

cartridge starter, two immense cartridges inserted just behind the main air intake. By the time I was ready to start I was expecting something really exciting. It was a few days before 5 November.

When I pressed the starter button, the cartridge gases ignited in the engine compressor and blew the spinner backplate into the front propeller, the whole thing flew to pieces and the odds and sods went into the engine and wrecked it; I got to Malta a week later, by Dakota.

For deck work, the combination of a 4110 horse-power Armstrong Siddeley Python engine and 14-foot eight-bladed contra-rotating propellers was unpromising. The inertia of the two-ton propeller system made engine response sluggish and under catapult acceleration fuel tended to drain away from the burners, causing flame-out, as in the early Gannets. This happened to Bruce Macfarlane, a New Zealander in 813 under its former C.O. Pridham-Price. Going off *Albion's* port catapult in the Mediterranean, his Wyvern crashed into the sea and the ship ran over him. His account reads:

'Catapulting is always a startling experience and I usually find myself off the bows before I collect my wits enough to be aware of anything and take control of the aircraft. In this case my first realization was a loss of power; I tried to open the throttle, but this was of course already locked in the open position.

'The next instant I hit the sea at about 70 knots, wheels down, of course, and flaps in the take-off position. I knew that the Wyvern had very poor ditiching characteristics and I had in fact witnessed a fatal ditching about 18 months ago when the Wyvern had entered the sea and disappeared immediately without any hesitation at all before sinking.

'This memory flashed through my mind just before hitting the sea and I felt that I had no chance of escape. The impact with the sea stunned me to some extent.

'When I had collected my wits again I was under water and it was getting darker. My nervous system seemed to have disconnected my body from my brain - except for my left hand. The yellow 'Emergency Canopy Jettison' knob filled my whole vision. I was grateful for its colour and position. I hit it with my left hand and the canopy became unlocked and green water poured in all around its edges. I did not notice the canopy actually go and it may have been more or less in position when I ejected. I pulled the ejector seat 'blind' handle with my left hand immediately after hitting the hood jettison lever.

'Tears on my flying overall and on my Mae West could have been caused by the ejection up through the canopy. I was wearing a crash helmet (bone dome) and the actual jettison seemed identical to the practice we had on the test rig. I then pulled the firing handle once more to fire the seat. I blacked out immediately and the next awareness was of being out of the aircraft. Ejection did not bring me out on the surface - from a position when I fired the seat perhaps 20 feet under and with the cockpit at about 30 degrees nose down.

'I learnt later that the ship had cut the fuselage in two - the tail and a collapsed fuselage tank had been seen to pass down the ship's starboard side. I assume I was out before the ship hit the aircraft. I was not aware of any collision with the ship. As soon as I collected my wits again after the ejection I became aware of being tumbled over violently in light green sea and becoming entangled in the seat and its yellow drogue chute. I had choked in quite a lot of water by this time and the prospect of drowning was no longer unpleasant - just like drinking fresh water.

'Eventually the tumbling eased and I thought I was going to live, and then, with the most bitter disappointment, I began to be dragged slowly down, deeper and deeper. I must have reached an advanced state of drowning as I was dreamy, relaxed, comfortable, but in a sad state, slowly 'floating' deeper. I had given up the struggle.

'Suddenly the tangle freed itself, a spark of life reached my brain - but the dinghy lanyard (fastening the dinghy to the Mae West) was still pulling me down. I followed my hand down and pulled the release and after two attempts it came adrift and I began rising. For the first time I had a desperate need for air; I tried to swim upward. I suddenly remembered my Mae West and I pulled the toggle to inflate it. I popped up like a cork, into the sunshine. I surfaced astern and to port, about 200 yards from the ship. The helicopter with the strop lowered was already there waiting for me.

'My overall conviction from this was that but for the ejector seat I would never have got out of the aircraft as the water pressure would have held the canopy on and I could not have lifted it. My experience on the 'practice' ejector seat rig was much appreciated. Crash helmet and inner helmet not only protected my face and head but my ears as well.'

By some miracle Bruce had nothing but a broken collarbone and minor cuts and bruises. Later research provided naval pilots with a safe underwater ejection option. The cause of Macfarlane's engine failure was fuel stoppage in the main supply pipeline carrying fuel forward from the tanks to the burners. This horizontal pipe was six feet long, and because fuel was *sucked* along it by a pump at the front, instead of being *pushed* by a pump at the back, catapult acceleration stopped the flow of fuel for about two seconds. The fault was easily corrected; the reader may well ask why the problem was not anticipated in an aircraft designed for carrier operation.

Wyverns landing-on were meat and drink to the 'goofers', off-duty members of the ship's company who assembled on the island decks to watch the flying and who thrived on excitement, as when Sub Lieutenant Jarret speared himself dartlike into *Eagle's* funnel. He survived with little harm, but *Eagle* had to return to Portsmouth with a R-R Python stuck in her funnel. However, when I got used to handling the engine I found that at a steady 100-102 knots the irresistible steamroller-like approach was as steady as a rock.

But the Wyvern was already obsolete – it took nearly seven years from maiden flight to operational use. In June at a Naval Air Staff meeting in Malta on the subject of *Strike Aircraft for the Royal Navy*, I said that what the Navy needed was a *single-purpose* aircraft, not like the Wyvern and Firebrand, designed to do everything and doing nothing well, but a genuine high-speed, low-level, long-range aircraft which could get *under* radar defences and deliver weapons from a

XK498, the fourth development Buccaneer MK.1 Deck trials, HMS Ark Royal, 15.11.1960. BCC/MOD via Crosley

safe distance. The notion of dropping torpedoes against surface ships, which I had been ordered to practise, should be scrapped. Three weeks later Blackburns received their first contract for the prototype NA39, later to become the Buccaneer, which fitted my prescription perfectly.

813 Squadron disbanded on 19 November 1955, but not before we had given a 'lecture' to an assembly of staff officers in the station cinema at Lee-on-Solent. This took the form of mock briefing for a dawn strike in the North Atlantic against four Sverdlov-class Russian cruisers advancing towards the Fleet in a winter gale. 813's Wyverns armed with torpedoes were going to try to stop them.

My pilots sat on the stage in their Mae Wests trying to look pale and subdued, eyes set and thinking of England. I, reading my briefing a few feet from a line of Admirals in the front row, was shaking with genuine fright. Further pathos was added when I came to deal with air/sea rescue arrangements if the Russians shot us down – sea temperature near zero and no helicopters. At this point one pilot pulled the inflation knob on his Mae West and started being sick in a bucket and from there on things degenerated until, at *exeunt omnes*, we took our leave from our Captain, who had done us proud. From there I made my way to Staff College for 'further education'.

The Wyvern's successor, the Buccaneer, had catapulting problems too. When a pre-production aircraft pitched-up off *Hermes'* catapult and crashed into the sea, killing both crew, the Buccaneer Certificate of Airworthiness was suspended until something fairly basic was done to eliminate all possibility of a repeat performance, and I became involved in this work with the Naval Test Squadron at Boscombe Down.

Comparing the Buccaneer with the contemporary Sea Vixen all-weather fighter, using the catapult at the Royal Aircraft Establishment at Bedford, we found that three seconds after launch the Vixen had gained twenty-six knots airspeed, the Buccaneer a mere three and a half, and that any attempt to climb would reduce even this small margin of speed towards stall and pitch-up. Fifty feet above the water, handling was so critical that before the next sea catapult trial something had to be done to make it easier.

Changes were made to the controls and flaps to increase lift coefficient, and undercarriage retraction was speeded up to reduce drag; but the most important innovation was the 'Hands-Off Launch Technique': flaps and trim were preset according to weight and loading, double-checked by the catapult officer, and the pilot *forbidden* to touch the controls until five seconds after launch! Proved in trials in *Ark Royal* in 1963, the 'Hands-Off' technique was used in all Buccaneer catapult launches from then on.

Without it, there would have been no Buccaneer Mk1s in service at all, and a much delayed Mk2. I was given £150 for the 'invention', which I spent on a skiing holiday to get away from my next job – flying a desk in the Admiralty.

Lieutenant J.A. Tayler,
Observer, Sea Venom, HMS *Albion*, Home Waters, 1955

We were the first Sea Venom Squadron in HMS *Albion* and things were not going well: the Squadron Boss had ditched twice off the catapult and another aircraft pulled its hook out and went over the bow. When at very short notice it was decided we should disembark to Yeovilton, nobody was surprised. For me the most important question was – what was I going to do with my *hamsters*?

Another Observer, Bob McCulloch, volunteered to take one, which eased the problem; I was late and had to dash down the flight deck with engines starting all around me, only just managing to pass the squirming creature in to him before his canopy clamped shut. My aircraft, pilot Ron Davidson, being first on the catapult, I strapped in in a great rush, and while I was sorting out my navigation kit the other hamster climbed out of my pocket and wandered forward out of reach. This was no time to go looking for him. As we shot down the catapult the little chap hurtled aft to hit the bulkhead somewhere behind us with an awful thump. He lay there with no oxygen mask, probably critically injured. What a way to go! At Yeovilton in the rush of arrival, customs and so forth, I have to admit I forgot all about him.

A few days later, a Safety Equipment rating sidled up to me with a heavy wink: 'Sir? I've had to write off your 'chute with those *oil stains*!' I followed him to the hangar. In those days, before ejection seats, we used our parachutes as seat cushions, and Hammy, having survived the adventure of his life, had joyfully recognized the scent of his owner's chair and eaten his way into the heart of the tightly-packed silk. He looked very much at home in the cockpit of our de Havilland Sea Venom all-weather jet fighter.

Lieutenant J.C. COWARD,

Pilot, Avenger, 814 Squadron, HMS Centaur, *North Atlantic, 1955*

Operating near the Arctic Circle north of the Shetlands with HMS *Albion* against a Canadian 'enemy' fleet, *Centaur* with two Seahawk squadrons and 814's Avengers had been experiencing arrester-gear problems. I was on my first operational tour, having embarked in the Mediterranean in February.

Just after sunset on 23 September 1955 I took off with a full load of Glow-worm rocket flares tasked to search for submarines and/or the 'enemy' fleet. I heard the last two day-fighter Seahawks slotting into *Centaur's* landing pattern as I trundled up the deck and off the bow, at which point the radio and intercom went dead. We soon got the intercom back, but without the VHF radio we were going to have to land back on.

Here I must introduce the other characters in the ensuing drama. My crew: Observer Tony Saunders - very good but prone to airsickness. When he got sick I opened the hood and he froze, but never complained. (We never used the heater, a fearsome petrol stove down in the rear cabin). Telegraphist Air Gunner (TAG) L/Tel Perkins, an excellent fellow who sat in the rear cabin and was primarily the sonobuoy operator. In case of intercom failure he could crawl up a tunnel to the Observer, who had a long cane with a paper-clip with which he could prod the pilot and pass messages. Finally the Avenger itself, slow but comfortable with plenty of fuel and an enormous weapon load, a lovely aircraft to fly. But the large American cockpit made it difficult to reach some controls without first unlocking the seat-harness with an extremely awkward left-handed lever behind the seat: there were five fuel tanks with tiny little gauges, and a fuel cock right down between the rudder pedals to switch tanks, usually when the engine coughed; and the lever for the cowl-gills, air-flaps around the cowling to control engine temperature, was out of reach the shoulder-straps locked. These big gills had to be open at slow speeds in the landing circuit, to keep the engine temperature down, but closed on final approach if you wanted to see the deck.

Back to the scene of action. My first need was to get rid of the rocket-flares. Arrested landings with live rockets were unpopular because they often came off the rails and slid up the deck. I tried firing them off but they wouldn't go: another electrical problem. I carried on with the Standard Operating Procedure for landing after radio failure, flying up the 'slot' on *Centaur's* starboard side rocking my wings, then across the bow into the landing circuit at 200 feet – only to get a wave-off from 'Bats' on final approach. On my next try there was no 'Bats', just a steady red light, so I climbed out to the 'wait' position nearby to await developments.

Tony noticed an Aldis lamp flashing at us and Perkins in the upper gun turret managed to read the order 'GO TO *ALBION*'.

We found *Albion* about 30 miles north, relieved that she had some lights on. Assuming she was steaming into wind, I descended slowly in total blackness to 500 feet, and from there down past the masthead light to get a rough altimeter check as I could not see the water. Round the circuit; hook, wheels, flaps down;

Avenger: '...slow but comfortable...' Lt Coward lands on, HMS *Centaur* 1955. Bats in foreground. Coward

torch out to check their little indicators on the panel; nicely set up downwind and – a red light from the ship.

More orbits overhead, until finally a green 'C' from below, the order to 'Charlie', i.e. land, and hoping that *Albion's* Batsman was OK in the dark – she was not a night operator at that time, and furthermore had recently got a Mirror Landing Sight which made batsmen redundant – I came down into the circuit, hauled round the final approach, prop in fine pitch making lots of noise. Suddenly the ship vanished. With a superhuman effort I reached the lever to shut the cowl-gills and she reappeared. Bats seemed to know what he was doing, and on the CUT signal I chopped the throttle, levelled the wings and heaved back on the stick into a good three-point landing. A wire jerked us to a stop. Two rockets came off their rails, shot off up the deck in a shower of sparks and slid overboard.

The 'powers' in *Albion* were not happy about the rockets, but otherwise everybody was very kind. We learned that the first Seahawk to land on *Centaur* broke the arrester gear and the other barely made it to a diversion field in Norway.

Our radio was fixed, but for the next three days the weather was too bad to fly. On 26 September we took off for *Centaur* after a pre-dawn briefing at which the Met Officer produced a blank chart and a warning of 'moderate sea state and a front out to the west somewhere'. With our task the same as before, we launched just before dawn and began a complex search pattern to try to find the 'enemy'. As time went by I occasionally caught a glimpse of big white horses down below the clouds and suspected the wind might have changed, but Tony, though cold and sick as usual, seemed unperturbed.

After two and a quarter hours, when we should have been overhead 'mother' at the end of our patrol, *Centaur* was nowhere to be seen. This was not unusual, but our radar showed nothing for forty miles around.

Lt Coward, second from right. Coward

Notwithstanding the Cold War and Russian spy-trawlers everywhere and constant warnings about radio security, I broke radio silence to call the ship – no reply. I tried *Centaur's* homer beacon, the 'YE' – no signal. Some time after taking off from *Albion* we had had another total radio failure; till now, not having found the 'enemy', there had been no occasion to talk to anyone.

Enter the TAG.. Perkins somehow coaxed his HF radio into life and to our great relief got a bearing from *Centaur*. She had heard our carrier-wave on VHF, *hoped* it was us and sent two Avengers down the bearing to find us. We met them coming out and they escorted us home, very late and low on fuel.

The official comment? – 'Didn't you notice the wind change at the front?'

Lieutenant Maurice Tibby,
Pilot, Seahawk, 803 Squadron, HMS *Centaur*, Moray Firth, 1955

For launching or recovering aircraft, a carrier must steam into wind, often at high speed in an undesirable direction, so all aspects of flying operations are constantly honed to reduce this into-wind time to the absolute minimum. A well worked-up ship and air-group could land aircraft at 25-second intervals, and to get the deck clear and arrester gear reset in this time required not only a high degreee of skill from pilots, but also maximum alertness and concentration from everybody on deck.

From the pilot's point of view this meant getting the hook up quickly without fouling the arrester wire, then accelerating rapidly off the landing area and into the for'ard deck park while raising the flaps and folding the wings. The previous aircraft were usually still manoeuvring into position when one came off the angle into the park.

Such was the situation on board *Centaur* on 6 September 1955 in the Moray Firth, when I landed an 803 Squadron Seahawk, raised my hook and flaps and accelerated smartly out of the wires with the wings beginning to fold: all normal procedure. That was the last normal thing that happened to me that day.

When I pulled the throttle back and braked it was soon apparent that the anticipated deceleration was not forthcoming. I applied the emergency brake but to no avail as the Seahawk, with locked wheels dragging and engine racing uncontrollably up to full power, ploughed into the for'ard deck park.

First contact was with the aircraft which had landed ahead of me, still folding its wings. My half-folded right wing struck it with an impact which swung me to starboard into collision with a third Seahawk which virtually broke my aircraft in half and, leaving the tail section behind, I plunged over the side at full power into the sea. All in less time than it takes to tell.

'...locked wheels and engine racing...' BCC/MOD via Tibby

'...first contact...' BCC/MOD via Tibby

I'm told the following few minutes were pure Hollywood as all aircraft behind me were diverted ashore, helicopters buzzed frantically and sea-boats were lowered. The ship began a head count to see who might be missing, and dazed

'...broke in half...' BCC/MOD via Tibby

'...and plunged over the side...' BCC/MOD via Tibby

flight-deck crews tried to come to terms with what had happened. Besides me, two others had gone into the sea: one squadron rating leapt clear overboard to save himself, and Sub Lieutenant Sam Janes, 803's Electrical Officer, not so fortunate, was struck by my Seahawk's nose and swept off the deck, landing in the sea sixty feet below flat on his chest and seriously damaging his lungs.

The remains of my aircraft hit the water on its side with its wings folded and before it sank I was able to scramble out with nothing worse than a badly bruised arm. The Planeguard helicopter picked us all up and returned us on board. Sam Janes was transferred to Inverness hospital where, after a few anxious days, he eventually made a complete recovery.

Tibby and his tail. Tibby

Lieutenant George Barras,
Pilot, Wyvern, 813 Squadron, HMS *Eagle*, Mediterranean 1956.

My first deck landing, in the early 1950s, was in a Harvard trainer aboard the USS *Monterey* off Florida as part of flying training with the US Navy in Pensacola, the next some time later in a Wyvern, an aircraft with an interesting reputation and not the easiest to deck-land. Although a very stable machine, from about a hundred yards out the long nose totally obscured the landing area of the deck, leaving the pilot to find the centre-line by keeping in the middle between the mirror landing sight on the left and the island superstructure on the right. It was a bit hit and miss as to which wire, if any, was caught, and there was a high proportion of 'bolters' (missed all the wires, go round again).

Compared with our efforts, the ease and precision with which other aircraft landed on deck was galling, but the reason became plain when I was instructing at Lossiemouth on Vampires and Seahawks and the Dutch carrier *Karel Doorman* came into the area and offered her deck for deck-landing practice. I jumped at the opportunity, and what an enlightening experience it was! Sitting in the front of a Seahawk you could see the whole deck, *select* your touchdown point and choose which wire you wanted! Now I understood why, after a string of Seahawks had landed one day aboard *Eagle*, we Wyverns had to ask for the Mirror landing aid to be switched on. They hadn't even noticed it was off. It seemed unfair they got paid the same as us.

Not long after the Suez cease-fire in 1956, flying a Wyvern on low-level intercepts from *Eagle* in the eastern Mediterranean, I smelt burning. I was alone,

HMS Eagle, 1955. Interim angled deck. 813 Wyverns aft. Foreground, 897/898 Squadron Seahawks: '...sitting right in the nose, you could see the WHOLE deck!' Barras

'...I eventually flopped on to the deck.' BCC/MOD via Barras

60 miles from the ship; everything looked normal and the engine was running fine, but when the cockpit began to fill with smoke I declared an emergency and turned towards 'Mother'. When the engine fire warning light came on, by the rules (fire warning confirmed by smoke) I should have ejected there and then, so I upgraded the emergency to a Mayday, tidied up the cockpit, lowered the ejection seat ready for use and pulled back the throttle to see if the red light would go out. It did, and I found that it would stay out provided I used just enough power to keep me in the air. Thus I wallowed slowly home and with much relief found the ship steaming into wind ready for me to flop on to the deck.

The engineers found a cleaning rag on top of the engine reduction gearbox, right under one of the fire-detector switches; hence the smell, the smoke, the fire-warning, and very nearly the loss of one Wyvern and a dunking for me.

Lieutenant G.J. 'Tank' Sherman
Pilot, Seahawk, Naval Air Fighter School, RNAS Lossiemouth, 1956.

On 9 February 1956, as a student at the fighter school at Lossiemouth flying Seahawks, I was being introduced to the mysteries of 'battle' formation – a loose flexible formation with pairs of aircraft about half a mile abreast covering each others' tails and able to respond rapidly to threats from any direction. I was flying Number 2 to Flight Lieutenant Dickie Wirdnam, on exchange from the Royal Air Force, in a three-ship formation instead of the usual four. After practising an emergency 'break' which left Seahawks all over the sky, he set up an orbit at 4000 feet, told us where he was and ordered us to rejoin him for a tail-chase.

I spotted him quickly and was closing with great gusto at high speed, pulling to the 7g limit to stop myself overshooting and get inside his turn, when there was an almighty great bang and my Seahawk flicked over to the right and started spinning extremely violently down towards the earth 4000 feet below. Thinking I had pulled too hard and gone into a high-speed stall and/or hit Leader's slipstream, I reacted instinctively with the time-honoured 'standard spin-recovery technique' – full rudder against the spin, stick fully forward...

At that moment the starboard wing came off.

The words of the Instructor in the Ejection Seat lecture rang in my mind: 'If you have to eject, DON'T panic. Proceed in a leisurely fashion – FEET Back, JETTISON the canopy, and PULL the blind'.

Feet came back OK. Next I pulled the black-and-yellow canopy jettison handle and – NOTHING! This was the second time in my flying career I had pulled a canopy jettison handle. Nothing happened that time either, but that's another story. By now I reckoned my sands of time were running out, the aircraft was mostly upside-down and gyrating crazily towards the spinning earth. I was going to have to eject through the canopy. My enthusiasm for this was dampened by the knowledge that the last guy to do so, and not so long ago, had killed himself because a shard of canopy disabled his seat barostat. I closed my eyes and yanked down the face-blind firing handle.

Starting with about minus 3g on the inverted aircraft, it was not an ideal ejection. Seahawk straps were renowned for poor vertical restraint. I was hanging well clear of the seat whose primitive 60-foot-per-second double cartridge gave me the biggest boot up the ass I ever had in my life, 22g out through the glass.

Six seconds later – a second for the drogue gun delay plus five more for the drogue to stabilize and slow the seat – I 'hit the silk', as the saying goes. I estimate the Seahawk's rate of descent when I left it was about 300 feet per second, and my parachute opened 100 feet above the ground.

As I hung briefly in space the plane spun past me and exploded in an impressive fireball close below. Banal thoughts of frying pans and fires passed briefly through my mind, but in the event I landed about ten yards clear of the inferno.

After a short pause a gallant Scots lady hove in sight and came to rest alongside. She had rushed over a couple of fields from a nearby farmhouse, pausing only to grab a bottle of whisky and a couple of glasses. When I told her alcohol was the worst thing in the world for shock, she hastily withdrew the bottle – until I said I was only joking.

Relaxing beside the fire, I soon found out what had happened Our Number 3 in the formation had cut off my tail with his wing, in the process shortening his own wing somewhat, and when he found he was unable to control his aircraft below 300 knots he decided to eject too. So, making sure he was over dry land, he pointed his Seahawk out to sea where it would do no harm and calmly and deliberately ejected. In fact he got it wrong on both counts: his lame aircraft immediately and predictably turned back, rolled over and dived into a field not far from mine; and the offshore breeze carried him out over the Moray Firth and dropped him in the water, from which he was rescued quickly by a fisherman who brought him in and landed him back near me. Lossiemouth's Search and Rescue helicopter arrived all too soon and broke up a very good party, but as I remember there was not much whisky left by then anyway.

Meanwhile Dickie Wirdnam was turning the air blue cursing the two would-be jet fighter pilots who were apparently unable to find him on a clear day in perfect visibility. He called exasperatedly on the radio; 'I am orbiting two very large bonfires – you MUST be able to see me!' When at last he put two and two together, he came down and gave us a wave.

Back at the ranch, the sun was setting on Scotland's short winter day as we two survivors alighted unsteadily from the helicopter to be greeted by the redoubtable Captain Percy Gick. 'It's too late to get airborne again now,' he said, 'but I've arranged for you both to fly on the first detail tomorrow morning. Meanwhile, see you in the bar in half an hour!'

Next morning I was indeed down to fly No. 3 on the first detail, but I awoke with not only a great hangover but also a backache so bad I could not get out of bed. I was rushed to Inverness Hospital with severe compression fractures of three lumbar vertebrae which prevented me from flying for six months. I thus had time to hop over to Denmark in pursuit of the love of my life who had gone there to escape me, and forty years later we are still very happily married - yet another story.

I had backache for most of those forty years. The doctors told me nothing could be done about it, and I chalked it up to experience – a small price to pay for being alive.

Lieutenant John Winton,
Assistant Damage Control Officer, HMS *Eagle*, Suez, 1956

At the time of Suez I was Assistant Damage Control officer in the carrier *Eagle*. Firefighting, pumping, counter-flooding, ventilation and water-tight integrity were my job, and as it turned out they were all to play a much more important part in events than I ever anticipated.

I cannot find it in my heart to feel the least affection for *Eagle*. Built by Harland and Wolff in Belfast, we sailors were convinced the shipbuilders must have locked a black leprechaun up somewhere inside her. She was chronically accident-prone on an almost operatic scale. Besides the fires and floods that kept my department on its toes, there would be the occasional 'cold shot' from the catapult to launch some hapless aircrew into the sea. Even 'goofing', a traditional spare-time activity, was fraught with danger as from time to time the flight deck was swept with a storm of lethal shrapnel from the contra-rotating propellers of an 830 Squadron Wyvern tipping on its nose while landing. An abiding memory of *Eagle* is of interminable broadcast warnings: 'Clear the Goofers! Wyverns landing on!'

Everything in the ship seemed designed to work in the most awkward way. Getting about was a nightmare; the ship's motto was *Arduus ad Solem*, which the sailors translated as 'Ard on the Feet'. Like the Red Queen in *Through the looking Glass*, we in *Eagle* seemed to have to run like hell just to stay in the same place, and if you wanted to get to somewhere else you had to run at least twice as fast.

Eagle was in Naples when Nasser seized the Suez Canal on Thursday 26 July, and sailed on Monday morning, 30 July, to embark and work up her Squadrons in a programme of intensive flying and exercising with other British and French ships. I cannot recall any particular sense of urgency or feeling that the ship might be about to go to war. In fact the Canal seemed to retreat further and further from our minds as the Mediterranean summer wore on.

Eagle lost a Seahawk pilot of 897 on 16 August. He crashed into the sea while night flying, and his body was picked up at dawn. And there were the usual *Eagle* alarms and excursions: an unattended Lansing Bagnall truck running off the flight deck into the sea; a flood in a Bofors magazine when a valve was opened by a Damage Control patrol – whose specific job it was to prevent such floods. On 5 September Lieutenant L.E. Middleton of 897 (of later fame as Captain of *Hermes* in the Falklands) had a fire in his Seahawk on take-off and ditched ahead of the ship, but was picked up safely.

And so life went on in typically *Eagle* fashion until a self-maintenance period in Gibraltar was unexpectedly cut short on 20 October and we sailed in haste at midday, embarking our aircraft that afternoon. For the very first time, there was a sense of anticipation, especially as we set off eastward at uncommonly high speed. Grand Harbour, Malta, on 26 October 1956 presented a sight not often seen – four British carriers, *Eagle, Albion, Bulwark,* and *Theseus,* the latter with Whirlwind helicopters of 845 Squadron. A fifth carrier, *Ocean,* was on her way with the Whirlwinds and Sycamores of the Joint Experimental Helicopter Unit, known as JEHU.

Tension was rising in the Near East. An impressively bedraggled-looking Egyptian destroyer passed close down *Eagle's* side on her way out of Grand Harbour on the morning of 29 October. Flying started at once. *Eagle* had two of the latest and last of the big hydraulic catapults, and true to form one of the first launches that day broke the main reeving wire on the starboard catapult, pitching a Seahawk into the sea ahead of the ship. Several tons of hydraulic ram machinery slammed unchecked into the bow with an impact that rocked the ship. On the quarterdeck at the time, I heard it clearly and felt the thump through the soles of my feet. The catapult watch-keeper was discovered standing at the top of the ram room access hatchway gibbering with fright. The Seahawk pilot, once again the unfortunate Middleton, surfaced after being underwater for more than three minutes.

With one catapult irreparably out of action, all now depended upon the port catapult, whose reeving wires were due for replacement soon – an eight-day task. Such was the state of the flagship of the Carrier Squadron Commander, Vice Admiral Sir Manley Power, as *Eagle* thundered eastward at the start of Operation MUSKETEER.

On 30 October the aircrew were issued with special equipment: pistols, survival packs, khaki clothing etc. The ship's company shifted into action working dress and we were issued with anti-flash gear, which I cannot remember ever putting on; then we were lectured by a fierce Royal Marine Major on survival techniques if we were shot down, getting some very helpful hints on edible fruit and berries, collecting firewood, telling which way was north if we didn't have a compass by noting which side the moss was growing on tree trunks, grid references, flares and so on.. The Major's main point, heavily emphasized, was that if we were captured we were only to give our names and ranks and, if very hard-pressed, the name of our ship.

'What happens if they cut off your privates?' a voice piped up from the back.

'Well,' said the Major after some thought, 'it *would* be a pity to let the occasion pass without comment.'

On what became known as D-Day, 31 October, operations against military targets in Egypt were authorized. *Eagle* flew Combat Air Patrols (CAPs) and reconnaissance flights all day, but the signal for offensive action never came. The radar plot began to show formations of RAF Canberras and Valiants on their way in to bomb Egyptian airfields. The highly-publicized RAF claims of how devastating these raids had been caused great irritation; in fact, for the effort involved they did very little damage.

The first Seahawk and Sea Venom strikes flew off early next day, 1 November, 'D+1', and as the day went on the carriers established a steady cycle, turning into wind and flying off strikes every sixty-five minutes; the attacks were extended inland and the turbo-prop Wyverns also took part. *Eagle* flew 138 sorties that day and the combined carrier squadrons claimed 71 aircraft destroyed and 92 damaged.

That evening, just before dinner, came the rather terrifying sound of the General Alarm and I rushed to my action station in Damage Control 'HQ Two' which duplicated the main Damage Control centre, 'HQ One'; if catastrophe befell HQ One, then we in HQ Two would take over.

We experienced a thrill of apprehension when a stoker from HQ1 told us we were about to be attacked by a flotilla of fast Egyptian E-boats, but nothing happened and soon we fell out from action stations, feeling rather sheepish. The radar echoes of fast-moving 'E-boats' turned out to be migrating flocks of Arctic terns.

By noon on D+2 all the main Egyptian airfields had been bombed and strafed, and when photographic evidence and debriefing showed that the Egyptian Air Force had been virtually eliminated, attention was shifted to transport depots, camps, vehicles and oil storages.

Although air opposition was non-existent, the Egyptian AA gunners improved with practice. A Sea Venom of 893 Squadron was hit, the observer injured and the hydraulic supply to the undercarriage severed. The pilot, Lieutenant Commander Wilcox, made a copy-book 'wheels-up' landing on board *Eagle*, but his observer, Flying Officer Olding, later had his left leg amputated above the knee. On 3 November a Wyvern was hit and the pilot, Lieutenant McCarthy, ejected into the sea only 4,000 yards from a shore battery. Fighters patrolled over him until a helicopter arrived from *Eagle* some 70 miles away.

On Sunday 4 November *Eagle* lost another Wyvern in a strike on Port Said when Lieutenant Commander Cowling was hit and had to eject. He, too, was picked up by helicopter.

By now, American disapproval was making itself apparent. Ships of the Sixth Fleet were operating so close that Admiral Durnford-Slater, the Task Force Commander, had to ask the American admiral to move over; he refused, but was obliged to signal the Pentagon: 'Whose side am I on?' Towering columns of black smoke rose from oil tanks ashore as *Eagle* pounded to and fro looking for enough wind for flying. Below decks all bulkhead doors were shut and the heat was intense.

On 6 November, after a bombardment by cruisers and destroyers, the Royal Marine Commandos, Royal Tank Regiment, and the French Foreign Legion went ashore in Port Said. In the first ever helicopter-borne assault landing, the whole of 45 Commando, some 435 men and 23 tons of stores, were landed from *Ocean* and *Theseus* in 90 minutes.

That day we lost a Seahawk of 897, when the late Donald Mills, who died at home on Christmas Day 1993, ejected over the desert east of the Canal; British and French fighters protected him until *Eagle's* helicopter arrived. A close friend of mine since the terrible day at Dartmouth when I was nominated to be Chief Cadet Captain on Sunday Divisions and he prompted me from behind on the correct orders to give the parade, his narrow escape brought home to me the true nature of the business we were in.

Rumours persisted throughout 6 November of the cease-fire which came into effect at 11 pm that night.

The feeling was that MUSKETEER as a whole had been well done, whatever the politicians said. *Eagle's* port catapult had done 631 launches since leaving Malta and was now somewhat frayed. Admiral Power and his staff transferred by helicopter to *Bulwark* on the 7th and *Eagle* went to Malta, returning for another extended period off Suez on 13 November.

When the General Alarm sounded just after tea on the 19th instinct told me it was for real, but as always in a real emergency it was almost impossible to find out what was going on. Down in HQ2 I was only slowly able to piece the story together: someone had been working on a Sea Venom in the lower hangar when its guns fired and set off a major fire. I was ordered to investigate.

The moment I reached the lobby leading to the hangar access-doors air lock, I knew this was the real thing. The vicious intensity of a big fire below decks, with fittings jumping off the bulkheads and burning heat in one's throat with every breath, is impossible to simulate or imagine.

The fire and emergency party in the lobby looked worried. The heat from inside the hangar was increasing rapidly, and suddenly there was a terrific crash as a cannon shell hit the bulkhead. Directly below me was a compartment known as Hell's Kitchen which contained flood and spray controls for several magazines, below that a bomb room, and then the Avgas storage (high octane petrol) with its cofferdam. Outboard of me were two Bofors magazines and just forward was the oxygen plant. Breathing the fiercely hot air become more and more difficult, and it became plain to me that we were fast approaching an explosion that might well blow most of the forward end of the ship off. The moment came when, like many before me, I said to myself, 'You've been drawing the Queen's money all these years, now's your chance to earn it'.

I told the fire and emergency party to get their gear together. We would start by spraying the hangar. I had no idea whether HQ1 had already ordered this drastic measure, but something had to be done, and quickly.

The hangar sprays were my department, six huge pumps in the bottom of the ship delivering I forget how many hundreds of tons of water per hour. A Mechanician – Hodge was his name – had maintained and cherished those pumps for nearly two years. They were started by pulling a chain in the access air lock and then turning a large handwheel valve. In the airlock I could smell paint burning. There was another terrifying crash against the inner door, right by my elbow. I pulled the chain, but the handwheel was too hot to grip. I got out a handkerchief and bound it round and tried again but it was stuck. Dear God, I thought, and lifted my foot and kicked it, whereupon it spun open and seconds later I could hear the drumming of water in the hangar like a mightly monsoon.

It made a fearful mess in the hangar, but we were flying again next day. We also held the funeral of Naval Airman Naylor of 893 Squadron who died in the fire. Damage Control had been all right on the night. In the absence of any official praise I let it be known discreetly that I thought Hodge had done extremely well, and that on a certain day at a certain time I proposed to tell him so, in HQ2.

At the appointed time I could not get in through the door. The place was packed. The entire off-watch Damage Control department was there – patrols, seamen, stokers, engine-room artificers, electricians and shipwrights. Stores people were there, hangar sentries, flightdeck people and all the squadrons were represented. There was no room for me so I stood at the door waiting to say my piece. But it wasn't needed. Someone began to clap, then another, working up slowly to a storm of applause. Poor Hodge, I can see him now. He went red, then white, and for an awful moment I thought he was going to burst into tears. Far down below the dash and glamour of the flight deck, I was proud to shake his hand with the rest.

Lieutenant P.H. 'Jan' Stuart,
Observer, Skyraider, 849 Squadron, HMS *Albion*, Home and Mediterranean, 1956-7

My introduction to the Skyraider was on 6 January 1956 when I joined 849 Airborne Early Warning (AEW) Squadron. I fell in love with it as soon as I climbed into the spacious observers' cockpit and saw the ashtray. This superb aeroplane could fly for four hours or more.

Normally at sea we were ranged right aft and did free take-offs with our 2700 horsepower often getting us airborne before we reached the island. On one memorable occasion, ranged for take-off aboard HMS *Albion*, the engine started, the intercom came alive as usual, but when I switched the radar to warm-up there was a blinding flash, the cabin filled with smoke and the intercom went dead. I couldn't tell David Burke up front in the cockpit what had happened, but we in the back scrambled out and made for the safety of the catwalk.

Increasing volumes of black smoke billowed from the Skyraider's back doors and blew aft in the slipstream, but David's eyes were on the nearest Flight Deck Officer, who in turn was looking up the deck at Flyco's traffic lights. I was contemplating a suicide dash across the deck among the thrashing propellers when at last for some reason David looked our way, made a classic double take when he saw his crew gesticulating from the deck-edge, stopped the engine and joined us as quickly as he decently could, leaving the smoking aircraft to the fire crew.

A very versatile aircraft, the Skyraider. In 1956 the Paratroopers who had gone in on Day One of the short and abortive Suez War to capture Gamil airfield signalled that their water supply was contaminated. They were thirsty, they said. First thoughts in *Albion* on receipt of the signal were to fit our four Skyraiders with long-range tanks full of water and fly it ashore; nothing could be simpler, but when the ship's Medical Officer vetoed the idea – he would not be able to pass the water as fit for human consumption, not even paratroopers – another solution had to be found.

Albion's Welfare Committee rose to the occasion by offering to send them canned beer, and as to how to get it ashore, what better than the back of our capacious Skyraiders? A quick check proved the beer capacity of the Douglas AD-4W to be about 1000 cans, and on 6 November at 1015 WV178 did a free take-off with me and a full load of beer in the back for the paras at Gamil. They were not slow in unloading the freight and getting to grips with the urgent business of slaking their raging thirst. My pilot, Squadron Boss Lt Cdr Noddy Fuller, went in search of his brother who was a Captain in the Para Brigade, only to find he had been shot in a very tender place by one of his own sentries and was lying spreadeagled in a hospital bed in the *Empire Fowey* in the harbour. The paras took us to visit said brother in a commandeered Egyptian Cadillac, and gave us each a captured Russian carbine as a souvenir.

For a while after this it was noticed that paratrooper water supply was becoming a recurring problem, but alas *Albion*, having done her duty supporting the Army in foreign parts, moved away.

Although the Skyraider's big radial was a lullaby of engineering, for reasons which were never explained it did have a habit of faltering now and again. Flying again with David Burke, from *Albion* in home waters this time, programmed for an area shipping reconnaissance in the Moray Firth, we were fired off the catapult at 1925GMT on 21 May 1957. Seconds later the engine stopped dead. In the ensuing deep silence I heard David say something like 'Oh dear!' I have no idea how long that magnificent airframe defied gravity in the bracing Scottish air, but after a bit there was a mighty roar of power from up front and we hauled around the circuit to land straight back on. Thank you David, our feet never touched the water.

'...a lullaby of engineering...' Skyraider WT 958, HMS Albion, Mediterranean 1956. Stuart

Lieutenant Commander John Hackett RN JP,
Senior Observer 809 Squadron, Sea Venom FAW21, HMS *Albion*, Suez 1956

Immediately the British Government declared a state of emergency on 2 August 1956 following Egypt's 'Nationalization' of the Suez Canal, 809 Squadron (Lieutenant Commander Ron Shilcock) based at RNAS Yeovilton began an intensive work-up programme in training for what might be expected in Egypt, especially day and night low-level intruder missions with Glow-worm rocket flares and Rocket-Projectiles (R/P). On 15 September the squadron embarked in HMS *Albion* (Captain R.M.Smeeton) together with 800 and 802 Seahawk squadrons and 849 'C' Flight's Skyraiders. A similar mix of aircraft was embarked in the carriers *Bulwark* and *Eagle*, the latter also having a squadron of Wyverns, while *Theseus* and *Ocean* operated helicopters only. Squadron work-ups continued through October, either at sea or disembarked at RNAS Hal Far in Malta.

By the end of that month all carrier Squadrons were ready for what had come to be called Operation MUSKETEER, whose two main objectives were to preserve freedom of traffic through the Suez Canal and to reaffirm Britain's overall position in the Middle East. When the opposition in Parliament under Hugh Gaitskell began attacking the Prime Minister's policy, we at sea felt strongly that we had been let down instead of being supported by the country as a whole.

All embarked aircrew now received five gold sovereigns to bribe the natives with if we were shot down, a paper Union Jack and a list of patriotic phrases in Arabic, a silk map of the area around the Suez Canal and a revolver. The gold sovereigns were to be returned at the end of hostilities, on pain of court martial. Censorship was imposed. Strictly against the rules I kept a brief diary of a memorable November 1956:

1st First strikes by Fleet Air Arm squadrons launched at 0520.
Attacked Almaza airfield at 0601 with 4 Sea Venoms. Aircraft on ground attacked and destroyed, thought to be MiG-15s. Flew four sorties during the day, three as CAP [Combat Air Patrol]. Suspect Subs. inside screen at night.

2nd Struck Inchas airfield at 0559 with 20mm cannon but little sign of life and no aircraft. Squadron also attacked Almaza. Sea Venom from HMS *Eagle* hit and one Seahawk lost in sea on landing on HMS *Bulwark* (Sub. Lieut. Chris Hall). Another 4 sorties throughout the day.

3rd Replenishment at Sea.

4th While flying CAP north of Nile Delta found and attacked one of three E-Boats with 20mm cannon. Severely damaged.

5th Flew 4 sorties of Cab-rank during the day in support of airborne parachute landing at Port Said. 6 Sea Venoms were launched every 2 hours. Attacked dug-in tanks with R/P, mortar positions, buildings and one truck left ablaze.

6th Anglo-French landings at Port Said. Attacked tanks and trucks south of Port Said, then CAP over Lieut Donald Mills whose Sea Hawk of 897 Squadron had been shot down near al-Qantara. (He was subsequently rescued by a Whirlwind from HMS *Eagle*).

7th   Flew armed reconnaissance down Suez Canal from Port Said to Ismalia; accurate anti-aircraft fire presumed to be from Russian radar controlled guns. HMS *Eagle* returned to Malta with unserviceable catapults. Cease fire announced.

8th   Sea Venoms and Seahawks flew CAP. Action station at 0600 for unidentified aircraft. Weather blowing up. Stood by from 1800 to 2100 to investigate ships leaving Alexandria. Censorship lifted.

9th   Refuelling at sea. Still blowing half a gale. No flying.

12th 30 days at sea! Egypt agreed to United Nations policing.

26th Left Port Said for Malta.

29th HMS *Albion* arrives Grand Harbour, Malta. Squadrons to Hal Far.

Albion arrived home on 5 March 1957. Looking back on Operation Musketeer some years afterwards I wrote, 'Historically and politically it may have been seen as a disaster, but for those of us who were engaged in it in the air or on the ground it was a job to be done with whatever resources we had at our disposal. When all the dust has settled what one remembers above all else is the comradeship and friendship of everyone concerned, as well as their total commitment. For me personally Suez was a rewarding experience which I still recall vividly and with emotion.

Lieutenant A.R. Robinson,
Pilot, Gannet AS Mk1, 820 Squadron, HMS *Bulwark*, North Sea, 1957

September 25 1957 was a beautiful day of calm seas, sunshine and tremendous visibility for several hundred NATO ships taking part in Exercise MAINBRACE in the North Sea. As a junior pilot flying anti-submarine Gannets in 820 Squadron aboard my first carrier, HMS *Bulwark*, I was briefed to 'get airborne and call HMS *Eagle* for instructions'.

This I did, with my regular observer Geoff Thomas and Telegraphist Farley, and we were delighted on such a magnificent day to be ordered to search all the Norwegian Arctic fiords between certain latitudes for 'enemy' ships. We set off at 3000ft, having shut down one engine, the normal way of extending the range of the Gannet, each of whose contra-rotating propellers was driven by its own engine; the aircraft would fly very adequately and economically on one engine, and the 'dead' one could normally be windmilled into life in a matter of seconds.

Far ahead, sixty miles beyond the stationary propeller, Norway's snow-clad mountains were clearly visible. A perfect day until half way to the coast when a friendly Skyraider equally full of *joie de vivre* made a pass at us, coincidentally my engine suddenly stopped, we lost height rapidly, the other engine refused to start and I carried out the smoothest landing I ever made, in the sea.

'...now got out and joined us...' Tibby

When the spray subsided we were sitting perfectly level in a calm sea and Geoff and I wasted no time in vacating our cockpits and walking out along the port wing, inflating our Mae Wests and preparing to board our dinghies, at which point we realized that Tel. Farley was not with us. Facing aft in his rear cockpit, and for some reason having turned off his intercom, the first he knew of our plight was when we started sliding along the sea. As the Gannet began to settle, Farley got out and joined us. Geoff darted back and retrieved his binoculars from his cockpit seconds before our aircraft dipped its nose and vanished on its way to the bottom of the Arctic Ocean.

Geoff and I were soon comfortable in our dinghies with our SARBE Search And Rescue Beacons working, but poor Farley, his second mistake of the day, had failed to roll up the waist-seal of his immersion suit properly and was not so happy when the icy sea quickly found its way in. However, the astonished and perhaps guilt-ridden Skyraider pilot immediately summoned help, and 45 minutes later one of *Eagle's* helicopters hauled us out of the sea and delivered us back to *Bulwark*.

Summoned to the bridge to explain what had happened, I was doing just this when an *Eagle* Seahawk pilot, one Barry Hartwell, floated down on the end of a parachute and dropped in the water close by. Our helicopter promptly returned the compliment by picking him up and delivering him back to his ship.

Lieutenant Bob McCulloch,
Observer, Sea Venom, 894 Squadron, HMS *Eagle*, Moray Firth 1957

In August 1957 *Eagle* was in the Moray Firth off RNAS Lossiemouth, preparing for the annual NATO 'autumn war', Exercise STRIKEBACK, usually held in foul weather up in the Iceland-Faroes gap. Appropriately, work-up operations were being made difficult by sea fog and a stagnant warm front.

I was airborne on 9 August in a pair of Sea Venom NF22s doing practice radar intercepts, when towards the end of the sortie the weather suddenly closed in. The only way of getting back on deck was going to be a primitive Carrier Controlled Approach (CCA), Air Traffic Controllers using the ship's radar to talk us down until we were close enough to see the deck and land.

Such was the theory. In fact none of the ship's radars was designed for such precise close-in work on a small fast-moving target, and not surprisingly we saw nothing of the ship on our first approach. Next time round, after a large missed-approach pattern that consumed a lot of fuel, in our eagerness to get aboard we probably went a little lower than we should, for very shortly after the controller advised 'Look ahead for the mirror...' *Eagle's* 150ft grey superstructure, bristling with aerials, flashed past our left wing-tip in the fog. It should have been on the other side. Half the line-up error and we would have flown square into the back of the funnel. I made our feelings known to the controller as pilot Bunny Warren powered us back up into the cloud and all aircraft were then ordered to divert and land ashore.

RNAS Lossiemouth being closed for runway repairs, RAF Kinloss a few miles along the coast was nominated as our diversion field. A major air base, Kinloss was equipped with precision GCA Ground Controlled Approach radar with which to talk us down on to their enormous runway.

Such was the theory. In practice Kinloss GCA operators were used to dealing with one or two slow-moving Shackleton maritime patrol aircraft movements a day. Eight or ten Navy jets, short of fuel, all clamouring for immediate landing in marginal weather, were another kettle of fish and things did not go smoothly. As far as Bunny and I were concerned, our fuel gauge told us we could not afford to take our turn in the Kinloss 'stack'. Cloud-base was 200 feet and getting worse. It was a matter of *sauve qui peut*. We would do our own approach. Using the sharp coastal echo on my AI-21 radar, I conned Bunny down below cloud over the sea and into Findhorn Bay towards the western end of Kinloss's east-west runway. But we shot past it in the mist without seeing anything until in desperation Bunny called for the runway control van to fire some Very lights. Seeing the glow of one of these, he did a very tight circuit, extremely low, and just managed to put the aircraft on the concrete before the engine stopped. Both tyres burst on touchdown. Our momentum was just enough to get us off the runway to let the others land, which they all did safely.

During the few days we spent ashore being splendidly entertained by the Royal Air Force, a notable event was an invitation to drinks after a formal Mess Dinner for the Royal Scots Guards, our odiferous flying overalls clashing wonderfully with their magnificent finery.

Back in *Eagle* the incident had stimulated the Boss of 894 Squadron, one Peter Young, and Senior Observer Ox Moore, into a bit of lateral thinking. Given that ship's radars were useless for getting aircraft down in really bad weather, and given that the AI-21 radar in the Sea Venom was specifically designed to track small contacts, which it did very well – pick-up range was about ten miles, and observers regularly conned pilots in as close as 100 feet behind the 'enemy' for a gun attack, close enough to see the red-hot turbine ring up the victim's jet-pipe – why not try using AI-21 for Carrier Controlled Approach? Like most 'inventions' it seemed so obvious that it was a wonder nobody thought of it before.

And so it was that soon after we got back aboard I found myself sitting in a Venom parked facing aft just behind the island, using my radar to 'talk down' a couple of Venoms on simulated CCAs. This was done by passing headings to steer to keep them on the ship's extended centreline, and also their range to touchdown and the height they should be at every half-mile as they descended. Giles Carne piloted the first Venom on the first AI21-controlled CCA. They rest, as they say, is history.

The trial was such an obvious success that during *Eagle*'s next short maintenance period at Rosyth a special 'shack' was built just aft of the island to house an AI-21 radar with associated communications, and very soon this hasty 'modification' was fitted in all RN fixed-wing carriers – the first dedicated CCA radar. Deservedly, Peter Young and Ox Moore were awarded a Herbert Lott Trust Fund prize for their contribution to Naval Aviation.

The only drawback was that to begin with we Venom observers, as well as flying, also made up the CCA talkdown roster, making for some very long days and nights. The only operational problem I recall was trying to sort out with the ship's Direction Officers, who fed the aircraft into our approach pattern using their own big radars, which 'blip' was which. It was fairly important to be sure you were talking to the right one. Do I hear somebody say, 'What's new?'

Lieutenant Jerry King and Sub Lieutenant John Winslow,
Pilots, Seahawks, 801 Squadron, HMS *Bulwark*, Oman, 1958

September 1958 found HMS *Bulwark* off Oman, where rebel forces in the Jebel Akhdar had upset a friendly Sultan. A Group Captain came aboard from Masira Island and told us that RAF Hunters and Venoms had failed to 'take out' the rebels who, as soon as they heard the jets, would unsportingly shin up rope ladders into deep caves in the rock, leaving bombs and rockets to explode harmlessly several hundred feet below. Would the Navy see what they could do?

According to the SAS contingent who did the 'mopping up' after us, our VT-fused bombs, set to explode at 200 feet, were very successful. Interestingly, while Lieutenant Fred De Labillière was dropping bombs, brother Peter, later

'...punched a steel rod and the first-stage drogue out through the canopy.' HMS *Bulwark*, off Aden, 18.8.58. BCC/MOD via Winslow

'...the Seahawk lost speed and headed for the water...' BCC/MOD via Winslow
'...hit the sea about a hundred yards ahead of the ship...' BCC/MOD via Winslow

Commander British Land Forces in the Gulf War, was on the ground mopping up.

I suffered a bomb 'hang-up' and fuel problems on one of these sorties and made an emergency diversion to a BP light-aircraft strip just north of Muscat. Having jettisoned the bomb I found the tiny airstrip with some difficulty and landed uneventfully, though with very little fuel remaining. The BP oilmen had the biggest fridge I have ever seen, full of gin, and entertained me for an hour while a relay of helicopters brought in barrels of jet fuel from the ship for my thirsty Seahawk.

After an exciting take-off – 'short-field' technique, flap half-way down the runway – I beat up the field for the benefit of my incredible hosts, who waved like mad, and headed out over the sea for 'Mother'.

Around this time another 801 Squadron pilot, Sub Lieutenant John Winslow, had an experience which is probably unique in carrier aviation. He was launched on *Bulwark*'s starboard catapult with his ejection seat not properly secured to the cockpit floor; the acceleration forced him and his loose seat up the firing rail whereupon the automatic seat mechanism, tricked into assuming that an ejection was in progress, responded by firing its drogue-gun cartridge which punched a steel rod and the first-stage drogue out through the canopy. This heavy drogue's normal job was to decelerate and stabilize the

80

seat before extracting the main parachute.

Three seconds later, just off the end of the catapult and fifty feet out over the waves, lacking the intelligence to realize that Winslow was still in the cockpit, the seat automatically released his safety harness. Normally the seat would fall away at this point, leaving him in his parachute.

Unable to overcome the drag of the drogue-chute, the Seahawk lost speed and headed for the water, and Winslow, sitting on an unsecured live seat with no safety straps, had no choice but to ride it down. When it hit the sea about a hundred yards ahead of the ship he was catapulted out of the cockpit, injuring his face, and narrowly escaped being run over by the ship. An excellent swimmer, he was picked up astern by the sea-boat and choppered off to the military hospital in Aden.

Visiting him a few days later, I found him in the next bed to *Bulwark's* Carrier-Borne Ground Liaison Officer, a Major Phelps, RA, who a little before this had been rudely ejected from his bunk in the middle of the night by the bow of an Egyptian freighter.

Winslow elaborates: 'The last thing I remember before ditching was reaching for the canopy jettison handle. The shattered canopy took me with it when it came off, pulling me out of the aicraft before it ditched, and I hit the water at high speed face first: my eyelids were nearly ripped off, my mask disappeared, my Mae West was shredded and I lost one tightly-laced boot.

'I came to under water blind and trapped in the parachute lines and was partially cut free by the chopper crewman, who also nearly drowned. He put the lifting-strop into my hands. I could hear the chopper and hung on to the strop trying to breathe, but suddenly the strop and I fell back into the water as the chopper cut the cable and moved out of the path of the ship which passed very close.

'I heard voices – the ship's lifeboat – and shouted, but not a sound came from my lips, and I realized I was drowning. A warm soft feeling of peace, sort of Mantovani playing in the background. I was finally picked up by the lifeboat whose Midshipman coxswain went berserk at the sight of so much blood and had to be flattened by the leading hand before they could get on with the job of rescuing me, something they cannot have done many times before: the third-degree burns on my buttocks, which puzzled the doctors for a while, came from having been tenderly laid on the boat's exhaust pipe in the bilges for the trip back.

'The bottom locking latch on my seat had been fitted upside down (Murphy's Law), and despite an immediate recommendation to Admiralty by the Squadron C.O. that the latches be modified, a year later it happened again – to the Squadron C.O., a very experienced test pilot. I was flying as his No.2, and as he launched, out came the drogue, and the same thing all over again. He avoided my fate by bracing his feet on the gunsight before ditching, then turning himself upside-down in the cockpit and kicking his way out of the submerged aircraft through the broken canopy – adrenalin is a wonderful thing!'

'...third degree burns on my buttocks...' Winslow

Lieutenant P.H. 'Jan' Stuart,

Observer, Whirlwind Mk.7, 824 Squadron, H.M.S. *Victorious* and *Centaur,* 1958-60.

In August 1958, 824 Squadron embarked in *Victorious* with a full complement of eight Whirlwind Mk.7s, but not for long. We left UK for the Far East having already lost three, XL849 XL848 and XK943, and XK838 splashed on the way to Malta.

Captain Charles Coke RN, a gentleman in every respect and perturbed by the number of Whirlwind accidents, decided shortly after sailing from Malta for the Canal that enough was enough. He would fly back to Malta and ring up Their Lordships to say he was going to ground 824 Squadron.

We were no more than fifty miles on our way when he asked our squadron Boss, Jim Trevis, to dig out a decent Mk.7 and fly him back to the island. I was Squadron Duty Officer that day and got the Captain kitted up in flying gear and brought him out to the helicopter. The Boss was already in the cockpit warming up the engine which, when we were about ten yards off, emitted an ominous cough. Captain Coke stopped dead and grabbed my arm.

'Is that the cough I keep reading about in these accident signals?'

'Yes, Sir,' says I, 'that's it.'

'In that case, my apologies to Mr Trevis. I will take the *ship* back to Malta.'

And so *Victorious* turned around and went back, the Captain made his phone call and our Whirlwinds were lowered over the side onto lighters and dumped ashore at Kalafrana.

I am not an aircraft engineer, but as a layman it seemed to me there was nothing fundamentally wrong with the Alvis Leonides engine; it was a good motor and did well in fixed-wing aircraft. But for an engine designed to run horizontal at about 60% rated power, it is asking a lot for it to perform as well at 85% lying on its back. After the 824 Squadron fiasco a long series of boring low-hover engine trials took place on Culdrose airfield: I have daily entries in my logbook from 18 March to 11 April 1959, doing just this, an hour and a half at a time. *Sacré bleu!*

By September 1960, when I was back in 824, the engines seemed to have been sorted out, but now there was another big frightener: the fuel gauges were so unreliable that Standing Orders required all aircraft to land with not less than 50lbs showing on each gauge. In *Centaur* in Indian Ocean temperatures, this reduced the Mk. 7's time-on-task on anti-submarine screen to a ludicrous forty minutes.

One day when I was grounded with a broken wrist and helping out in the Ops room, I heard John Nevill-Rolf, out ahead on the screen, calling to say his gauges were close to '50-50' and he was returning, only to be sharply told by a more senior pilot, also airborne, not to be so chicken.

'You can't be that low on fuel!' he was told. 'I've still got plenty ....er...MAYDAY MAYDAY MAYDAY!' And so another Whirlwind Mk7 went to the bottom of the sea.

You could say that the Whirlwind Mk7 was a typical Treasury Aeroplane, built to save dollars. The original Mk2, with the American Wright Cyclone, was a honey.

Midshipman W.J.V. Walker,

Observer, Skyraider, 849 Squadron 'B' Flight, HMS *Victorious*, North Atlantic, 1959

As a brand new Observer, I joined 849'B' Flight in the summer of 1959, flying Skyraiders from HMS *Victorious* in the Airborne Early Warning (AEW) role. The Douglas Skyraider AD-4W was powered by a single Wright Cyclone engine and carried a 200-mile-range AN/APS-20C downward-looking radar; its primary use was to give the fleet early warning of low-level air attack, but it could also provide strike-direction and surface surveillance. It was crewed by a pilot and two observers, the senior of whom was concerned with the primary role whilst the No.2, unfortunately me at this stage of my career, was responsible for navigation.

At 0530 on 22 September 1959 I was in the first aircraft launched from *Victorious*, flagship of a task force in the opening phase of a large NATO exercise in the North Atlantic, our task being to direct ground-attack Scimitars on to a bombing range on the Norwegian coast near Bodø at 67° 20′N. Like all other aircrew we wore immersion suits and a crude and heavy emergency locator device called 'TALBE' (Talk And Listen BEacon). Our Skyraider had full drop-tanks for a briefed sortie length of 7½ hours and, after many hours directing successive waves of Scimitars onto their target, I gave pilot Barry Hartwell a southerly heading and we started back south for 'Mother'. Confident of picking her up very soon on our magnificent radar, I began to think of large meals and hot baths.

But it was not to be. When we got to *Victorious*' predicted position it was as if the whole task force had never existed. No carrier, no escorts, no aircraft, and a total and eerie silence on the radio. Nothing even on the 'YE' Beacon, a rudimentary but usually totally reliable radio homing gadget for pilots. One or two small radar contacts, probably fishing boats, were the only other signs of human presence on the planet. A hasty search proved futile, and after about half an hour Barry announced that we had enough fuel to investigate one more radar contact, and if it wasn't a carrier we would have to ditch in the sea alongside it. The radar blip came slowly down the scope and turned into a Russian trawler. Fuel gauges on zero, Barry warned, 'Stand by to ditch!'

Once all the splashing and fuss was over, we boarded our dinghies and tied ourselves together in the approved fashion. The Skyraider's tail slid out of sight leaving two aimless-looking drop-tanks bobbing about on the surface. We were alive and unhurt and the sun had come out. Not too bad so far. A big swell was running, and although we could see nothing at the bottom of the troughs, when we bobbed up to the top there was the comforting sight of the Russian churning his way towards us. To my horror, after getting close enough for a good look, it turned away and started heading fast towards the horizon. Even now I find it difficult to describe my feelings at that moment. The elation of survival drained away leaving me cold and frightened. After what seemed a lifetime the Russian hove back into view and manoeuvred alongside, and to my indescribable relief the crew started shouting and throwing ropes.

I should pause here for some contemporary history. In 1959 the Cold War was approaching freezing point, the world's political thinking starkly polarized between Moscow and Washington and, in the course of a world propaganda tour, Bulganin and Khruschev, Premier of the USSR and First Secretary of the Russian Communist Party respectively, had recently been given a spectacularly bad reception in New York. Tension between East and West had never been worse.

However, in a tiny dinghy in what felt like the middle of the Atlantic, politics seemed unimportant – until, that is, you are fished up dripping on to a trawler's deck to be faced by a grim-looking Russian pointing a large pistol at you.

'Amerikan!' he growled menacingly.

'Who, us? No! ENGLISH!'

The effect was magical. The Russian's face split into a broad grin and he put away his gun.

'Ha! English! VODKA!'

The whole crew could not have been kinder. They hadn't much to offer, but everything they had was ours, including the captain's own quarters. Between them they mustered a few words of English, and when they found we were fellow sailors and therefore *real* friends, they were delighted. *Really* delighted! They hadn't picked us up straight away because they had to report to Moscow and obtain official permission to save us.

After twenty-four hours they transferred us to their depot ship, the *Atlantika*, and two days later the Royal Navy in the form of HMS *Urchin*, diverted from fishery protection off Iceland, reclaimed us. The *Atlantika*'s crew offered us their only two books in English, one ghastly political novel, and, without a word of a lie, *Three Men in a Boat*.

The subsequent Board of Enquiry found that whereas we were briefed that the Task Force would be advancing north at twenty knots throughout our sortie, great minds in high places decided it should go west at fifteen knots instead, and nobody thought to tell us. Pythagoras could have told them that was going to put the fleet about 180 miles south-west of where I expected them to be, so I got off the hook. But I believe some heads did roll.

A couple of months later, Barry Hartwell got his feet wet again, this time flying on his own with a load of mail in the Mediterranean, when his Skyraider's engine quit suddenly. Although for some reason his safety harness was not done up, he braced his feet against the instrument panel before hitting the sea and climbed out unhurt.

Lieutenant Commander Tom Stride,
Flight Commander 848 Squadron, Whirlwind Mk.7, HMS *Bulwark*, 1959

In May 1959, summoned urgently from Malta, where I was in 848 Squadron working-up with No. 40 and 45 Commandos for embarkation in the Navy's first commando carrier, HMS *Bulwark*, I reported to the Conference Room in the Royal Naval Barracks in Portsmouth for a 'planning meeting'.

I knew only that the subject of the meeting was urgent and 'classified'. A Royal Marine guard stood at the door and examined my papers. Inside were

Bulwark's planning team: Commander (Air) and the Operations Officer, the C.O. and Intelligence Officer of No 42 Commando, Captain Franks, Royal Navy, Commanding Officer HMS *Bulwark*, in the chair. A sealed envelope lay unopened in front of me while Captain Franks emphasized the need for total security.

He then outlined the operation we were to plan, and in due course execute, namely a helicopter-borne Commando assault, in the course of *Bulwark's* passasge to the Far East, on the Jeabel Akhdar in the Oman. When we had found out where this was, the Chairman filled in the background. It had been decided, he told us, that the time had come to put a stop to the activities of a band of revolting tribesmen who had terrorized the area for years, killing and wounding many troops and natives.

The Commandos then presented their plans, which had obviously taken a long time to prepare but were basically simple. Plan A, attack by day, and Plan B attack by night.

This was followed by the Met Officer describing the terrain and climatic conditions, both of which could be summed up as unfriendly to helicopters. Jebel Akhdar was a range of steep-sided bare-rock mountains between 8000 and 10,000 feet in height, and because of a twist of local climatic conditions the temperature at the top was usually about the same as at the bottom, around +30°C.

Armed with this information, I was allowed to open my sealed envelope. Its contents were disappointing. 848 Squadron in Malta was perforce working-up with American-built Sikorsky S-55s, designated the Whirlwind Mk.22, because the British-built Whirlwind Mk.7s, which would be used in this assault, had not yet been delivered. I knew little about the Mk.7 and would have expected my envelope to contain at least a copy of the standard blue-covered 'Pilot's Notes', but the only papers of any use were some 'Performance Graphs' provided by the Admiralty. I shot an enquiring look across the table at my Commander (Air) who, neatly demonstrating the art of delegation, merely shrugged.

A cursory glance at the performance graphs was enough to set the alarm bells ringing, and a more careful study, applying forecast temperatures to the average height of the Jebel Akhdar, revealed that the proposed task was out of the question. I was considering how to break this news to the asembled gung-ho audience when the Chairman announced, 'And now we'll hear the Air Plan.'

I prefaced my remarks by saying that my estimates were based on the information provided in my envelope, as I had no experience of the Mk.7 Whirlwind. By day, I pronounced, allowing for the ship being 30-50 miles from the target, the Whirlwind Mk.7 would carry one Marine, with rifle and kit, to the high point of the mountain range. By night, in slightly lower temperatures, I suggested the payload might be increased to $1^{1}/_{2}$ Marines.

After a short stunned silence I was told, 'Check the figures again!', but there was no altering the awful truth that, as far as this operation was concerned, 'The Whirlwind Seven won't get you to Heaven!'

Escorted for security purposes by *Bulwark's* Major of Marines, I was despatched to Westlands at Yeovil where the Whirlwind was made, to verify the Admiralty graphs. A conclave of experts, sworn to secrecy, examined them and announced that they were actually on the generous side, being in their opinion 5-10% too ambitious when it came to load-carrying. The Major and I returned to Portsmouth for a re-convened planning meeting where I was asked to present the Amended Air Plan.

I took a deep breath and announced that using the *manufacturer*'s figures, the daytime payload must be reduced to one unarmed Marine, whilst at night we might just manage one Marine with a rifle.

A prolonged silence greeted this news, which at a stroke dashed hopes of glory and gongs, aspirations of flag rank and brass hats all around the table. Discussion moved to other questions, such as 'Whose bright idea was this in the first place?', to which nobody would own up.

As a postscript to 'The Raid that Never Was', I can report that some time later a Whirlwind Mk VII Squadron from another carrier *was* tasked to carry out a reconnaissance of the Jebel Akhdar. The two aircraft they lost in forced-landings through lack of power had to be destroyed by RAF Venoms to prevent them falling into enemy hands and being used against us. And the revolt was finally put down by the SAS.

Early troubles with the Whirlwind Mk.7 required a *second* long period of Intensive Flying Trials to overcome problems with its Alvis Leonides engine. The Royal Flight refused to accept it, preferring to continue with the American Sikorsky. Its performance in both the anti-submarine and Commando role exposed its acute limitations; on warm windless days, even in northern waters, it was pretty useless as an anti-submarine vehicle, and as Lieutenant Commander (Flying) of *Bulwark* in her second commission I vividly remember how it took a Squadron of them three whole days, in good weather and without any enemy opposition, to put the Commando on the beach.

In my opinion the Whirlwind Mk VII was a *débâcle*. But some good may have come of it. All subsequent helicopters were thoroughly evaluated and tested *before* entry into service.

CHAPTER THREE

THE 1960s

Introduction

By 1962 the two light carriers *Bulwark* and *Albion* had converted to the Commando role, each equipped with a 600-strong Royal Marine Commando and a squadron of Whirlwind Mk.7 and later Wessex Mk.1 helicopters. *Bulwark* with No.42 Commando was on-scene in the Persian Gulf within forty-eight hours of Iraq threatening Kuwait in 1961, closely followed by *Victorious* and *Centaur*. Both Commando carriers were heavily involved in the Indonesian Confrontation (1962-66). Two dedicated Assault Ships with large helicopter decks, *Fearless* and *Intrepid*, entered service, and the twin-engined 16-passenger Wessex Mk.5 was introduced in 1965, the year which saw the end of the long-serving Dragonfly. In 1963 the Fleet Air Arm received the Wasp, a good purpose-built small-ship helicopter which by the end of the decade was an integral part of the weapon systems of most frigates and destroyers.

Eagle, Ark Royal, Victorious, Centaur and *Hermes* were now equipped with Scimitars, Sea Vixens, Gannets, Skyraiders and Whirlwinds (the latter an anglicized S.55 with a highly unsatisfactory Alvis engine). The nuclear-capable Buccaneer low-level strike bomber was introduced in 1962, another excellent aircraft initially hampered by unsatisfactory engines. In the Buccaneer Mk2 which entered service with Rolls-Royce Spey engines in 1965 the Navy at last had an effective anti-shipping and nuclear strike aircraft whose crews for many years stood ready for one-way missions against Soviet targets. An AEW version of the Gannet superseded the Skyraider, and turbine Wessex helicopters replaced the Whirlwind, ending the need for aviation gasoline at sea.

At 46,000 tons, the two Fleet Carriers were a reasonable size for the big jets, but *Centaur* and *Hermes*, at 27,000 tons, were small. The 'mirror' made deck-landing easier, but it could not prevent bad landings: accident rates, particularly at night on the small carriers with primitive flight-deck lighting, rose to unacceptable levels in the first half of the decade but were quickly reduced to near-zero by the re-introduction of the Landing Safety Officer, a senior and experienced pilot on deck – without bats – monitoring all approaches with authority to 'wave off' any that looked unsafe. And generally, as metallurgical science caught up with design, engines and aircraft became more reliable.

In this decade, as well as honing skills for the ever-threatening Third World War, Royal Navy carriers and their squadrons met tasks in Kuwait, East Africa (flood relief), Borneo, Tanganyika, Yemen, Aden and Mozambique

Centaur went to the scrapyard in 1966, followed by *Victorious* in 1967 after a serious fire. The Navy's big hope for the future, a new large carrier designated 'CVA-01', was announced in 1963; its cancellation in 1966 signalled *finis* for conventional fixed-wing carriers in the Royal Navy, leaving only *Eagle*, *Ark Royal* and *Hermes* to continue this role to the end. The simple 'mirror' was improved by the US Navy and sold back to its inventors as the more robust – and expensive – Projector Sight. Cruisers *Blake* and *Tiger* were converted to Helicopter Cruisers with four helicopters each; *Engadine* commissioned as a Helicopter Support Ship; six Naval Air Stations remained in commission.

The Fleet Air Arm Roll of Honour contains the names of those who lost their lives in flying operations in the 1960s. The numbers are:

Pilots	101
Observers	55
Aircrewmen	11
Others	26

Lieutenant A.D. Hare,
Pilot, Sea Prince, 750 Squadron, RNAS Hal Far, Malta, 1960

Like any naval airfield, Hal Far's runways had an emergency arrester-gear system to stop aircraft with tailhooks overrunning – one or two cables, or 'wires', stretched across the runway at the upwind end, held a few inches off the concrete by rubber bobbins spaced along the wire.

But being hard rubber and quite large, these bobbins could be a hazard in themselves if struck by an aircraft nosewheel at any speed; the ensuing high-frequency 'shimmy' was sometimes severe enough to damage the airframe. And the Sea Prince, with its twin nosewheels, was particularly sensitive in this respect, so great care was always taken to avoid the bobbins. At night, if only Sea Princes were flying, the wires would usually be removed altogether and Squadron Standing Orders required pilots to check before landing to see if this had been done.

Observer training being the Squadron task, one night six of us took off in a long stream for a Night Navigation Exercise. First back was Vic Cockburn, an aged aviator of about thirty-five, and I was a close second. I heard Vic enquire about the wires and ATC telling him they had been removed. It is germane to note that the Sea Prince was one of the first naval aircraft to be fitted with a landing-lamp, which some pilots, like Vic, thought pansy and didn't use. I did.

I was cleared to land after him, touched down and ran down the runway with my landing-lamp blazing – and just as well, because it enabled me see Vic's totally unlit Sea Prince stopped dead among the arrester wires, which had not been removed, and to avoid smashing into him.

He had hit a bobbin at speed and the resulting shimmy was severe enough to activate the crash switch which disconnected all his electrics, including radio and navigation lights, and shut down his engines, and the first ATC knew about this was when I told them.

The shimmy was so bad that it shook Vic's false teeth out on to the cockpit floor, and having lost his torch in the confusion he was still on his hands and knees looking for his teeth when the crash and rescue crews arrived. The Sea Prince's fuselage was badly wrinkled and I don't think it ever flew again.

'...and shook his false teeth out on to the floor...' Thomas

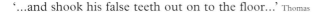

Lieutenant John Eatwell,
Observer, Sea Vixen 892 Squadron, Buccaneer 800 Sqdn, HMS *Victorious*, 1960; HMS *Eagle* 1964

A vicious storm south of Sardinia two weeks before Christmas 1960 caught *Victorious* with a normal range of aircraft on deck, most of which were hastily moved amidships and chained down. But one of 892's Sea Vixens, XJ484, parked about as far forward on the port bow as it was possible to get, proved inaccessible as conditions rapidly worsened and the flight deck was put out of bounds. So there it had to stay. *Victorious*'s single rudder jammed hard over to one side and one of her engines failed, resulting in the ship going round in circles in giant seas, plunging the angled deck on the port side under water every time we came beam-on to the storm. It is a recorded fact that many of the fish in the wardroom aquarium expired and finished belly-up from sea-sickness.

When the weather abated, the first priority was to get XJ484's radar down to the workshops for drying-out and servicing. When the radar was taken out of the nose, the weight of water trapped in its booms tipped the aircraft up on its tail.

With spare parts flown aboard in a Skyraider, the ship's rudder was mended and the good news soon circulated that we were on our way home for Christmas, the Squadrons to fly ashore to their home airfields, in our case RNAS Yeovilton. But of course XJ484 was in no condition to fly and had to be craned over the side on to a lighter and taken to RNAS Lee-on-Solent near Portsmouth. Her salt-drenched airframe was visibly corroding away and it was vital to get her to the Navy's main Aircraft Repair Yard at Sydenham, near Belfast in Northern Ireland, as soon as possible.

And Belfast being three hundred-odd miles from Lee, and no sea transport being available for several months, it was decided she must be flown.

Pilot John Carey and I drew the short straw and made our way down to Lee. XJ484's undercarriage was rusted permanently down and the drop tanks unusable, which meant a pit-stop for fuel at RNAS Brawdy in South Wales. Checking that the ejection seats at least had been serviced and were in working order, we took off at 1215 on 11 January 1961.

John complained that all the controls were 'spongy' and, slightly more worrying, there was a marked control restriction to movement of the all-flying tailplane which moved up and down between the two vertical fins. A booster-pump failed, trapping 1000lbs of useless fuel in one of the wing tanks, but we landed safely at Brawdy, refuelled and headed out wheels-down across the Irish Sea for Belfast. The controls were 'spongier', and the tailplane restriction worse. A second fuel booster pump failed, trapping another half a ton of unusable fuel, but after a gigantic circuit we duly put down safely at Sydenham.

There were deep score-marks on the inside of both fins. Apparently XJ484's whole tail had been twisted by the battering she had taken in the storm and we were lucky the tailplane hadn't jammed solid in the air. In short, she was a crock. I don't think she ever flew again

At the end of March 1961 HMS *Victorious* arrived in Singapore and disembarked her aircraft to the various airfields. 892's Sea Vixens went to RAF Tengah and, as our period there coincided with the opening of the new Singapore International Airport at Paya Lebar on Easter Saturday, it was decided to mark the occasion with a Joint Flying Display.

892's contribution was to be a formation fly-past at high speed, followed by a low-speed pass with everything hanging down, wheels, flaps, hooks etc – an easy ride for me down in the 'coal hole', with John Carey doing all the work.

All went well until after the first fly-past when the Boss called 'Airbrakes...GO!' to slow us down for the next part of the show, at which point John and I shot out ahead of the formation, definitely not slowing down. No airbrake. In fact both General Services hydraulic systems had failed. As GS hydraulics also worked the undercarriage, flaps, brakes, hook, wingfold, in fact everything that moved except the flying controls, all of a sudden our Easter Saturday jaunt suddenly took on a different tone.

We quickly set about trying to get the wheels down with what pressure remained. The main legs took an age, but eventually locked down and gave us 'two greens', although another aircraft told us the doors were hanging open. The effort exhausted the system completely, leaving us no nosewheel, flaps or brakes, and unsure whether the main gear would collapse on touchdown; an earlier 'drooping doors' accident off Cape Town suggested it might.

Tengah's runway having monsoon ditches like tank traps down each side, and 1000 yards of soft new concrete at one end, which was 'out of bounds', after some discussion their Command offered us the 'safe' option of taking our Vixen out over the sea and ejecting; but this, after taking such things as sharks and sea-snakes into consideration, we declined; we started dumping fuel for a landing.

Without flaps, it was a fast approach and both tyres burst as soon as the wheels hit the ground. Thinking the undercarriage was collapsing, I pulled the hatch jettison lever – I had always wanted to see if it would work. John's reaction time was the same, for my hatch and his canopy ended up side by side on the runway. The main gear didn't collapse but when the nose dropped and started

'...Gyron Junior engines...' HMS *Eagle*, off Singapore, Buccaneer Mk 1 of 800 Squadron did a 'bolter' (missed the wires), engines failed to accelerate, crew ejected about one second before the aircraft hit the water both picked up uninjured. BCC/MOD via Giles

scraping nastily along the concrete just below my feet it got very noisy. The 'goofers' thought the flame and sparks around the nose-frame quite spectacular. It seemed a very long time before we eventually came to rest, well down into the forbidden area of soft concrete.

This incident, causing a lot of extra work in the middle of the Easter holiday, put a severe strain upon the Royal Air Force's sense of humour. For this, and for the neat grooves in their new concrete, we were of course deeply sorry.

Seasonal holidays weigh less heavily against the exigencies of global naval operations. As Christmas 1964 approached I was with 800 Squadron at RNAS Lossiemouth, preparing to embark for the Far East in HMS *Eagle*. However, one of our Mk.1 Buccaneers, XN951, had other ideas and remained stubbornly unserviceable in a corner of the hangar. On 1 December the rest of the squadron flew off to *Eagle* in Lyme Bay, leaving XN951 in the hands of Lossie's Station Support Unit engineers, and Don Richardson and I stayed behind to try to coax the old rogue into the air, when she was ready. We were told to be in Malta by 6 December, with or without her, to catch the ship en route to the Suez Canal.

The usual snow and ice engulfed Lossiemouth, and when at last, late on 3 December, the news came that our aircraft was ready to fly, the prospect looked extremely doubtful. It was dark. All flying had stopped. Taxying was impossible and tractors could not get enough grip on the ice to tow a fully-fuelled Buccaneer. Undeterred, we got in and shut the hood and a refuelling bowser towed us out to the end of the runway where we started up and took off at 2000.

After a night-stop at Yeovilton and in-flight refuelling over France, during which XN951 behaved impeccably, we arrived at lunchtime next day at RNAS Hal Far in Malta. High Frequency radio conditions were so good that we were able to talk to *Eagle*, which was off Gibraltar, and to report our arrival to Lossiemouth, 1700 miles north.

The Mediterranean weather was pure delight, but a priority signal instructed us to fly out to the ship on her way past next morning. However, as Sunday dawned another priority signal arrived grounding all Buccaneers because of cracks in the turbine blades of their Gyron Junior engines; all engines were to be inspected internally using a brand new gadget called an 'endoscope'. But Hal Far had no endoscope, so was XN951 going to avoid that Far East cruise after all? No! She was excused the endoscope, for 'one flight only', to get her aboard, and so at about 1130 we landed into the wires on *Eagle*'s flight deck.

At which point both engine fire-warning systems operated, all hell broke loose and we hurriedly shut down and got out. This was XN951's final tantrum. The endoscope examination revealed cracks in both turbines, and since several Buccaneers had already failed this examination and there were only four new engines on board, she was put up the far end of the lower hangar and became a 'Christmas Tree' supplying spares for all the others.

There she remained for the next nine months until *Eagle* came home, when she was again made serviceable – for 'one flight only' back to Lossiemouth, during which she of course behaved impeccably.

Lieutenant C.K. Manning,
Pilot, Sea Venom, 738 Squadron Sea Vixen 893 Sqdn, RNAS Lossiemouth 1960; HMS *Centaur*, Persian Gulf, 1961

It was my jet transition course on Sea Venoms at Lossiemouth, and the time had come for Night Formation Flying. A staff pilot and I would go off in the dark and I would practise close formation on him using only dim blue 'formation lights'. Leader briefed the take-off: 10-second interval, he just left of the centreline, me just right, and we would join up once airborne. It had been snowing, but the runway was clear, they said.

Out on the runway on a moonless midwinter night, there was nothing to be seen but two tapering rows of runway lights. Leader called 'Rolling, Rolling, GO!' and moved off with a muffled roar. I started counting, caught a brief glimpse of red-hot turbine up his jet-pipe, then his tail-light was off down his side of the runway in a haze of jet fumes.

Nine...Ten!. Off brakes. Full throttle. I concentrated on staying midway between the runway lights accelerating past my ears – no landing-lamp in those days, we were playing war. Everything went splendidly until I tried to lift off at 120 knots, when there was an explosion and the aircraft slewed heavily right. Too fast to stop and too low to eject, I had to keep flying, right-wing-heavy and yawing left but the engine going fine. When I went to raise the wheels a red light came on and the controls stiffened, a normal consequence of hydraulic failure: the powered controls had disengaged, leaving me in manual control with the aircraft doing its best to roll over on its back to the right.

I got up to 5000ft and held it steady while Leader looked me over using his green nav-light. He reported my starboard undercarriage leg was missing, plus a lot of the flap that side, and I was bleeding hydraulic fluid.

Standard Operating Procedure for damaged aircraft at Lossiemouth being to head out over the sea and eject, they scrambled the rescue services and told me

'...a moonless midwinter night...' Sea Venom, 738 Squadron, RNAS Lossiemouth. Thomas

that when everything was ready they would radar-vector me out to the selected spot in the Moray Firth.

Well, 4 January 1960 was my 28th birthday. I had been married thirteen days, to the widow of a Navy pilot with a small son. The world outside my cosy cockpit was black as Hades and icy cold; Scotland was covered with snow and parachuting into the sea at night, even if ejection seat and parachute worked as advertised, carried a good chance of entanglement and drowning. I opted to land on the airfield and started dumping overload fuel from the tip-tanks and burning down to minimum before landing, the salvage and rescue vehicles gathering below on the airfield in clusters of winking yellow lights. Somebody told me they had found my missing leg, and that I seemed to have hit a pile of frozen snow.

Once committed to landing I had no need of a parachute, which would only be a hindrance in a crash-landing, so with 400lbs of fuel remaining, working by feel, I turned and squeezed the parachute Quick-Release Box (QRB). Early ejection seats had the parachute straps inside the safety harness that held you into the seat, with a QRB for each, and a new freedom of movement told me I had opened the wrong one, which left me sitting unattached on an armed ejection seat, but still in my useless parachute. And since doing up QRBs is a two-handed job, and I needed one hand on the stick to stop the Venom rolling on its back, I was going to have to land that way.

I made what I thought was quite a good landing, closed the fuel cock as the right tip-tank hit the concrete in a shower of sparks and flame which my course-mates later told me was the best part of the show, and had no further control over events. The Venom slewed to the right across the runway lights and out into the snow-covered bundu. There was a lot of room that side of Lossie's main runway and my only worry was the wingtip digging into a snowbank and setting up a cartwheel. I think I blew off the canopy at this stage. When everything stopped moving I climbed out carefully (live ejection seats are lethal) and stood in the snow beside the sizzling wreck of what had recently been one of Her Majesty's All-Weather Fighters.

The 'explosion' was my starboard undercarriage hitting a bank of packed snow, product of the afternoon's 'snow-clearing' operation, eight yards in from the right edge of the runway.

Notwithstanding this, the next year I was in 893 All-Weather Fighter Squadron flying Sea Vixens aboard HMS *Centaur* when she became part of a Task Force hurriedly assembled for what was nearly the 1961 Gulf War.

Somewhere off Kuwait, pitch dark and very hot, *Centaur* was getting ready to launch a night patrol. We, my Observer Dennis Brown and I, were tensioned on the port catapult when our Sea Vixen went unserviceable, the launch was cancelled and I folded the wings and shut down while a tractor took us by the nose to get us off the catapult. Before switching off the radio I heard an airborne Vixen being told to divert ashore to Kuwait airport. After a tight dumbell-turn the tractor had us facing aft and began towing us back down the deck. We could feel the screws shaking as the ship heeled into a turn.

Dennis and I were still tightly strapped in, ejection seats armed, and would stay that way until the aircraft was parked and chocked; but for some reason, somewhere between the catapult and jet-blast deflectors, right on the end of the landing area, the tractor stopped and we sat there facing aft in the middle of the deck. In those days the only aids for night landing were flush-fitting deck-edge and centreline lights shining aft, and looking aft I could not see these; but way down the deck I could see a pair of marshalling wands waving, and then I noticed a pair of navigation lights out to my right looking exactly like an aircraft turning in to land – the diverted aircraft coming round for an overhead departure, I thought.

As he got closer I could see him clawing right all the time to keep up with the ship's turn, and I thought, this looks a bit silly; it was too dark to be playing around at low level like that if you didn't have to. But closer and closer he came with the Flight Deck Officer, for he it was, Lieutenant Commander 'Monty' Mellor, standing on the centreline giving the 'wave-off' with his wands. When the tractor driver got off and made for the catwalk I must have felt my first stab of doubt.

But nobody ever lands on a carrier deck without the ship being at 'Recovery Stations' – ship into wind, arrester-gear ready, deck clear; fire, rescue and salvage crews at the ready and the landing finally sanctioned by an aft-facing green light on Flyco. So the aircraft rapidly approaching the back-end of the ship couldn't possibly be *landing...*

At the last possible moment 'Monty' hurled his useless wands at Flyco and dived for the catwalk. I froze. I remember unfastening my harness although there was no time to even start to get clear. Even if the aircraft coming over the round-down caught a wire there was a good chance of a head-on crunch because of the pullout distance; if he didn't, we would all go out in a spectacular ball of fire.

He hit the deck short and slow in a shower of sparks, caught No.1 wire and stopped. His black radome was a few feet the other side of my tractor, gleaming in its headlights. When his engines wound down leaving a very long silence on the deck it came to me that I had said nothing throughout to Dennis, who, being unable to see anything from the Observer's cockpit, was blissfully unaware that in the last few seconds he, like me and several others, had come close to sudden death. Not that there would have been time to escape if I had said anything, but I think about this from time to time.

Having for some reason not received the order to divert, the other pilot waiting to land had arranged his approach as per Standard Operating Procedures to arrive over the round-down at his briefed 'Charlie Time'; no radio calls were required unless this time changed. But as far as the ship was concerned, flying was over for the night.

We owed our lives to two things: the Sea Vixen's 128-knot landing speed put a severe strain on *Centaur's* arrester gear at Gulf temperatures, encouraging some experienced pilots to land as much as five knots slow – hence the short-pull-out; and this particular pilot was far and away the most reliable deck-lander in the Squadron, a dead cert to catch the first wire every time at night.

Lieutenant J.F. de WINTON,
Pilot, Sea Vixen, 893 Squadron, HMS *Ark Royal*, Davis Strait, 1961

Most of my memories of flying at sea are of the '50s and '60s, a period covering the introduction of the large twin-jets aboard our comparatively small carriers, and the efforts to make this mixture work. A bitterly cold pitch-black winter's night on the edge of the Arctic Circle provided plenty of opportunity for things to go wrong and stick in the memory – especially since, given my intention in the heat of the moment to storm up to the bridge and assault the Captain, it could well have put an early end to my naval career,

I was a Lieutenant in 893 Squadron, the third Sea Vixen Night Fighter Squadron to go to sea, and *Ark Royal* was engaged in a series of 'Arctic Trials' in demanding and unpleasant conditions. These included 'non-diversion' flying, meaning that should a problem arise affecting one's ability to land back aboard the ship, there is nowhere else to go – serious business, particularly at night over near-freezing water.

Having briefed for a 2100 launch, my observer and I went out on deck to man our aircraft which should have been just outside the island door in that part of the deck called 'Fly 2'. It was in fact on the end of a tractor being towed up to the starboard catapult, immediately in front of the bridge below the Captain's window, and we couldn't get in until it had been positioned and chocked.

With twenty minutes to go to launch time, I climbed into the cockpit and found the ejection seat in the fully-up position and no electrical power to lower it. Warnings and alarm bells kept flashing on and off as the flight deck crew endeavoured to plug in the ground-power lead, and while this was going on I was unable to use the aircraft's battery to motor the seat down or even close the canopy to protect myself from the freezing gale of sleet and spray coming in over the port bow. I was rapidly getting numb with cold, watching out for brake signals as the aircraft was repositioned over the catapult, and using my torch to try and strap in. This intricate procedure required careful routeing of harness straps, equipment connectors and leg-restraint cords, and inevitably I got one leg cord wrong and had to start again.

When at last the power came on and I got the seat down and closed the canopy, I foolishly thought my troubles were over. However, the first low-pressure air-starter the ground-crew tried didn't work. They found another one and I got both engines started, but when I spread the wings they wouldn't lock, and while I was 'head down' in the office sorting this out I missed the marshaller's final signal to release the brakes for the last part of the loading procedure, catapult tensioning.

Flyco told me on the radio to release the brakes, which I did, but too late. It was a 'misload', and as another Vixen went off the port catapult, a tractor and towing-arm were attached to push us back to reload. This time all went well. I felt the catapult tension and got the wind-up signal to go to full power for the launch. I pushed the throttles forward.

'Stop the launch!' called Flyco in a peremptory tone on the radio.

The launching officer's wand signalled me to throttle back. Tensioned on the catapult, this was not a welcome order, especially on a night like this, but reluctantly I pulled the throttles back. Next, 'Cut engines'. Then he signalled 'Flaps up' and 'Fold Wings', but of course with the engines running down there was no hydraulic power. 'Too blanking late!'

Seething with pent-up adrenalin and frustration, I was all set to storm up to the bridge to have it out with the Captain, because the impression given by Flyco's transmissions was that he thought the whole fiasco was my fault and had finally lost patience with me. Fortunately, my C.O. intercepted me at the island door, and given that my intended victim was on his rapid way to the highest military position in the land, probably saved my naval career.

In a better frame of mind the next night, I got airborne normally, had an engine fire many miles from the ship and had to land on one engine.

Lieutenant P.J. Taylor,
Observer, 824 Squadron Whirlwind Mk.7, HMS *Centaur*, Indian Ocean, 1962

At 0820 on 30 January 1962, somewhere near Singapore at 2°20′North, 104°26′East, a Whirlwind Mk.7 lifted off from the deck of HMS *Centaur*. I was the observer, the pilot was Lieutenant Dave Bridger, and the Underwater Controller was Leading Seaman Bean. Because the Whirlwind 7 was so grossly underpowered in the tropics, the aircraft was stripped of 'unnecessary' items like doors, windows, tail fairing, landing light, etc.

We were peeling away from the deck when the tail-rotor drive failed, the

'...I found myself kneeling on the ceiling...' HMS *Centaur*, Indian Ocean, 30.1.1960. Stuart

Whirlwind spun round a few times and we hit the sea.

DO NOT UNSTRAP UNTIL ALL MOTION HAS CEASED AFTER THE AIRCRAFT HITS THE WATER was the cardinal rule for surviving a helicopter ditching, hammered into everybody again and again at the countless safety briefings and drills that I, as the Squadron Safety Equipment Officer, arranged and supervised; nevertheless I unstrapped as soon as we hit the water, so when the aircraft nosed over and hung upside down, poised for its plunge to the bottom of the ocean, I found myself kneeling on the ceiling.

Thus I was last out by a long way. I then got stung by what I am convinced was a *huge* jellyfish, and when picked up by the SAR helicopter – another Whirlwind Mk 7 – forgot to disconnect my dinghy lanyard, which could have been *very* serious if the dinghy had caught in the sinking wreckage. Safely back on deck, we all three took the customary route down the bomb lift to the sick bay flat, where I ducked out of the lift-shaft too soon, struck my head on the steel bulkhead and nearly knocked myself out and, having managed to walk this far, had to be dragged semi-conscious into the sick bay.

824 was my first Squadron, and I think we lost eight aircraft in the time I was with them, including the mid-air collision over Cornwall on 10 March 1961, in which I was involved.

Recollections of 815 and 814 Squadrons later, in *Ark Royal* and *Hermes*, are extremely vague. Perhaps it was the fear that makes 824 and *Centaur* so memorable – that or the cockroaches.

Lieutenant George Barras,
Pilot, Wessex Mk.1, 815 Squadron, HMS *Ark Royal*, 1962

The Royal Navy's first Wessex HAS Mk.1 Anti-Submarine Squadron, 815, embarked in *Ark Royal* in early 1962 for a Far East tour which followed the familiar groove through the Med and Suez Canal, a stop at Aden and on to Singapore, where we were to disembark for a period at RNAS Sembawang. There, instead of sending the usual small shore-detachment, it was decided to make an evolution of it and fly the entire Squadron ashore, so a couple of aircraft were converted to the trooping role and all the way across the Indian Ocean we practised load-lifting with concrete blocks and the new Semi-Automatic Cable Release Unit (SACRU) hook.

The first aircraft ashore was full of air and ground crews, and I was to follow them in with

'...bills for the lost property.' BCC/MOD via Craig

98

their baggage – in the first underslung load. Flying XM 843, I lifted the load and was moving to port over the ship's side when there was a bit of a bump. 'You've lost it!' Flyco called.

IT was the cargo net full of suitcases, toolboxes and stores. We set about trying to rescue some of the suitcases bobbing about in the ship's wake, assisted by the Planeguard helicopter with its 'Sproule Net', but with limited success before I had to leave for the shore. Word of the tragedy had preceded us and a group of anxious Squadron personnel awaited, hoping their cases were among the survivors. The saddest sight was Jock English, whose hopes were raised when he spotted his suitcase only to be dashed when he picked it up: it was missing both its bottom and its contents.

It was found that distortion caused by our intensive practice sessions prevented my hook from locking. SACRU hooks were rapidly modified and subsequently used with great success, but it was a long time before I stopped receiving spurious bills for lost property.

Lieutenant Brian Davies,
Test Pilot, RAE, Boscombe Down, 1962

I was not directly involved when a Gannet AEW Mk.3 came to Boscombe Down in 1962 for handling trials, but since it was the only 'Mark' of Gannet I had not flown, I persuaded Nick Bennett, who had been doing the tests, to let me fly it before it left.

A problem shared by all Gannets, but in which the AEW3 excelled, was directional control on the ground. Without nosewheel steering, the pilot had to use the old technique of braking one main wheel to swing the aircraft in that direction; with the cumbersome Mk.3, precise manoeuvring on a carrier deck could only be achieved by a nose-steering arm held by a Naval Airman walking backwards a few feet in front of its deafeningly noisy contra-rotating propellers – a job for strong nerves, especially on a slippery pitching deck. It had been deemed too costly, at £3/4m, to equip the entire Gannet fleet with nosewheel steering.

My Mk.3 was parked between two hangars, and after familiarizing myself with the Pilot's Notes and cockpit layout I started her up; the two propellers a few feet in front of me spun up and disappeared, I waved away the chocks and started to taxy. Back aft in what was known as the coalhole, because they could only see out sideways through two tiny windows in the entry hatches, were my 'crew', two test observers along for the ride to play with the radar.

Emerging from between the hangars I had to use a lot of left brake in a hard left turn towards the V-Bomber Dispersal, a huge concrete apron bisected by the taxiway, with a row of transport aircraft and V-Bombers, now dead ahead of me, on the far side. Soon I needed another left turn to get onto the taxiway, but when I eased my foot down on the left brake actuator, a button on the rudder pedal which sent an electrical signal to the hydraulic brake unit telling it how much brake pressure I wanted, nothing happened. I was now heading towards a line of V-Bombers under the considerable ground-idle thrust of the Gannet's two engines.

I pressed hard on the left brake button to no avail and, as I was by now too close to swing right without hitting the nearest Vulcan, reached behind the seat and pulled up the Manual Override Brake handle which applies full pressure equally to both wheels, like a parking brake. The right wheel instantly locked, slewing the Gannet violently right; I shut down both engines and waited to be squashed under the Vulcan's nose looming over my cockpit. The Gannet's still-spinning propellers hacked viciously into the Vulcan's thin skin; bits of Vulcan flew everywhere, and when everything finally stopped the shredded ends of a thousand brightly coloured electrical cables hung from a jagged hole in the Vulcan's side. The silence was deathly.

When I tried to inform my 'crew' what had happened, there was no reply: experienced flight-test observers, they were long gone.

I took off my helmet and started the long awkward climb down the steps in the side of the Gannet's fuselage. Small groups of people stood around in animated conversation – like a cocktail party without the drinks, it struck me

'...bits of Vulcan everywhere...' BCC/MOD via Davies

incongruously. A black staff-car drew up: Boscombe's Superintendent of Flying, a Group Captain.

'What happened?'

'Port brake failed, Sir'

'Hop in. I'll drive you back to the Squadron.'

We drove off, exchanging a few pleasantries before a pregnant pause.

'How many hours have you got in the Gannet?'

'Well, I haven't actually flown this mark yet, Sir.' He paled, so I added, 'but I do have fifty hours or so in other marks, and they're basically all the same.' I explained the Gannet's peculiar brake system and told him that the failure of the left brake to work on either normal or override systems indicated something wrong with the brake unit itself.

He in turn told me the injured Vulcan had arrived at Boscombe Down that morning after a six-month programme of modification, to test the Blue Steel stand-off bomb, and the bit I had chopped out of the forward pressure bulkhead was exactly where most of the new instrumentation was – hence all the pretty coloured wires. Another Vulcan would now have to be modified, he told me, setting the programme back six to nine months at a cost, he guessed, of about £4 million.

It came to light that a new type of brake unit had been fitted since the Gannet's last flight and the engineer, either because he misread the manual or the manual had not been updated, had 'backed off' an adjustor nut two whole turns from fully tight instead of the *two flats* (about one-third of a turn); my initial hard left turn had shaved off the surface of the new pad, which from then on couldn't reach the disc, so the brake was totally useless.

The Navy's Gannets never did get nosewheel steering.

Lieutenant Maurice Hynett,
Pilot, Scimitar, UK/Mediterranean, 1963

I was that most piteous of creatures, a pilot on a ground tour – 'Scimitar Simulator Officer' at RNAS Lossiemouth in the north of Scotland, instructing in 'Flight Procedures and Emergencies'. The boredom of the job was overwhelming. This morning as usual I had dealt with my programmed students by 1130, but I had a terrible cold and was about to go home; I had told my wife I would come home for lunch and then go to bed.

I was on my way to the door when the phone rang. Duty overcame inclination and I picked it up. Somebody wanted a pilot to deliver a Hunter to Yeovilton.

I hadn't flown a Hunter for ages, my nose and sinuses were blocked solid and I felt awful, but no ground-tour pilot ever refuses an offer to fly. The Hunter was only a lady's-shopping sort of aircraft and a dose of oxygen would probably do me good. At 1255 I was parking the Hunter on the concrete beside Yeovilton's control tower, 400 miles south.

Summoned over the radio to report to Commander (Air), Yeovilton's Boss Flier, and, expecting to be bawled out over some minor infringement, I tried to strike a politely defiant pose when I got in front of his desk up in the tower. But his appearance made me uneasy. He looked slightly ingratiating, a bad sign in a senior officer. I sensed he wanted something.

'Heard you were on the way,' he said. 'You fly those – ?' He pointed down across acres of concrete at a lone Scimitar strike-fighter parked among Yeovilton's Sea Vixens.

'Used to, Sir,' I replied in matching monosyllables.

'One of 803's. They left it behind to be mended. Needs to go to Malta. Now.'

There being no time to obtain Diplomatic Clearance, I wouldn't be able to land in France and would have to refuel in flight to make the distance; and the fact that I had never done air-to-air refuelling did not deter Commander (Air). He whistled up a tanker pilot to give me a quick briefing, and at 1410 I was airborne in 803's Scimitar.

Over Paris at 40,000ft, well above all civil traffic in those days, I came up behind the bat-like Sea Vixen tanker, apparently motionless against the black stratosphere, the funnel-shaped drogue, or 'basket', gyrating gently in the slipstream on the end of its hose. It was uncanny to have the metal-ribbed object so close in front of the windscreen. I could count the stitches in the padding around the two-foot mouth of the basket, tantalizingly close to my nose-mounted probe. My mini-briefing had included a severe warning against trying to 'stab' the probe into the basket with bursts of power. 'Line up a few feet back and ease into it with a slow steady overtake – slow walking pace,' he said. Trouble was the drogue would not keep still; my first attempt clouted the side of the thing and the second failed altogether. I now know that nobody ever refuels as high as this if they can avoid it, certainly not with L-plates like me, because the rarified air makes control so difficult.

But it was either get my probe in that basket or return to Yeovilton with my tail between my legs, so I chanced everything on a forbidden burst of power, got straight in, pushed forward a bit until the green light came on at the back of the 'buddy' pod, and for the first time in my life saw fuel gauges rising in flight. I disengaged 150 miles south-east of Paris with brimming tanks. Ho-hum, next stop Malta.

I began to muse about carrier flying, and carrier life. My favourite was boosting off the catapult at dawn for some bombing or rocketing and coming back for a deck-landing before breakfast. It seemed ages ago. Deck-landing! The peak of the pilot's art, it needed constant practice. A couple of weeks off and you lost the touch. Happy days! French controllers passed me on to Italians, and thence to Malta Control and RAF Luqa. I coasted out over Sicily and saw Gozo, Comino and Malta in the heat haze far below.

It was 1605, one hour fifty-five minutes from Yeovilton. I changed frequency again to RNAS Hal Far, got my clearance and set up a fast descent with airbrakes out and throttles closed, expecting to be on the ground in five minutes or so. I had 2,500lbs of fuel, about twenty minutes flying.

Passing 10,000ft in descent with the canopy steaming up nicely in the warm Mediterranean air, a new voice came up on Hal Far's frequency:

'Navy 327 this is X-ray Tango. Confirm this is the 803 aircraft from

Yeovilton?'

'327 that's affirmative.'

'OK 327. Come to Mother.' 'Mother' is your home carrier. They couldn't be serious?

'327 Say again!'

'Come to Mother. Position thirty-two miles east of Delamara Point. You can land straight aboard. We have a ready deck. .'

Thirty-two miles was four minutes flying.

'327, fuel state Chicken plus ten,' I told him, meaning I had to be on the ground in ten minutes.

'X-ray Tango Roger.'

I turned seaward, the carrier picked me up on radar and soon I saw the creaming white wake, *Ark Royal* herself carving through the calm blue water at the speed of a motor-car, then the 'dayglo' orange stripe down the centre of its angled deck, and then I hit the deck and to my immense relief felt the seat straps bite into my shoulders and we stopped.

I went through the old familiar routine, hook up, flaps up, fold the wings, as if I had never been away. They told me afterwards I caught the target wire, No.3. The time was 1620.

In the helicopter taking me ashore to Hal Far I had time to start worrying about my wife and what she had done with my lunch. And that reminded me about my cold. What cold? It had completely gone.

Lieutenant R.W. Steil,
Pilot, 845 Squadron, Wessex, Borneo 1963

On 26 September 1963 I took four Commando Wessex helicopters from HMS *Albion* to Sibu airport in Sarawak to provide support for the Gurkha Rifles engaged in security and anti-insurgent patrolling. Rebel bands from Indonesia, infiltrating across the nearby border to carry out lightning raids, could be back up one of the many well-defined jungle tracks and over the border in 45 minutes, so rapid reaction was essential for the Gurkhas to intercept them. We went to 10-minute readiness throughout daylight hours with platoons of Gurkhas on standby at their Company HQ.

Two days later when the longhouses at Selepong were raided by a gang estimated at 15-20 strong, we were too late to catch them but roped in a platoon of Gurkhas to an ambush position near the border on their most likely return track, using the opportunity to make the first operational drop of dummy parachutists, or 'Freds', cunning devices with a delayed-action 'battle noise' kit. We dropped the latter along the border to confuse the enemy. Instead, the noise of the 'Freds' confused the Gurkhas and the raiders got away.

We picked up a Chinese rebel killed by the Field Force Police at Selepong, delivered to the aircraft strung by wrists and ankles to a pole, half his head missing and a line of bullet holes across his body; then we dropped a dozen

'After that I decided to arm my aircraft...'
BCC/MOD via Steil

police at Sungei Sawa in the south-east of our region to recover the body of a policeman killed in an ambush ten days previously and whose relatives now wanted the body, or at least the head. I decided the time had come to arm my aircraft, mounted a Bren gun on sandbags in the back and got the Gurkha Adjutant to try it out. He found it quite accurate over a small arc of fire and said it could work very effectively along a track. I took along some grenades, and with a little practice was able to drop these fairly accurately too. However, despite the fact that one enemy platoon ambushed by the Gurkhas had a .300 Browning Medium Machine Gun – lethal to helicopters – and 800 rounds of ammunition, I was informed by Brigade Headquarters that armed helicopters were not, at present, to be used, and that was that.

Jungle-covered ridges ran east-west across the operating area, the valleys invariably full of cloud until mid-morning; then from mid-afternoon towering thunderstorms built up with incredible rapidity. Maps were rudimentary. On one occasion, having landed some troops in the bottom of a valley near the border, a thunderstorm 'closed the door' behind me. Just before the cloud came down on to the hilltops all around, which would have sealed me in altogether, I slipped out the other way. At another landing-zone in heavy rain my wingman's windscreen-wiper failed and I had to drop my troops, find him, and lead him in to the landing site in close formation.

Considering the equipment they had, often just machetes and kukris, and the size of the trees, the Gurkhas were very good at hacking a landing site out of the 150-ft high jungle canopy; and after I had persuaded them that a vertical 'tube' up through the trees, just wide enough for a Wessex all the way down with perhaps five feet to spare all round, was not *quite* enough for safe operation, they were even able to add approach and exit lanes – 'for our comfort and convenience', as it were. I was hovering over one of these DIY landing-sites, lifting out a platoon which had been lost for five days, when my aircrewman, seeing the Gurkhas scattering, surmised something was wrong and gave me the 'GO UP!' signal. Just in time: a tree they had been cutting fell the wrong way, tearing out our cable and hook. Shingle banks along the rivers made useful landing-sites, but would be submerged after heavy rain. When we discovered a prepared landing-site in one area 'staked' by the enemy with ten-foot poles, we roped down a platoon of Gurkhas who at dusk that evening very successfully ambushed and killed twenty-six of the perpetrators, capturing two powered longboats.

The Wessex's range and lifting capability were much affected by the temperature and the altitude of some landing sites: to take off with the standard payload of eight troops plus kit (200 lbs each) and enough fuel for the average round-trip invariably meant overweight running take-offs from base. And fuel planning could be quite complex, as when twenty-four men had to be pulled out of an ambush site 2000ft up a mountain 70 miles away – *all at the same time* because any small group left behind would be vulnerable to attack. With 850lbs of fuel and no allowance for bad weather, the three Wessex involved could each lift eight men; with 950lbs of fuel, only seven men; and with 750 lbs they would not make it home. On this occasion a thunderstorm near base resulted in two of them landing short anyway, to be refuelled next morning and flown in.

We got on very well with the natives, trading shotgun cartridges for fresh fruit, vegetables and meat, ate very well and slept in their village, a pleasant twenty-minute longboat ride down-river from our base. Unlike many, I thoroughly enjoyed my two detachments in Borneo carrying out one of the Royal Navy's traditional tasks, supporting the army in foreign parts.

Lieutenant P.G.N. Hoare,
Pilot

According to Chuck Yeager's memoirs he got five victories in one mission in 1944: two German FW-190s saw his P-51 in their 6 o'clock, broke inwards and obligingly collided, after which he shot down three more. Hard to match? Read on.

It was about 1963, and time for the Sea Vixens' annual Firestreak air-to-air heat-seeking missile practice, live firing with inert warheads at pilotless Meteor targets over Cardigan Bay. You weren't supposed to *hit* the target: a close miss, lethal with a live warhead, would prove the system adequately. Drone Meteors were expensive.

Our hero's first Firestreak went straight up the drone's left jet-pipe with spectacular results. On his next sortie, with a new Meteor, another went up its right jet-pipe. Two down. The Firestreak was proving more of a hittile than a missile – excellent for morale, especially in view of the opposition we faced in the Sixties.

Back to the ship in Lyme Bay, our hero cocked-up his deck landing, missed the wires, bolted up the deck off-line, smashed into a Vixen and a Scimitar in the deck park, staggered into the air and ejected.

Five in one day, though not on the same mission. No medals, but a lot of form-filling. I don't think anybody was hurt. By the way, it wasn't me.

Lieutenant Willie Hare,
Pilot, Sea Vixen, 890 Squadron, HMS *Ark Royal*, South China Sea, 1963

It was one of those set-ups beloved of the Grim Reaper – a black humid night in the South China Sea, my first aircraft had gone 'u/s' and I was in a hurry to get the spare airborne on time. Out of one cockpit into the other, hasty strap-in, start up and rush through the pre take-off checks – all from memory in those days – and I missed one out, *'Set Cabin Temperature Control'*. Vital? Not usually – only on pitch-black, humid nights on the catapult.

Loaded on the cat, I ran up to full power, checked the engines and indicated ready to launch by switching nav lights from flash to steady. The launching officer's green wand swept down. It takes 2-3 seconds for the cat to fire. Ahead through the windscreen I could see nothing. My eyes were fixed on the artificial horizon in the middle of the instrument panel, but suddenly the cockpit filled with thick mist and the panel was totally obscured.

I couldn't cancel the launch. I had maybe a second before the cat fired, so I took my hand off the throttles and made a quick grab down on the left console to spin 'Cabin Temp Control' (1) clockwise to 'Full Hot', where it should have been.

But in doing this, my thumb caught an adjacent dimmer rheostat (33) and rotated it fully anti-clockwise, putting the panel lights out. And in my haste to get my hand back on the throttles my sleeve caught the handle of the connector on the side of my seat which carried my radio, intercom and oxygen, and pulled it out.

The cat fired and I was off down the catapult track and out over the invisible sea, blind, deaf and dumb, rotating the Vixen literally by the seat of my pants into what I hoped was a healthy climb away from the water. Within seconds the condensation cleared and my very alert 'looker' had his torch shining on the instruments, after which things looked up.

'...make a quick grab down on the left console...' Sea Vixen Pilot's Notes

Lieutenant K. Brent Owen,

Pilot, Scimitar, 803 Squadron, HMS *Ark Royal*, North Atlantic 1963-64

In 1960 when the Royal Navy and the RAF accepted me for pilot training within days of each other I had no difficulty in choosing between light and dark blue; it was carrier-flying for me! – and preferably fighters. And I was just in time to get a slot on 803 Squadron flying the last single-seat fighter the Royal Navy expected to have, the twin-engined swept-wing beast called the Scimitar.

At 40,000lbs it was the heaviest single-seat shipboard fighter in the world at the time, and flying it from WWII-designed carriers was a marginal operation at best: in a neat coincidence of mathematics, of 76 Scimitars built, 38 crashed. Starting life as a high-level interceptor, a tendency to fall out of the sky at high altitude led to its becoming a 'Low Level Strike Fighter'. Its redeeming features were unrelenting power, acceleration, and a phenomenal 540 degree-per-second rate of roll. Unlike the Hunters I flew in training, which had caused me a few moments of deep thought, as on my first solo when the engine blew up, but never seemed actually intent upon harming me, the Scimitar tried several times *quite deliberately* to do me serious mischief.

There being of course no dual-control Scimitars, one's first flight was a lonely affair. 'The acceleration is *amazing*! You won't get the gear up before 10,000 feet on your first flight,' Old Hands warned. 'Don't ever do *this*..... Don't ever do *that*!' All very intimidating. They would be watching my first Scimitar take-off, so I figured a way to show them how fortunate they were to have young Owen joining their illustrious Squadron. The big problem seemed to be the fierce acceleration, so I would tame the beast by the simple expedient of using only *partial* power. Anyone who knows anything about flying will not be surprised at the result. I found the resulting violent wing-drop at lift off *highly* stimulating – as did the spectators – and after firewalling both throttles it was indeed 10,000ft before my eyeballs stopped spinning and I got the gear and flaps up.

803 were popular at air shows in the summer, leaving the winter for carrier flying, usually in the North Sea, the North Atlantic and the Sub Arctic where *Ark Royal* was never warm and her deck rarely dry. The Scimitar's 'wet' wings were constantly weeping fuel. On my way out to an aircraft once when the ship was heeling in a turn, I slipped on a patch of fuel and slid on my back right across the 'non-skid' deck into the scupper, sixty feet above the waves. Taxying, let alone flying, in these conditions was a stimulating exercise. I once held the world speed record for losing a canopy, just over 600 knots very close to the sea, the sort of thing that made one consider a career in banking.

One morning, immediately after being catapulted in appalling weather, I was told to climb to 45,000 feet and conserve fuel as 'deck movement is now out of limits for flight operations.'! I was the only one airborne, with no airfields in range, and to make matters worse, like most of the ship's company I was suffering some looseness of bowel, the effect of fuel-oil in the drinking water. This was much aggravated by high altitude, and my need increased as the ship charged around looking for a calmer patch of water. I began to worry if my bowel would stand the 4g push on my lower belly from that big harness buckle if I ever did get back on deck. Circling slowly at 45,000 feet, nothing but cloud and sea for hundreds of miles, fearful images of 'bowel failure'on the flight deck crowded my mind, confirming US Navy pilot Paul T. Gillcrist's view (in *Feet Wet*) that 'most naval aviators would rather die in a ball of flame than screw up in front of their buddies.' Suffice to say the sphincter held, and I was hero of the day!

Great times; but when Prime Minister Harold Wilson announced what amounted to unilateral disarmament in 1964, I decided to go, so disgusted with the 'Wilson Gang' that I went instead across the Atlantic to American Airways where I have been for the past thirty-plus years. From time to time, in the comfort of my Captain's armchair, sipping coffee while the co-pilot does the difficult bits starting up my Boeing 767, I recall with a shiver those cold damp Scimitar cockpits in the drizzle of first light on *Ark Royal*'s flight deck. Cold War? It certainly was!

Lieutenant Commander I.F. Blake,
Pilot, Commanding Officer 892 Squadron, Sea Vixen, HMS *Centaur*,
Indian Ocean 1964

The dangers of flying were largely what created such a strong sense of camaraderie among the aircrew, and groundcrew, of a Squadron. And flying itself was fun, the kind of excitement associated with risky sports: my first ever deck-landing in a Supermarine Attacker of 800 Squadron, on HMS *Eagle*'s straight deck in 1954, was probably the single most frightening experience of my life – and the most exhilarating.

With the introduction of the angled deck it stopped being so frightening, unless the ship was moving a lot in rough seas – and of course at night. Deck-landing in the dark was vastly more nerve-racking, one reason being the lack of depth perception, like trying to gauge the distance of oncoming headlights on an unlit road. Approaching the carrier's sketchy and sometimes highly mobile array of tiny shaded lights at 130 knots required total concentration and absolute precision all the way down until you hit the deck, because you never knew how close you were. There was never time to enjoy a night deck-landing.

The peak of my career was commanding 892 Squadron, fourteen De Havilland Sea Vixens and about 400 men. The Sea Vixen was a twin-boom night fighter, descended from the Sea Vampire and the ill-fated DH110, of which an American once remarked 'only the British could build an aircraft with that much thrust and keep it subsonic at full throttle!'

In January 1964 the Squadron was aboard HMS *Centaur* off Aden when the Tanganyika army mutinied and took over the country, forcing President Julius Nyerere into hiding. When he appealed to the British government for help, the Admiralty instructed *Centaur* to embark an additional Squadron of helicopters and a Royal Marine Commando and sail for Dar es Salaam. Arriving in the

Zanzibar Channel in the middle of the night, we were met by a boat carrying the ex-British Army General who had run the Tanganyikan army for some years. He seemed desperately sad at what had happened. The army had not taken over the country, he told us, but they had mutinied and taken over the barracks in Dar es Salaam, another inland at Tabora, and a third at Nachingwea in the south.

Our clandestine arrival was well timed: the men in the Dar barracks had been celebrating and could be relied on to sleep late, and to have terrible hangovers when they did wake up. At the briefing in the chartroom, it was decided to put the Royal Marines ashore at dawn by helicopter to occupy the barracks. I was impressed by the assessment of military parity: ten to one – ten Tanganyikan soldiers equal one Royal Marine commando. Hangovers probably stretched the odds even further, for at dawn it was all over very quickly. The Royal Marines called to the mutineers in the guardroom to come out, and when they didn't they fired a bazooka into the building, killing two of them. The remainder of the barracks surrendered without further argument.

The next step was to repeat the exercise at Tabora, which was less straightforward because it was out of helicopter range and the Royal Marines would not have the benefit of surprise. The Royals solved the first problem by commandeering a Viscount airliner for transport; and it was proposed that 892 Squadron could make up for the lack of surprise by providing air cover for their landing and approach to the barracks.

Tabora being over 400 miles inland from Dar es Salaam, this was an interesting challenge for a night-fighter Squadron. In fact, laden with rocket-

'...embarked the six hundred men of 45 Commando...' HMS *Centaur*, Indian Ocean, 1964. BCC/MOD via Blake

pods, and having to descend at Tabora and fly around the barracks burning fuel at low level for some time, it was theoretically beyond our capability. It was only made possible by some careful calculations, and a flight profile which in a real war zone would have been absurd.

The operation took place on Saturday 25 January 1964. It relied on precise timing, since with our UHF radios we had no way of communicating with the Royal Marine Viscount in the air. I took off with four aircraft loaded with 400 gallons of overload fuel, and pods of 2-inch Rocket Projectiles which would make a threatening show, and could indeed be fired into the barracks if it came to it. We climbed at full throttle to a cruising altitude of 42,000 feet, then at the critical moment throttled back to idle and started a long glide. Fighter aircraft glide surprisingly well and the Sea Vixen was no exception; even with rocket-pods and drop-tanks it would cover nearly two miles for every thousand feet of altitude, using very little fuel, neatly extending our operational radius by the eighty miles we needed.

We passed the Viscount just short of the airfield and made noisy circuits while it landed, then made low passes over the barracks until my fuel gauge told me it was time to go, following the same unorthodox flight profile to return to *Centaur*. My log-book records the 2 hours 15 minutes flight time, but not the nervous strain suffered by Commander (Air) waiting on the bridge to see if we had got our fuel sums right. As it turned out, all four Vixens got back with around 800lbs fuel, enough for two circuits, and the ship was ready into wind. Long before we landed, the Royal Marines had taken over the barracks without incident.

Two days later we repeated the performance at Nachingwea, a straightforward trip two hundred miles south, and the revolution was over.

Thirty years later at a lunch in Vienna, where I was working with IBM, I mentioned this incident to a professional portrait painter called David Hankinson. He knew all about it, he told me; he was Captain of the frigate that escorted *Centaur* down from Aden and provided shore bombardment! Our host was both amazed and amused by such a coincidence, the more so since he too was in Dar es Salaam at the time, working for the World Bank, and remembered very well the relief of the population when the Royal Navy came to the rescue.

Lieutenant Paul Barton,
Pilot, Hiller 12E and Whirlwind Mk.7, 845 Naval Air Commando Squadron,
Borneo 1964.

It is not widely known that the Hiller 12E light helicopter, used for basic training in the Navy before the Gazelle, enjoyed a brief period of front-line glory in the first stage in the development of the 3rd Commando Brigade Air Squadron, 1964-65. The idea was born in 1963 in discussions between the Flag Officer Flying Training and the head of the Army Air Corps. When Rear Admiral Percy Gick suggested that Army Air might have something to teach Navy Commando Helicopter Squadrons, Brigadier Napier Crookenden's response was enthusiastic, and so it was that in March 1964, having learnt the Army way of flying at Middle Wallop, I found myself on my way to Borneo in HMS *Bulwark* with Mike Thompson and two Hiller 12Es, *en route* to join 845 Squadron, already engaged in the Borneo-Indonesia 'Confrontation' with Wessex Mk.Is.

The two Hillers we landed at Sibu on 6 April 1964 were robust little three-seaters with a Lycoming engine, cruised at 70 knots and could fly for two and a half hours on a 38-gallon tank of gasoline. Our army training had included many new skills and it did not take long to find out how useful these would be...

On 10 April a call for help came from an SAS patrol in trouble up near the border. Their need was urgent, the terrain inaccessible to the Wessex, so without further ado I set off in the Hiller 110 miles up the mighty Rajang River for Nanga Gaat – the first of many such journeys – refuelled, picked up a 'guide', Lieutenant Rod Robertson, and continued another 55 miles to a forward operating base at Long Jawi for more fuel and briefing. I was agape at the increasingly fantastic scenery and, there being no useful maps of the region, very glad of the company of an experienced jungle pilot. Rod was also, incidentally, the closest friend I ever had, tragically killed in a mid-air collision over Nanga Gaat some time later.

An RAF Valletta was in communcation with the stranded patrol, who had shot their way out of an encounter with an Indonesian patrol on the border, losing some vital supplies in the process. They were exhausted, unsure if the enemy were still nearby, and needed to get out fast. They said there was no hope of a Wessex getting down to them, there wasn't enough room.

The Wessex came along to help us find the missing men and we established their rough location thirty miles beyond Long Jawi. The terrain was awe-inspiring and, for a single-engined helicopter, intimidating – steep, cluttered primary jungle slopes up to 5000 feet with, to me, no identifiable features apart from the main border ridge. After a second refuelling at Long Jawi, and much helped by the Hiller's carefree handling and excellent visibility, we pinpointed the casualties, whereupon I rendezvoused with the Wessex at the nearest landing site a mile or so away to drop Rod and returned to set about the hairiest bit of flying I have ever undertaken, before or since. No amount of 'Confined Area Landing Practice' on Salisbury Plain, or at St Erth in Cornwall, could have prepared anyone for this..

At the bottom of a seemingly impossibly deep, dark hole in the primary jungle, the SAS had felled trees to create a Hiller-sized opening in the 200ft jungle canopy. At the bottom of this was my minuscule landing-site, which was going to require an almost vertical descent of nearly 1000 feet, with the last 300 feet absolutely vertical down through the foliage.

For the uninitiated, extreme care is needed when descending vertically in a helicopter because of a mysterious phenomenon known as 'vortex ring' which can induce a sudden uncontrollable descent; fully aware that if this happened going down that deep rock hole I would have no room to recover, I started down into it with a circumspection bordering on terror.

All went well, but it was a very uncanny feeling at the bottom, descending inch by inch on to the jungle floor with the rotor tips feet from the surrounding tree

'...holding our breath for the last ten minutes.' Barton

trunks, by no means sure I wasn't about to be shot at, or that I would be able to lift the patrol out without running out of power or hitting something, in which case we could all be here for ever.

I discovered the three-man patrol still had a hefty amount of kit which was going to mean three lifts up to the ridge site some 2500 feet above, all the time at full power with no chance of survival if the engine failed, not to mention the chance of the noise attracting the Indonesians back.

I lifted one man and a pile of kit, staggered vertically up and up and up, barely climbing with the throttle hard on the stops and the Lycoming yammering at full power. That magnificent engine! Never missed a beat. Once out of the gorge, I could creep the speed up into forward flight for the short transit to the ridge site.

Three lifts took the best part of an hour and went without a hitch, and my intense relief at pulling out of that eerie hole for the last time, transferring the last man and re-embarking Rod to navigate me back to Long Jawi was tempered only by knowledge that all that time at full power had left me very low on fuel and there was absolutely nowhere to land en route. I put the Hiller down at Long Jawi after 125 minutes airborne with the fuel needle on zero, Rod and I holding our breath for the last ten minutes.

This 'Mission Impossible' won the Hiller its spurs in Borneo and, in the course of 6¼ hours airborne on my fifth day on the job, taught me more than a little about the task that lay ahead.

By the mid-'60s I was having the time of my life flying 80 hours a month with 845 Squadron; Hillers, Wessex 1s, and a pair of old Whirlwind Mk.7s somebody had found in a hangar in Singapore. Our forward base was at Nanga Gaat, an idyllic spot 110 miles up the Rajang River from Sibu. There were fuel dumps at Song, about half-way between the two, and further on at Kapit, so when I was told to take five Royal Engineer topographers up to Nanga Gaat in a Wessex it should have been a routine trip.

However, there being no Wessex available, the task fell to one of the old

Whirlwinds, a quick calculation showing that with the five 'Dapper Mappers' (topographers always looked so smart) at 'standard' weight, the Whirlwind could lift off with 400lbs of fuel, just enough for the 55 miles to Song. So in they piled, big boys, and with a lot of kit, I thought. The Alvis coughed into life, I taxied to the runway and lurched somewhat sluggishly into the air from a running take-off. For a fully-laden Whirlwind this was not unusual, but when I only got 55 knots in the cruise instead of 70 it was plainly going to be a bit tight getting to Song. Undeterred, like Ernest K. Gann in his Liberators, I fine-tuned the engine up to 60 knots, just enough to make it with the statutory 100lbs landing allowance, or thereabouts.

Song was hotter and higher than Sibu. The Whirlwind did her best, but during the landing I was not fully in control: to put a helicopter down neatly on a sixpence you need more power than weight, which plainly I did not have. So I now had a problem: without a runway, I was not going to be able to lift five Mappers out of there with enough fuel to get to Nanga Gaat. I could top up at Kapit, but having landed so messily at Song I was reluctant to be any heavier than absolutely necessary when I got to Nanga Gaat, whose landing sites were on the side of a hill; an overshoot there would be disastrous.

Then I remembered Song's other landing-pad, just big enough for a single helicopter, at a height of 300 feet close to the river bank. If I put 300lbs of fuel in where I was, I reckoned I could cart my Mappers piecemeal up there, then get them all aboard and roll the aircraft over the cliff, as it were, an 'unofficial' technique that might be called Gravity Induced Airspeed Aquisition Profile or GIAAP.

As I finished hand-refuelling with the wobble-pump the rain started, a real tropical cataract. I rammed a new cartridge in the starter breech and shinned up into the cockpit before I got absolutely drenched, switched on the battery master switch, fuel cock, booster pumps, prime, magnetos, pressed the button and was rewarded with a futile hiss from the starter.

I understand that the design for the Mk.7's starter was the winner of a joke competition in *Boys' Own Paper*. It had a rotary six-cartridge breech in which you could never put more than one cartridge at a time, otherwise they would all go off together, with outstanding results. The gas from the 12-bore cartridge forced a piston up a cylinder, causing the engine to turn over and, hopefully, burst into life. Because of a tendency to disassemble itself with great violence, it was housed in a special blister panel to catch the bits and pieces.

My starter piston was simply jammed, and the solution was equally simple – hit it with a hammer. It was best to use a hide-face hammer, otherwise the whole thing could fall apart. Failing a hammer, a chock usually worked, but I had no chocks either, as they were too heavy to carry around. Option three was the flight-deck boot, a heavily reinforced but amazingly comfortable item of kit which made a very effective hide-face hammer; my passengers were thus treated to the spectacle of their captain leaping out of the cockpit in a fit of rage into a Niagara of rain, hopping around in the mud on one foot and clouting the starter with a boot with enough force to rock the whole aircraft. I couldn't have got any wetter if I'd fallen in the Rajang River.

The beast started and, pausing long enough to get my boot back on and let my rage evaporate along with some of the water, I ferried the Mappers to the top site, finally piled them all in, applied full power and – didn't move. Fortunately the Whirlwind's manual throttle allowed some judicious over-revving and, with a snatch on the collective lever and a good push forward on the stick, I persuaded it to drop off the edge of the pad to prove my 'GIAAP' theory. It worked.

Having already used a lot of precious fuel shuttling up to the launch pad, I was now prey to the liveliest misgivings about making Nanga Gaat, but nevertheless pressed on past Kapit and arrived safely, albeit with a bit of a thud: built like a brick outhouse, the Whirlwind could take a lot of such punishment provided all four wheels hit the ground at the same time.

I weighed my Mappers – not so Dapper now – before they departed on their business; they came out well above the 'standard' 200lbs a copy, more like 300, which explained all my troubles – a quarter of a ton too much army in the back. In future I always tried to use the scales *before* a flight.

But also I learned to respect that old warhorse which in some 1500 hours over the jungles of Borneo, the mountains of Scotland and the oceans of the world, never seriously let me down. Unusual I know, but I haven't a bad word to say about the old 'Whirly 7'.

Lieutenant Commander G.J. 'Tank' Sherman,
C.O. 845 Squadron, Wessex Mk.1, Borneo 1964

From 1963 to 1965 during Indonesia's confrontation with the newly-formed Malaysia, I commanded 845 Squadron flying Wessex Mk.1 helicopters in Sarawak, North Borneo, tasked to support military operations in the West Brigade Area, which was about twice the size of Wales.

Our base was about fifty miles inland up the mighty Rajang River at Sibu, the principal town of Sarawak's Third Division, rugged country with no roads and very few airstrips; the weather was unpredictable, there were no navigation aids and flying was normally confined to daylight hours. Flying at night *might* be possible, we agreed, but it would have to be a serious emergency.

Just before midnight on Tuesday, 1 March 1964 the Gurkha detachment at Song, about a hundred miles up-river from Sibu, radioed to say an Iban tribesman was very seriously injured. Could we get him to hospital?

I went to the radio and asked the Gurkha, 'What is the weather like at Song?'
'It is clear.'

Experience told me this was highly unlikely. The local climate had only two dependable features: there was very little wind and low cloud blanketed the whole country every night.

'Can you see the stars?'
'No. We can see no stars.' As expected: total overcast.
'Is it raining?'
'No. It is not raining.'

'Can the man wait until the morning?'

'No. He will die by then.'

I balanced an unknown tribesman's life against the very real risk of taking a helicopter a hundred miles inland over unmapped cloud-covered terrain and then back out to Sibu. There was no way of knowing how bad the weather was. Cloud base at Song might be five hundred feet – or fifty. And it was likely to get worse as the night went on.

'Will he die anyway?' I asked.

'We do not think so if he is rescued now.'

'OK. Expect me in about an hour.'

Five minutes later I was airborne in drizzle and, finding the cloudbase lowering rapidly, decided to abandon the direct route to Song and fly up the river. So began the most nerve-racking trip of my life. Before long the cloudbase was touching the 200ft trees lining the river banks and for the best part of an hour I felt my way upriver in almost total blackness between water and cloud, trying to keep contact with the left bank where Song lay.

The visibility at Song was so bad I would have missed it had they not heard me coming and waved flaming torches in the mist. This was the Gurkha's idea of 'clear weather'! I crept in and landed in the *padang* in front of the school.

I was unsure if I could face the journey back – until a doctor climbed into the cabin and told me on the intercom that he would be travelling with the patient, and we had half an hour to get him to hospital or he would die.

To return down the river was out of the question: for one thing I couldn't bring myself to do it, for another I was short of fuel. I was going to have to climb out on instruments and fly direct to Sibu at a safe height above the surrounding hills – about 3000 feet.

It was a viciously bumpy ride in black, turbulent cloud, navigation no more than dead-reckoning, i.e. intelligent guesswork, and my main problem was how to be sure I was close enough to Sibu to let down safely. To make matters worse the engine started surging and I had to take out the governor and revert to manual throttle control. The doctor kept up a running commentary on his patient, a 17-year-old, casualty of a longhouse feud with one hand almost severed at the wrist by a parang.

When my 'navigation' told me we should be in the vicinity of Sibu, I forced myself to reduce power and descend in the cloud, knowing that if I had got my sums wrong the first we would know about it was when we hit high ground. The descent took a very long time. As the altimeter slowly unwound I was glad doctor and patient in the back didn't know what was going on. I was reflecting on the fine line between heroics and stupidity when I saw the lights of Sibu ahead in the gloom.

An ambulance rushed the Iban to hospital where the brilliant Chinese surgeon Wong Sungkei mended him as good as new, which of course made it all worthwhile. But I still can't decide if I was a hero or a fool. Either way, a young man's life was saved by a crazily inaccurate Gurkha weather report, a slightly mad Royal Navy helicopter pilot and a brilliant Chinese surgeon – all in the best tradition of Sarawak's amiable multi-racial society.

Lieutenant H.W. Thomas,
Pilot, Scimitar, HMS *Ark Royal*, Moray Firth and South China Sea, 1965

February 11 1965. Two years' training for this day – my first deck landing. For the last two weeks, three of us on the training course at Lossiemouth had been practising with our Scimitars on the Dummy Deck, a mirror landing-sight on the edge of the runway and a painted carrier centre-line. The mirror shone a beam of yellow light at $3^{1}/_{2}°$ up the approach path, and all the pilot had to do for a perfect deck landing was to keep this yellow blob – the 'meatball' – level with the bars of fixed green lights either side of the mirror, keep on the centreline, and hold his speed within a knot or two of a 'datum' which varied according to weight. We had got quite good at it.

I cannot recall being the least bit nervous. The three of us climbed aboard our powerful 'beasts', started up, taxied out to the runway and took off, and in loose formation headed north for *Ark Royal*, somewhere in the Moray Firth.

I thought it seemed to be taking a long time to get to where the ship was supposed to be – the weather was a bit hazy – but at long last our Leader, an RAF exchange pilot called Gilroy, saw the carrier and called the *Ark*, who immediately gave instructions to join the landing circuit. We promptly began our approach to the ship, but about two miles out with the carrier now clearly in sight, Flyco told us to report our position; he could not see us, he said. We were nearly on top of the carrier when our third student, a lieutenant R.N., called 'That's not *Ark*, it's *Karel Doorman!*' To be fair to our Leader, to whom at that stage one aircraft carrier must have looked much like another, nobody had told us there was also a Dutch carrier in the Firth that morning.

Not far away, the Royal Navy's largest warship, 46,000 tons with a crew of 2500 men, was steaming fast into wind with a clear deck and a planeguard helo on station, and after being acidly invited by Flyco to join and commence our DLPs (Deck Landing Practice) at our earliest convenience, we flew neatly up 'the slot' on the ship's starboard side in echelon and timed our break to arrange ourselves evenly around the landing circuit.

Downwind abeam the ship at 600ft, I pushed the button to lower the undercarriage, selected flap, calculated my All-Up Weight and passed it to Flyco, checked the audio-airspeed, released my dinghy lanyard and leg-restraint cords, and tried to do everything as briefed. From here the ship looked unbelievably small, but there was too much going on to be nervous. Half-way round the final turn I picked up the 'meatball' and the Deck Landing Control Officer started talking. I straightened up on final approach looking down the ridiculously short white-painted centreline with him talking all the time: '...keep it coming...you're a little high...a little low...you're fast... you're slow...etc, etc' A very experienced pilot, he could tell my speed within a couple of knots from the Scimitar's nose-angle.

No finesse is required for deck landing – you just drive straight into the deck. The undercarriage is, by design, very strong. After three respectable touch-and-go's with the hook up, bouncing mightily off the deck and roaring off at full

'Hook Down!' This was IT!.. Thomas

'...barrelling in over the round-down at 135 knots...' Thomas

power, Flyco called me: 'Zero Three Four - hook down!' – this was it! Next time, far too busy to think about being nervous, I came barrelling in over the round-down at the back end of the ship at 135 knots hook down, glaring at the mirror all the way until the wheels hit the deck. The hook caught a wire and I came to a sudden, screaming, juddering 4g stop! From nowhere a Marshaller appeared and started waving; brain and memory re-engaged and I realized he wanted me to throttle back (which I had omitted to do), then raise the hook to drop the wire. This done, I remembered to switch off the blow and fold the wings as he motioned me forward. A quick burst of power to get moving, and he passed me on to another Marshaller who guided me into Fly One – the parking area at the very front of the ship.

This was another initiation. Unlike ashore, where they are advisory, flight deck Marshaller's signals are mandatory; only he can see how close you are to the edge, he not you is responsible for any mishap, and you have to trust him. I felt at times that my right wheel was no more than a foot from the edge. I was the first of the three down and he parked me as far up front as possible.

A blast of cold salt air hit me when I motored back the canopy. The crewman put the seat safety pins in and I tried to stand up and get out, only to find my legs had turned to jelly. I took a few deep breaths, climbed out carefully and proceeded with what I hoped was a nonchalant air down the trembling steel deck to the 'island', helped along by a thirty-knot gale in my back.

So far so good. We still had to get back to Lossiemouth and, unlike later pilots, we did not have the benefit of 'taster' shots on the shore catapult at Bedford; *Ark's* cat was to be another first.

A few decks down in a briefing room the Flight Deck Officer gave a very thorough briefing on catapult procedure and, an hour and a half after landing, we were climbing back into our Scimitars, ranged down aft on the port side.

'Now I *was* nervous.' Thomas

Now I *was* nervous. Was it really possible for that invisible contraption under the deck, which incidentally seemed to be leaking a worrying amount of steam, I thought, to get me and my twenty-ton monster up to flying speed in a mere 110 feet? I kept telling myself that it wasn't like going to the moon, people were doing it every day.

START UP! Flyco's light changed from red to amber, the chocks and lashings were removed and I gingerly followed the instructions of a Marshaller who took me up the deck and handed me over, sheep to the slaughter, to the catapult man. This expert inched me up the catapult track until my wheels hit the loading chocks, signalled 'Brakes On', and there I sat while half a dozen 'loaders' dived in underneath. Two of them should be hooking up the wire launching strop while down the back end others were lying flat under the jet-pipes attaching the 'Holdback', a short steel wire strop, one end fixed to the deck, the other to a T-bar under the aircraft.

Job done, the loaders scrambled out and gave 'thumbs up', the Flight Deck Officer signalled the catapult engineer to take up the tension and the launching shuttle took up the slack in the launching strop, raising the Scimitar's nose until the back-end thudded down on the tail-skid. From where I sat, high in the air, the distance to the end of the deck looked about the length of a cricket pitch. The aircraft was now bar-taut between shuttle and holdback.

Somebody held up a board: 'CHECK: FLAPS - BLOW - BRAKES OFF' and the Flight Deck Officer started winding me up, circling his green flag above his head. The engines screamed up to full power as I pushed the throttles fully forward and a heavy trembling shook the aircraft. Flag still circling, the FDO

118

looked ahead to make sure there was nothing in the way, at the catapult engineer for a green light, at Flyco for a green light, and finally at me. This is it! After showing the back of my hand against the perspex to indicate 'Ready to launch', I hastily jammed my elbows into my stomach in the approved fashion and forced my head hard back against the trembling headrest.

In what struck me, under the circumstances, as a quaintly courteous gesture, the FDO swept his green flag all the way down to the deck, at which instant the engineer in the control howdah would be slamming his fist down on a big red button marked 'FIRE'.

Nothing happened.

'Expect a delay of a couple of seconds,' they said. Well, I had time to readjust my elbows at least twice and take several more squints at the RPM gauges, and was beginning to move my head to see what was going on when after a jolt and a fractional pause my Scimitar and I were hurled off the bow and into the air. The sensation was indescribable. Nothing could have prepared for it. I blacked out momentarily before I found we were flying, my brain caught up and I got the wheels and flaps up and looked for my two buddies. We had to do three more of those before returning to Lossiemouth.

There was much to talk about that night in the wardroom bar among ourselves. Oddly, nobody else seemed much interested, but to me, that was the day I became a Fleet Air Arm pilot.

Well at least I had made a start.

Later that year I thought myself very privileged to be chosen to take one of 803 Squadron's Scimitars from *Ark Royal* to Hong Kong's Kai Tak airport two days ahead of the ship's visit. Hong Kong and Kai Tak were exciting names to a first-timer like me. *And* flying in meant an extra two days ashore.

'...a delay of a couple of sceonds,' they said...' Thomas

119

But come the day, 28 September, climbing into Scimitar XD333, I wondered if it was such a good idea. The skies in the South China Sea were black and ominous, it was raining hard and the ship was rolling and pitching quite alarmingly in a gale and heavy seas. Four Scimitars and four Sea Vixens were disembarking to Kai Tak, and as a concession to the weather it was decided that each Scimitar would 'buddy-up' with a Sea Vixen whose observer with his splendid radar set would shepherd the pair through the storms, avoiding the mountains around Hong Kong: the Scimitar had no radar or navigation aids whatsoever.

When the Flight Deck Officer dropped his flag I was looking straight down into the dirty green sea, but during the seemingly endless delay before the cat fired the bow lurched up again, and when I went off the end all I could see through the streaming windscreen was that ominous black sky. I joined up with my buddy Vixen, piloted by Lieutenant Pat Randall of 890 Squadron, and he led off towards Kai Tak at low level.

The cloud progressively lowered until, as we came up to the coast, it was just about down on the sea. Survival instincts stirring, I tucked in close to Pat. Not far ahead was a fair amount of 'cumulo-granitus', i.e. solid-cored cloud, and I thought 'Radar or no radar, if Pat goes into cloud at this height, I'm leaving!', but plainly he didn't entirely trust the radar either, for as the first tendrils of mist flicked over my canopy I felt the 'g' come on as we pulled up. We levelled off at a safe height to hear our Vixen 'Wing' leader calling Kai Tak.

'Kai Tak this is Navjet 139 plus seven jets. Request radar vectoring for landing.'

'Navjet 139 this is Kai Tak. Regret it is not possible for you to come here. We do not have towing arms for your aircraft.'

'Navjet 139, Roger.'

After a long pause while Leader thought this over: '*Ark Royal* this is Navjet 139. Returning to you, Unable to land Kai Tak. Stand by for ETA.'

'Navjet 139 Negative! Landing-on is impossible. Ship now pitching in excess of four degrees.'

At four degrees of pitch the back end of the ship was going up and down about sixty feet, periodically rising above the glideslope, meaning we might fly aboard through the picture windows of the Admiral's day-cabin in the stern. Leader explained all this to Kai Tak who not only refused landing permission, but also, despite being informed that we were nearly overhead and had to land because we were all going to run out of fuel in the not too distant future, offered no help whatsoever with our first pressing need, which was to get down below cloud without running into high ground.

Clinging leech-like to Pat's wing, I caught a glimpse of sea through a hole in the cloud and he took us down in a tight spiral. Safely underneath, all around was grey sea and cloud, no land. Back up at a safe height, weather clutter and the profusion of small islands off the Chinese coast made it hard for Pat's observer to be sure where we were, but he did a good job and when he said we were over Hong Kong we saw ships far below through another hole in the cloud.

'Tally ho!' cried Pat, racking into a tight starboard turn, 'Hang on!', and down we spiralled again, me clinging on to his wing for dear life.

To my intense relief it *was* Hong Kong harbour and at 800 feet we picked out the runway lights, made our approach and landed safely at Kai Tak in heavy rain. I am not sure whether we got landing clearance, but we were going to land anyway. Two others got there ahead of us, the remaining four landing shortly afterwards without mishap.

We were met by some RAF officers who had watched with amazement as Sea Vixens and Scimitars appeared out of the murk from all points of the compass. They told us why Air Traffic Control were so unhelpful: a few years earlier some Sea Venoms had come in from a carrier in a similar circumstances and scattered themselves all over the airfield, closing it to civil traffic for some hours and causing airliners to divert. Fortunately for all concerned there were no airliners anywhere near Hong Kong when Navjet 139 et al came in from the sea that day.

'Is this such a good idea...?' Thomas

Lieutenant Commander Jim Purvis,
Senior Pilot, 803 Squadron, Scimitars, HMS *Ark Royal*, Far East, 1965

Soon after I was lucky enough to be appointed Senior Pilot of 803 Squadron, we were on our way in *Ark Royal* to the Far East where throughout the 'Confrontation' with Indonesia a large fleet was maintained. *Ark* was long overdue for major refit and key equipment on the flight deck was prone to fail at crucial moments: we came within five minutes of losing six Scimitars in the middle of the Indian Ocean when the arrester gear hydraulics failed. There were no airborne tankers in those days, and Commander (Air) was planning to take one Scimitar into the crash-barrier and order the other five to eject, but the engineers got the wires fixed just before we ran out of fuel.

Although the Scimitar has been described as the RN's most exciting aircraft to fly, it was a brute to maintain; despite the prodigious feats performed night

'...the RN's most exciting aircraft...' Lt Neil Rankin engages barrier, HMS *Ark Royal*.
BCC/MOD via Thomas

Catapult launch, HMS *Victorious*, Mediterranean, 9.11.1960. Left, Lt Purvis in parachute. Right, Scimitar XD329

'Usual routine, Sir? Dry clothes to the sick bay?' Both BCC/MOD via Purvis

after night in the hangars by our maintenance men, we got barely enough flying time, which led to problems – five ejections and five more write-offs in ten months in the Far East. I telephoned our Leading Steward Taylor from Flyco one day to tell him Lieutenant Williams had just ejected:

'Usual routine, Sir?' he replied, Jeeves-like. 'Dry clothes to the sick bay?'

Of the ejections, Paddy Waring's was the most spectacular. Having lost an engine on a test flight and diverted ashore, he lost all hydraulics (and therefore control) on the last stage of the approach to Changi and ejected as the aircraft hit the runway. It bounced, rolled and landed upside down in a ball of flame; he landed hard on the concrete in his 'chute, and although he was able to walk down to the blaze and reassure the rescue crews that he was all right, I recently learned that he is confined to a wheelchair as a result of the damage he sustained that day.

Another Scimitar was left at Changi by Peter de Souza when a fire warning light came on and the C.O., Jack Worth, confirmed he was on fire; spurious warnings were routine, so you always got somebody to check. Pete pointed the aircraft away from habitation and ejected over shallow water, landing unhurt and paddling ashore in his dinghy. On the way he met a young girl and offered her a ride, which she gladly accepted; local headline 'GLAMOROUS BLONDE SAVES NAVAL PILOT!' The water being too shallow for a salvage vessel, whilst the accident investigators were puzzling out how to recover the wreck the local Chinese, with sampans and oil barrels, got at it and within a day or two most of it was on sale in Singapore's scrap market.

Despite the many problems, including the Labour government's sudden cancellation of the Navy's carrier building programme, morale in both Squadron and ship remained amazingly good. *Ark Royal* was a happy ship. 803 pilots felt we had the most enjoyable and satisfying flying in the Navy. In later life, working in industry, I would look back and wonder how it was that an organization with so much defective and unreliable equipment, constant fires and emergencies, a 70-80 hour working week and abominable living conditions managed to run so efficiently and maintain such high morale. It was certainly true of our aircraft carriers that 'man is splendid in adversity', but above all else there was the sense that what we were doing was immensely worthwhile.

Lieutenant Commander Chuck Giles,
Senior Pilot, 801 Squadron, Buccaneers, HMS *Victorious*, Suez Canal, 1965

The Buccaneer Mk 1 had no air-to-air combat capability whatsoever, and only a modest Electronic Warfare kit. Combined with the very moderate thrust provided by its Gyron Junior engines, particularly in tropical climes, this made us extremely vulnerable to any form of fighter threat. Well, totally defenceless really.

Pondering this on the way up the Red Sea approaching the Suez Canal, I idly put it to our Air Weapons Instructor, Jack Smith, that behind every palm tree along the edge of the canal there would likely be a Soviet telephoto lens, and what a pity we couldn't hang something like a Sidewinder on one of our Buccaneers on the flight deck as we went through. Something to spread alarm and despondency among our potential enemies.

Jack took this seriously. He got his armourers to make a 'Sidewinder' out of beer cans welded end to end, painted white, complete with fins and a most convincing nose-cone. Entering the canal I was delighted to see the gleaming new missile on a wing pylon of the most prominent Buccaneer in the range, a perfect photo-opportunity for Russian spies.

But alas, unknown to me – and, surprisingly, to Jack – Suez Canal regulations forbid warships in transit to display weapons of war. And unfortunately our Commander (Air), Ivan Brown, who knew his stuff, saw the 'Sidewinder' on his way to lunch that day – and it had to go.

But it got three hours' exposure to Soviet lenses and who knows, the beer-can missile may have caused an urgent reappraisal of the Buccaneer threat in the enemy camp. On the other hand they may have thought we were completely mad.

Lieutenant Tony Tayler,
Observer, Buccaneer, Royal Naval Test Squadron, Boscombe Down, 1965

Operational crews train intensively on any new aircraft type, and all of a Squadron's aircraft are near-identical. The Naval Test Squadron at Boscombe Down was very different: pilots were expected to fly any aircraft after reading Pilot's Notes and maybe getting a brief from an old hand, and test observers were usually expected to find things out for themselves.

The Buccaneer which I climbed into one cloudy day in 1965, after four or five trips on the type, was loaded with four inert 1000lb bombs for an exercise which had been cancelled due to low cloud. Neither I nor the pilot had yet flown in a Buccaneer with an armament system fitted. Our mission was merely to practise the Buccaneer's special bomb-delivery profile known as Low Altitude Bombing System or LABS, by going through the motions. We didn't need the bombs; but in the pervading urgency of the height of the Cold War there wasn't time to unload them.

LABS was designed to allow safe delivery of a nuclear bomb by ensuring that the strike aircraft was not consumed in its own nuclear fireball: after a high-speed low-level approach you pulled up at three miles and, at about forty-five degrees nose-up, 'tossed' the bomb on to the target, completing the half-loop and exiting fast in the opposite direction as low as possible. Timing of weapon release was by computer, the crew's job being to get to the release point at the right speed, height and climb-angle.

After take-off we were directed to an empty piece of sky somewhere over Somerset and commenced a series of 'dry runs', for which the two tons of inert bombs in the bomb-bay were no more than a slight inconvenience. But for some reason we got no computer commands in the pilot's Head Up Display (HUD) and, after several abortive runs, were obliged to pause and try all the likely-looking switches around both cockpits, including the bomb doors, until at last we got a picture in the HUD. All systems go..

At the release point on the next 'dry-run', we felt four heavy thumps. I looked over the side. We were over full cloud cover and I could see nothing of the ground, or the bombs. Down there somewhere was a fair-sized country town.

On arrival back at Boscombe the bomb bay was empty. And it was quickly established that the Master Armament Safety Switch in the rear cockpit, of which up to that moment I knew nothing, was 'LIVE'.

After a short interview with the Boss, my pilot and I received individual copies of the following instruction:

You are to submit to me, by 0900 on Thursday 1st July 1965,
a report on the circumstances in which bombs were dropped
from Buccaneer XK 525 on Friday 25th June 1965

G.R. Higgs Commander

After that a deathly quiet descended on this affair. The bombs disappeared into the ether. No Board of Inquiry. No Court Martial. Yet.

Later in 1965, when I went with the same pilot to collect a 'modified'

Buccaneer from the makers at Brough in Yorkshire, we naturally took a keen interest in the 'Mods' and checked through them with the engineers; strangely though, they could not tell us anything about a certain 'Mod xxx', saying that no Buccaneer had yet flown with it fitted.

This Mod, we later learned, stemmed from a tragic accident involving Commander Des Russell, who ditched in a Scimitar alongside a carrier after parting an arrester wire, became trapped in the cockpit and sank in full view of Press and TV crews. The subsequent urgent demand for some way of getting aircrew out of ditched aircraft, even injured or unconscious, entailed many years' work at the Royal Aircraft Establishment at Farnborough, including some very brave experimental underwater ejections by navy doctors; it produced a modification to the ejection seat which sensed when the aircraft was underwater, fired the seat at half charge, pushed the occupant out of the cockpit and inflated his Mae West.

A careful search of our modified 'Bucc' revealed in both cockpits a new lever with two positions marked respectively SAFE and LIVE, and having no idea what the levers did, we put both to SAFE and took off for Boscombe Down. We had to fly high above the civil airways until about twenty miles out, then make a rapid descent, during which there was a fierce hiss and an alarming smell of cordite. 'Mod xxx', confused by the rapid pressure increase, had fired my seat at half charge to initiate underwater ejection.

The mysterious levers being SAFE, the charge vented harmlessly, I am pleased to report. Set to LIVE, my seat would have released all my straps, including the parachute, before pushing me out through the canopy to be bisected a split-second later by the Buccaneer's 400-knot tail fin.

Teething troubles like this were soon overcome and 'Mod xxx' proved its worth many times over. For me, I have to say, in later deck-landing trials aboard USS *Lexington* and HMS *Hermes*, precisely the conditions for which it was designed, I could somehow never bring myself to put that lever to LIVE. That *hiss* lives on in my nightmares.

Lieutenant Commander J.M. Milne,
Observer, Wessex Mk.1, 819 Squadron, HMS *Ark Royal*, Moray Firth, 1965
HMS *Bulwark*, Mediterranean, 1972

On 28 February 1965 in the Moray Firth, when *Ark Royal*'s Whirlwind Planeguard helicopter went unserviceable, an 819 Squadron Anti-submarine Wessex which happened to be doing a running turn-round on deck was ordered to take over Planeguard duty for the next fixed-wing launch and recover. I was observer of the Wessex.

It began snowing as the rescue diver clambered aboard with his air bottles; the ship started turning into wind and by the time we reached Planeguard station about 200 yards off the port quarter we were flying in thick snow, 75 feet above the sea with the main cabin door on the starboard side shut. I was in my seat on

126

the port side of the cabin, the aircrewman and SAR diver beside the main door, wearing despatcher harnesses, when without warning the engine quit – intakes choked with snow – and we plummeted into the water and rolled over to the right.

The Wessex had just been fitted with an improved observer's escape window on the port side, and the next moment I was standing on the side of the aircraft looking down into the cabin through the hole where my window had been, astonished to see diver and aircrewman involved in what appeared to be a strenuous tussle.

The diver, I learned later, wanted to get the main cabin door open so he could use his underwater-breathing equipment, whereas the aircrewman, a normal air-breathing creature, naturally wanted to keep it shut. Thinking that one or both had been stunned or injured and deciding I must try and help them out, I took a step back, promptly falling back into the cabin through the rear window, which was not designed to be stood upon. I hastily re-evacuated the half-submerged cabin, via the rear window, at about the same time as the aircrewman, having decided it was more important to get out than win the argument, came out through the other one. We jumped into the water with our pilot, Tom Bowler, inflated our dinghies and climbed aboard and after a while the diver, having had a worthwhile swim, popped up to the surface and joined us.

The ship had disappeared, the sound of her engines fading away in the snow. We tied our dinghies together and I activated my SARBE Search And Rescue Beacon, a small personal radio carried in the life-jacket.

The only witness to our ditching was a Midshipman on the quarterdeck who had the good sense to ring the bridge, and the mighty *Ark* circled back in the snow, having called another Wessex back from the screen to help pick us up.

Before long the carrier's bow emerged eerily from the gloom and she gently turned and stopped beam-on to launch a sea-boat, just as the screen Wessex arrived. The diver flatly refused another ride in a Wessex and declared he would wait for the boat. The rest of us preferred the devil we knew and were back aboard in minutes, none the worse for wear. Wessex XM931 sank in twenty-nine fathoms and is still there.

I wrote a letter of thanks to Burndept Ltd, the makers of SARBE, and some months later was delighted to be presented with a silver 'Sarbe Tankard', awarded, I believe, to all aircrew who use their Sarbe 'in anger'.

Far from the Moray Firth, on a summer day in the Aegean Sea in 1972, HMS *Bulwark* lay at anchor after a hectic morning's flying. There was to be a maximum effort that afternoon in support of Royal Marines ashore, but for now all was quiet. People up from below decks to enjoy the sunshine strolled among ground crews pre-flighting 845 Squadron's Wessex 5s all over the flight deck. Far off on the hazy horizon lay the square bulk of US carrier *Ranger*, flying fixed-wing support for the troops ashore, and somewhere in the vicinity there was a US helicopter carrier like *Bulwark*.

Unusually in a non-flying period, Lieutenant Commander (Flying) was in Flyco when an American voice came over one of his speakers.

'*Bulwark* this is *Ranger* Two Five. I'd like permission to do a pass down your port side in a coupla minutes, Sir. Do you have any traffic?'

And assuming this was a helicopter, Lieutenant Commander (Flying) replied, '*Ranger* Two Five no problem. We have no traffic. Give me a one-minute call.'

'Much obliged Sir, and we're one minute to run.'

One minute later there was a shattering explosion.

In the upper levels of the ship the shock felt like an explosion below decks. Down in the engine room they were so sure there had been a major crash or explosion on deck they started emergency procedures. All down the flight deck Wessex windows blew out and clattered to the deck. I was in the Operations Room just inside the island behind a closed steel door which was sucked from its mountings by the force of the blast. Nobody in the Ops room or anywhere else below decks had the slightest clue what had happened. Some sudden disaster had shattered the comparative tranquillity of a lunchtime break in our little mock war, and for a while in the ensuing dusty silence it was as if the ship's heart stopped – until an unusually sheepish Lieutenant Commander (Flying) came on the Tannoy to explain: one of the USS *Ranger*'s A-5 Vigilante attack bombers had just flown down the port side, doing about Mach 1.5.

With shock-waves like that, I thought, who needs *bombs*?

Lieutenant K.J.McK. Ayres,
Pilot, Wessex MkI and Wasp, RNAS Culdrose 1966, RNAS Portland 1969

For a trainee anti-submarine helicopter pilot, two hours' 'night dipping' – hovering 30ft above the water with a sonar transducer on the end of a cable hunting non-existent submarines - was bad enough. All you needed to turn it into sheer misery was an instructor you actively disliked

It was one of those totally black nights over a flat calm sea that require a very high level of concentration. We were about an hour into a two-hour sortie, me doing all the work and sweating in my immersion suit. Instructor 'T' had given me a hard time from the moment we met in the briefing room and the ear-bashing increased exponentially as the sortie progressed, made worse by the fact that the strictures he was heaping on my miserable head were mostly well deserved. The crew in the back kept very quiet.

We had just completed a 'jump' from one spot to the next and settled in the hover over the sonar cable when the stream of invective from the left-hand seat unaccountably dried up. Stealing a glance, I was delighted to see 'T' engrossed in the difficult manoeuvre of trying to have a pee, and having a great deal of trouble.

Since you couldn't get up and walk around in the cockpit, the Wessex's designers had thoughtfully provided each pilot with a sort of funnel affair on the end of a rubber tube, which was quite straightforward; but the same could not be said for the corrresponding facility on the immersion suit; the tightly-laced little widger provided for personal relief was neither quick nor easy to use. The more 'T' struggled with it the happier I got, until there was a grave danger of a guffaw.

The widger won. 'Break dip and return to base!' he snapped.

'But there's still an hour to go –'

'Don't argue. Return to base!'

The flight back to Culdrose was wonderfully peaceful. I caught myself humming under my breath. I didn't hurry. In fact, 'T' being such a stickler, I carried out all the procedures with extra care and precision. He unbuckled his harness and was out of the door before we stopped rolling, scurrying out from under the rotor. But to my surprise he suddenly halted beside the Marshaller.

Typical, I thought: watching for me to make a mistake in the shut-down drill. But when all was done he was still there. I walked over, removing my helmet.

'I thought you wanted a pee?'

'I did!' he responded grimly. And as we walked in silence to the Squadron office I could hear the squelching of his boots.

At RNAS Portland in 1969 I was flying one of two Wasps doing deck-landings on training frigate HMS *Undaunted* for the benefit of trainee flight-deck crew. The other pilot was one 'TT'; we were both solo, my regular aircrewman, Charlie Gracie, being on deck helping the trainees.

I had just made my sixth landing, 'TT' somewhere round behind me in the circuit, when I heard his MAYDAY call. This was a regular occurrence at Portland in those days, but it always set the adrenalin going. I waved away the 'chain gang', who under Charlie's supervision was about to anchor me to the deck, and signalled Charlie to get aboard, fast. He had no helmet or flying gear, but our own ship having just completed the notorious Portland Work-up, he didn't hesitate; he jumped in.

Lifting off *Undaunted*'s deck I saw 'TT's Wasp splashing down in the sea in a great cloud of spray about 500 yards on the starboard beam. His flotation gear didn't work and by the time we got there the Wasp was inverted and sinking. Charlie already had the hoist wire down. When 'TT' popped up like a porpoise the hook was dangling in front of his nose and we had him aboard within seconds. He looked all right, but I headed inshore in case he had any injuries, thinking 'that's a beer he owes me'.

He had no injuries, and I got no beer.

'Bloody fool!' was his greeting when we decanted him dripping onto the concrete. 'You didn't even give me time to get my SARBE going!'

This meant, of course, that he couldn't claim the silver tankard presented by the manufacturers of SARBE, the rescue beacon we all carried in our life-jackets, whenever their product was used in a rescue.

In the heat of the moment, I hadn't thought of that.

Lieutenant Commander Bob McQueen,
Commanding Officer, 899 Squadron, Sea Vixens, HMS *Eagle*, 1966.
RNAS Yeovilton, 1968

In the course of my 700-odd fixed-wing carrier landings in the comparatively safe environment of the angled deck, several refinements were introduced to improve the art of deck-landing and make it safer.

One was the 'Donkey's Tail', a vertical string of lights dropped down over the ship's stern to extend the very short line of lights indicating the deck centreline. For the pilot on approach at night its effect was magical, for the slightest deviation from the true centreline immediately showed up as a kink in the donkey's tail, allowing much more precise line-up control than before; and as a Sea Vixen landing at 130 knots on one of the smaller carriers like *Centaur* or *Hermes* could not be more than two feet off-centre without the risk of hitting something, this was important.

Even more momentous was the introduction of the LSO or Landing Safety Officer, previously the 'batsman', who had been pronounced redundant with the introduction of the mirror landing sight. Initial problems with the big fast jets forced a re-think on this and the LSO reappeared in the form of a senior pilot, of such experience that even I as a Squadron C.O. could not question his judgement, monitoring all landings from the deck-edge with the power to 'wave off' any dubious approaches. And because his assessment of each landing was posted up in stark colour on a board in that most public of places, the Squadron briefing-room – red for dangerous; yellow, passable; green, good; and green star,

'...dare one say, a little tame?' LSO in foreground. Manning

teacher's pet – deck-landing became competitive. The LSO, stalking the crew-rooms with his clipboard preaching the one true faith, standardization, was at first resented by some of us more senior and experienced pilots, but there was no escaping the very public verdict of 'The Board', or the fact that deck-landing safety improved tremendously, to the extent that most pilots including myself were soon catching the target No.3 wire on the centreline every time. Dare one say – a little tame?

However, other things could happen to spoil a pretty row of 'greens'.

On 2 March 1966 I returned to HMS *Eagle* in my Sea Vixen with my observer, Mick Comber, flew a good approach and thumped satisfyingly onto the deck in just the right place to put my hook into No.3 wire. Ho hum, another boring green stamp, I thought. So certain was I of catching a wire that I pulled the throttles back; but this was a mistake, for as the engines wound down there was no familiar snatch from the arrester-cable, instead we trundled unimpeded at high speed up the short centreline. I slammed the throttles forward to try and get some power on before we dropped into space, but we reached the end of the deck at something well below the Sea Vixen's advertised stalling speed, fell off and sank towards the water. I ordered Mick to eject.

I had always been very cynical about the so-called pressure-wave or air-cushion effect that was supposed to support heavier-than-air machines flying very close to the ground or water, but I am now a fully-paid up member of the Air-Cushion Club. For an age while the two Avons spooled up from idle, airspeed so low that we should have fallen out of the air, we creamed along just above the waves throwing up, I am told, a most impressive wake, until at last the engines kicked in and we regained flying speed. My final arrival was a good No.3 wire, on the centreline, but despite all my pleas the LSO put a richly-deserved and conspicuous yellow stamp on the end of my proud row of greens.

I was told that after hitting the deck in the right place my hook bounced clear over the 3rd and 4th wires. This did not happen often with the Sea Vixen, but I for one was never caught out again.

And what happened to Mick? Despite being able to see very little from his recessed cockpit, he said he decided to stay while we kept flying; and when he announced he was happy to continue flying as my observer I put a stop to the bar-talk as to whether he should be court-martialled for disobeying an order.

On 1 July 1968, a day when big pink hailstones were reported falling on Wales, I climbed out to the west from RNAS Yeovilton in a Sea Vixen for some high-level intercepts with observer John O'Gorman. We were climbing to 40,000 feet, so would be well above the thick black cumulo-nimbus I noticed up ahead on take-off by the time we got to that part of the sky. But after several minutes in cloud we ran into turbulence that shook the aircraft so badly it was hard to read the instruments, which anyway seemed to be going crazy, the mach needle going up over Mach 2, the altimeter stuck, airspeed and vertical speed completely 'off the clock'.

Mindful of an old training movie about flying in thunderstorms, and hoping the gyros were still working, I tried to hold a constant altitude and decided, possibly wrongly, to turn 180 degrees to get back out of the storm. This seemed to take an age, but eventually the turbulence eased and the pressure instruments gradually resumed more normal readings. I carried out a stall check, dumped fuel and returned to Yeovilton, landed normally and taxied in to the Squadron dispersal.

Our nose radome was punctured in several places with holes the size of a fist and the deep dents all along the leading edges of the wings looked as if they had been inflicted by a team of demented blacksmiths with heavy hammers. I shall never forget the look on the marshaller's face as we taxied in.

That summer thunderstorm was in an air-mass straight up from the Sahara, hence the gigantic pink hailstones which we flew into at Mach 0.85 or about 430 knots. Our pitot tube, which measures air pressure for the instruments, had speared a hailstone and choked with ice, hence the mayhem on the instrument panel. The aircraft was a write-off.

Lieutenant Chris Craig,
Pilot, Wessex HAS 1, 820 Squadron, HMS *Eagle*, South China Sea, 1966

Fifteen minutes to take-off and there was a catapult delay. It was night, there were jets to launch and Gannets to recover and I was flying the Planeguard Wessex. Right at the back end of the flight deck, when the green light from Flyco at last allowed us to lift off out of the choking funnel-smoke it was an immense relief to get airborne; the delay had cost a lot of valuable fuel.

With nothing visible beyond the windscreen and vertigo threatening, co-pilot Rob Hughes and I concentrated on our instruments; in the back, observer Mike Pringle set up his nav computer and young Ricketts the aircrewman readied the rescue hoist. Soon we were slipping along 125 feet above the water in a blind race-track pattern on *Eagle*'s quarter, full of the knowledge that the water here is 12,000 feet deep and four naval Wessex have been lost in the Far East in the past year, with eight dead. I handed over the controls to Rob to sharpen up his instrument scan.

Orange tongues of flame showed Vixens and Buccaneers going off the catapults until the last tiny glowing stub flickered and died, quenched in the suffocating blackness. Jet launch complete. Switching frequency, we heard the returning Gannets on talkdown and watched the first one all the way down onto the deck. Safely hooked on, he turned his lights to dim. Good. I eased stiff muscles against my locked harness. Tedious..

'Mayday! Engine failed. Ditching....' Understated and controlled. Very British.

I told Rob to stay on instruments and fixed my eyes on the flashing lights of the terminally descending second Gannet, the most important thing being to get a precise 'on-top' of the ditching: to get into position to winch up the survivors in these horizonless conditions we were going to have to fly a very precise circuit on instruments.

When we arrived overhead, the floating Gannet's lights were flashing eerily in the water. 'Mark the plot!' Mike Pringle in the back took charge. 'Stand by departing...On top...Now!' He talked us round the circuit, four smooth turns back into wind, then the autopilot would bring us safely down to the hover at winching height, just short of the ditching position. The autopilot lived up to its dubious reputation over smooth seas like this and needed some assistance. The Gannet's lights had vanished. 100 feet...75...50...at 30 feet above the invisible water the vibration level rose, the rotorhead shuddered and circulating salt spray enveloped the helicopter as we entered the hover. If we had got it right, the ditched aircrew should be a hundred yards in our 11 o'clock position; if not, they could be anywhere. These waters are full of sharks.

I took the controls and crabbed the aircraft slowly forward. The crosswires on the drift indicator were the only indication of the aircraft's movement. There were no lights in the water, but a couple of miles ahead *Eagle* had finished her emergency turnback and was now coming straight for us. 'I hope she can see us on her radar,' I was thinking when Rob and I were blinded by one of her searchlights. Struggling for control of helicopter, nerves and temper, I crushed the transmit button and yelled, 'Put that bloody light out! Do you want all of us in the water?'

The light died and in intensified darkness we resumed our creeping search, Mike and AB Ricketts at the cabin door with the winch ready. At last a weak red 'minflare' arced up into the night off to our right at one o'clock. Mike was soon able to see a tiny winking sea-cell light and started talking us in for the final approach, a technique we had practised a thousand times.

I decided to use the new rescue floodlights fitted only two days before, told Rob to switch them on and found myself in a sparkling glitter-bowl of recirculating seawater, disconcerting at first, but through the silver mist of spray I could now see the life raft, one survivor in it and another alongside hanging on.

Two minutes later the hanger-on was safe in our rear cabin, but the other one, whose dinghy, relieved of the braking effect of his waterlogged colleague, slid away under the force of our downwash, spinning and skidding in all directions every time we came near him, was not so easy. Time after time we tried, burning precious fuel. 'Why doesn't he get out of his dinghy?' Rob wailed. 'Would you?' I replied, thinking of the sharks.

Soaked with sweat and increasingly worried about fuel, I struggled to follow Mike's instructions: 'Come left...forward...right...missed him! Left again...Oh Gawd!...Come back and left,' until suddenly he was cut off. After a brief silence, Ricketts came on, clear and positive: 'Lt. Pringle's mike has failed. I've taken over his intercom lead...' and he continued conning the helicopter until, ironically, our destructive downwash eventually solved the problem of the skittish dinghy by waterlogging it, and our second dripping victim was soon on his grateful way up on the winchwire. A few minutes later we were back on *Eagle's* deck with bare minimum landing fuel. The survivors trooped off to the sick bay. Typically, the fickle moon chose that moment to appear and lighten the horizon.

A little later the Squadron Senior Pilot breezed into the greasy-spoon Aircrew

Refreshment Bar as I was tucking into a full-plate fry-up in my sweat-stained overalls.

'How'd it go, Chris?'

'Routine,' I told him. 'No problem.'

HMS *Eagle*, South China Sea, 1966. BCC/MOD via Craig

Lieutenant Allan Tarver,
Pilot, Sea Vixen, 890 Squadron, HMS *Ark Royal*, Indian Ocean, 1966

On 22 March 1966, west of Sumatra, 890 Squadron began a series of trials with 500lb and 1000lb bombs fitted with VT (variable timed) fuses, set to explode at a predetermined height above the target for maximum blast and shrapnel effect. We would drop one VT bomb at the start of each sortie, aimed at a smoke float in the water a safe distance from the ship.

The first morning's sorties passed uneventfully, the fuses behaving as advertised. I was No 2 in a division of Sea Vixens programmed for the same routine in the afternoon, and made my way with my observer, John Stutchbury, to our Vixen parked on the port after corner of the flight deck. I was at the top of the ladder with one foot in the cockpit when someone tugged my leg. It was division leader James Patrick with his observer Colin Lightfoot. Their aircraft was still in the hangar and might not be ready; James had to have a day trip before flying that night, so we were to swop aircraft.

John and I got into the other Vixen in the hangar and came up on the lift in time to launch with the division as planned, except that James was now leading in 'my' aircraft and, having started from right down aft on the flight deck, he was last off the catapult.

The planeguard Wessex dropped a smoke-float target a couple of miles off the port beam and, in due course, the rest of us having dropped our bombs with the expected result, I pulled out of the bombing circuit watching Leader over my shoulder as he peeled into his dive.

But instead of coming off his wing the bomb appeared to explode on its pylon. The aircraft disappeared in a ball of flame and smoke. A shower of wreckage cascaded down towards the ocean. After a few seconds one fully-developed parachute emerged from the smoke but sadly the harness hung empty. I can see it now: *Ark* starting her ponderous turn towards that smudge of dirty smoke and that drifting white parachute, all that remained of 'my' aircraft.

Flight Lieutenant Tom Eeles,
RAF Exchange Pilot, Buccaneer, 801 Squadron, HMS *Victorious*, South China Sea 1967.

The first Royal Naval Squadron in which I was privileged to serve was also the first to receive the new Buccaneer S Mk.2, and as is the custom with new aircraft there were many things that didn't work properly on this new wonder jet; the Rolls-Royce Spey turbofan engines in particular were in a state of constant modification, so the number of engine changes undertaken in the close confines of *Victorious's* hangar must have run into treble figures. Nevertheless, the engineers performed miracles, driven hard by 801's fearsome junior Air Engineer Officer – an impressive individual known as Split-Pin. In all respects this officer represented the epitome of a Viking looter and rapist, sporting a huge bushy red beard and drinking vast quantities of anything that came to hand.

At the end of one mammoth series of engine changes, it was decided to reward the indefatigable Split-Pin for his efforts by offering him a trip in the back seat.

Now Split-Pin had never flown before, let alone from a carrier deck in the South China Sea in the back of a Buccaneer S Mk.2 strike jet, sandwiched between two of his own brand new Spey engines, and after being strapped extra-tight into his ejection seat by two of his own ratings it is safe to assume he was hot, nervous, very uncomfortable and probably wishing he was back in the hangar in his white overalls. The purpose of the sortie was, naturally, to carry out a double engine test flight.

Shortly after engine start he asked me whether the aircraft was serviceable.

'Of course not!' I unwisely joked. 'None of the cabs you lot of useless engineers muck about with are ever *serviceable*.'

Much relieved to hear this, and without telling me, Split-Pin undid all those uncomfortable straps, put the safety-pins in his ejection seat and sat back in anticipation of a short taxy up into the deck park, where he could get out and scurry back down below.

Taxy forward we did, but to Split-Pin's increasing puzzlement and consternation the aircraft was marshalled on to the catapult; flight-deck crew dived underneath and attached the bridle and hold-back, the tension came on, the tail-skid thumped on the deck and the nose reared up, engines winding up to full power in a very good imitation of a Buccaneer about to launch.

'What's going on?' Split-Pin squawked. 'I thought you said we were unserviceable!!'

'Certainly not,' I told him. 'Only pulling your leg.'

'But – !'

Down went the green flag and off we went down the catapult..

Split-Pin didn't contribute much to the conduct of the engine test schedules, spending most of the sortie trying to get his straps reconnected. By the time we got back in the landing circuit he had the lap-strap done up, but sadly he never did manage the shoulder straps and thus smote his forehead a mighty blow on the coaming when we caught a wire and decelerated from 135 knots to zero in

'...consternation...the aircraft was marshalled onto the catapult...' BCC/MOD via Eeles.

'...and thus struck his forehead a mighty blow on the coaming when we caught a wire.'
BCC/MOD via Eeles

a couple of seconds.

But his image as a Viking marauder, though slightly dented physically, remained safe because, from that day to this, nobody ever knew what happened. What did this teach me? Be very careful what you say to engineers.

In 1970, still on exchange, I was back at RNAS Lossiemouth instructing on the old Mk.1 Buccaneer with Gyron Junior engines. As I recall, the study-pack issued to students on arrival in 736 Squadron included a Martin-Baker tie: it

HMS Victorious, South China Sea, 1967. BCC/MOD via Eeles

was not a question of *if*, but *when* you would be entitled to wear it.

But I believe Ivor Evans and I were the only two to eject on a student's *first* trip. He was one of the RAF pilots training with the Navy for the RAF's new Mk.2 Buccaneer Squadrons, and the old Mk.1 Buccaneers dragged out of retirement for these courses were decidedly tired. For example, their Gyron Junior engines, never user-friendly, were extremely difficult to accelerate in a crosswind on the runway; you often had to point directly into wind, brakes on, to persuade the engines to accelerate up to full power, then turn to line up with the runway as you started the take-off roll. The acceleration was so sluggish that this evolution never presented any difficulty. There were no dual-controlled Buccaneers, so the instructor in the back was reduced to the capacity of adviser-cum-consultant.

Ominously, on Ivor's first trip he had great difficulty with the port engine on the runway; but he finally got it wound up and off we went. All went well until we came back for circuits and landings and he came in too high on his first approach. At about 200ft I told him to overshoot and go round again, but when he pushed the throttles forward for full power all we got from the port engine was a lot of loud bangs and choking noises. With commendable alacrity for a pilot on his first flight on type, Ivor lifted the wheels and got the airbrake in, but

'Isaac Newton's First Law…' BCC/MOD via Eeles

with landing-flap down and the 'blown' ailerons and tailplane bleeding large amounts of air from our one good engine, Isaac Newton's First Law soon kicked in and it very rapidly became evident that this sortie was not going to end satisfactorily without the help of Mr.Martin Baker's rocket-assisted deck-chair.

I had loosened my shoulder harness to see ahead round the top of Ivor's ejection seat, and this was no time to start tightening straps. Shouting EJECT EJECT!, I pulled the firing handle between my legs, and after a big bang I was looking down through my feet at the airfield grass coming up fast. I arrived on terra firma like a sack of spuds from a second-floor window. .

After establishing that I was alive and that my back hurt, my next priority was to get my SARBE Search And Rescue BEacon going to qualify for the silver tankard that Burndept Electronics gave to all aircrew who used their excellent product in a rescue. When an asbestos-suited fireman appeared in my field of vision I told him rudely to go away as I still hadn't got the beacon working yet. Given that I was sprawled in the middle of Lossiemouth airfield he clearly thought I was delerious, took it gently from me and made soothing noises until the ambulance arrived.

Ivor also jumped out successfully. The hapless Buccaneer flopped on the airfield, narrowly missing some people mending a radar aerial, and slithered to a halt on its belly; the cockpit section broke off and a fire started. The big fire tender, when it arrived after getting bogged down in the grass, squirted foam all over it trying to extinguish the fire and shut down the starboard engine, which perversely continued running at full power for quite a while. A putrid smell drifted away on the wind and gave rise to serious complaints from lunchtime drinkers in the Wardroom.

I spent an uncomfortable three weeks lying flat on my back getting my

'Thank you, Sir James, for the rest of my life'. BCC/MOD via Eeles

vertebrae back in place, drinking smuggled whisky and annoying the nurses. Ivor, whose straps were tight, was back flying in a couple of days.

A few years later, a married and more responsible officer altogether, I visited the Martin Baker factory and met that great man Sir James Martin. I think I speak for every ejectee when I say thank you, Sir James, and all at Martin Baker, for the rest of my life.

Sub Lieutenant Tony Ogilvy,
Pilot, Buccaneer, 800 Squadron, RNAS Lossiemouth, 1967

800 Squadron was working up at Lossiemouth prior to embarkation in HMS *Eagle* when I joined them as a newly-promoted Sub Lieutenant on my first front-line tour. Being just a kid, they teamed me up with Dave Brearley, otherwise DB, a veteran observer with one tour and one ejection under his belt, his job being to keep us both alive while he patiently worked my skills towards operational competence. So went the theory.

At the end of one uneventful night sortie we set up for a GCA (Ground Controlled Approach) to Lossiemouth. I will try to keep the technicalities to a minimum, but the Buccaneer's controls were a bit quaint and need some explanation. After you'd slowed up with the airbrake you remained airborne by the grace and virtue of various so-called 'lift augmentation devices' – drooping flaps and ailerons, and a tailplane flap which moved in the opposite direction – all with air from the engine blown over them and 'ganged' selector switches to ensure that all the bits and pieces moved together without affecting the trim. Thus the first notch on the switches gave you 15° flap+10° aileron droop+10° tailplane flap or '15-10-10', the second notch produced '30-20-20'. Full airbrake was also needed for landing, and of course the hook at sea. Anyone seeing a Buccaneer on approach to landing was in no doubt he was looking at the mother of all landing configurations.

Tiny 'Droop' and 'Blow' gauges, almost invisible at night, told the pilot how it was out there, and further spice was added by a marked lag in the thrust response of the big Spey bypass motors. The airbrake was essential to keep the engines at the top end of the power range where they gave plenty of 'blow' for lift-augmentation; and if you were unwise enough to pull the power off too soon, the blow stopped and the whole twenty-ton contraption fell out of the sky like a manhole cover. This produced some truly memorable deck arrivals.

But back to my GCA. Five miles from touchdown at 1500 feet, with undercarriage down and '15-10-10' set as described above, I made the selection to '30-20-20' for the glideslope – and, *tout suite*, the aircraft was standing on its nose pointing straight down at Aves village.

DB in the back dropped the *Pig Breeder's Manual*, his staple reading from 20 miles out on GCA, and asked some pointed questions. I rammed both throttles wide open, thumbed in the airbrake, flipped up the flap/droop switches and told him to eject, which he did with commendable alacrity, out through the canopy, filling my eyes with dust and rubbish sucked up from the bottom of the cockpit. I could just make out 1000 feet on the altimeter and we were still pointing at the ground.

I reached for the firing handle between my legs, but at that instant both Speys suddenly hit full thrust, the nose reared up, the flight-path changed for the good, and it became clear that the crash was off, for the time being anyway. DB, old hand as he was at this sort of thing, and already on the ground after a short Martin Baker let-down, was expecting a boom and fireball but instead heard the healthy roar of two Speys pulling safely away into the night. And he was not a happy man.

The tale now splits into two contrasting survival stories.

With the roar of slipstream and engines in the cockpit it was barely possible to converse with the tower, let alone convey a tricky message. 'Yes, the observer has gone. He ejected. That's right, ejected as in Martin Baker. I lost control but I have it back now - more or less. Over.' That sort of thing. When I managed to get a good look at the aforementioned 'mini-dials' I found that the tailplane flap had failed, so selecting '30-20-20' had given me '30-20-nothing' and hence the uncontrollable nose-down pitch. By pure instinct I had done the right thing with the switches, and the engines spooled up and hit full power just in time to get me out of the dive. I really loved those Speys.

Using standby switches I got a sort of landing configuration and put the aircraft on the ground where the Watch Chief, paperwork and hassle written all over his face, was waiting at the Squadron. I was feeling guilty enough already when I made the mistake of motoring back the canopy, the way we normally do to get out. Or rather the remains of the canopy: I had reckoned without the six-foot steel tube poking up out of DB's cockpit, the remains of his ejection seat. Hood motors are notoriously powerful, and the graunching of reinforced plexiglass splintering on metal sticks in my mind. Definitely not one of life's champagne moments.

Meanwhile, a young lady sound asleep in her bed near Aves was awoken by repeated cries from outside her window. Peering out she saw below, standing in the moonlight with his parachute canopy billowing in the breeze, Lieutenant David Brearley, Royal Navy, pleading thus: 'Naval aviator in a spot of bother...just been abandoned by some low-life space cadet who as soon as I catch up with him is going to learn the true meaning of pain...please come down...don't be afraid...etc, etc.' Amazingly she reached for neither her phone nor her shotgun, but went down and let him in. They breed them tough in Morayshire.

DB and I patched it up in the sick bay over a bottle of the local white wine; he ended up hiring the girl's house; the Watch Chief hit me, but I did become a member of the Buccaneer Single Seat Club, of which I think there are only two other members.

Writing this has reminded me that although, anywhere above 400 knots and below 10,000 feet, the Buccaneer was probably the finest purpose-built attack aircraft ever built, below 200 knots in the 'landing configuration', things were always interesting.

Nunquam non paratus est.

Lieutenant Jan Greener,
Observer, Wessex Mk.1, 820 Squadron, HMS *Eagle*, Moray Firth, 1968

On 30 August 1968 HMS *Eagle* was working-up in the Moray Firth, 820 Squadron engaged upon a series of Combined Anti-Submarine Exercises (CASEXs) preparing for the big annual NATO exercise in the autumn. I was flying in Wessex 065 (XS 888)with pilot Lieutenant Peter West and sonar operator Petty Officer Chicko Henson, plus a Royal Air Force cadet sitting up front with the pilot for the experience of 'flying navy'. The exercise started with three helicopters screening ahead of the carrier to detect submarines.

About an hour into the sortie I asked Chicko if he could smell fuel.

'I've got a cold,' he replied. 'Can't smell anything.'

We carried on with our work.

Fifteen minutes later the pilot asked if we could smell fuel in the back. I told

'I was flying Wessex 065...' BCC/MOD via Greener

him I got a whiff some time ago but thought I was mistaken. I got Chicko to open the cabin door on the starboard side and check underneath for fuel leaks. We were in the hover at about fifty feet with the sonar in the water. He saw nothing, but left the sliding door open to clear the fumes and strapped back into his seat.

A few seconds later the engine cut dead.

Pete barely had time to exclaim 'S—- we're ditching!' and send out a brief 'Mayday', and I was just able to jettison the observer's window, my escape route on the port side, before we hit the water.

It was in fact a surprisingly gentle landing and I was beginning to unstrap when I remembered the 'First Rule of Ditching':'DO NOT UNSTRAP UNTIL THE ROTORS HAVE STOPPED AND ALL MOTION HAS CEASED.' I refastened my straps and sat back to wait for what seemed an eternity until the noise stopped.

There was little more drama. The big air-bags attached to each wheel auto-inflated perfectly on contact with the water and the helicopter floated upright with no water entering the cabin despite the open door. I motioned a white-faced Chicko to get out; he jumped into the sea; I grabbed my dinghy pack and climbed nimbly out of my window and stood on the port torpedo carrier trying not to get my feet wet. The RAF cadet was still up in the left-hand cockpit seat; I invited him to join me and showed him how to inflate his dinghy by operating my own. When it was nicely inflated I jumped in and it capsized.

Remembering the correct drill, I righted the life raft and climbed back in, only to be caught by a stiff breeze and blown back towards the wallowing helicopter. A protruding aerial speared the buoyancy chamber and the dinghy folded up and sank around me. Dripping and furious, I clambered back onto the helicopter.

The RAF cadet had by now inflated his own liferaft, boarded it without getting wet, and was paddling manfully away towards the horizon as though he had been doing this sort of thing all his life. The back of the helo was settling, so I climbed up into the seat recently vacated by our intrepid cadet. Pete West was trying to radio the ship since no one appeared to have noticed our predicament. Excited radio chatter about a submarine contact had blocked our 'Mayday' call and the helicopter safety lookout on the ship thought we were still in the hover, though 'a bit low' as he said later.

It seemed hardly necessary, there being so many ships and aircraft close by, to use our SARBE personal rescue beacons; but there was a rumour that if it were instrumental in a rescue, the manufacturers gave the rescuee a silver tankard, so I jumped back into the water and, after putting a little distance between myself and the helicopter, set the thing beeping. Then it occurred to me I might collect additional tankards by deploying the many other seldom-used lifesaving aids ingeniously fitted to the Mae West, and I was soon floating in the middle of a patch of bright green fluorescene dye-marker flashing my polished steel heliograph at all and sundry. I got my sea-cell light, mini-flares and whistle ready in case it got dark.

'A Gemini inflatable hurriedly launched...' BCC/MOD via Greener

'...getting a ring on the rotor-head...' BCC/MOD via Greener

'...a few minutes later "065" would have exploded.' BCC/MOD via Greener

My SARBE was, truly, the first indication anybody had that we had ditched, and within a couple of minutes the two other Squadron helicopters were overhead and *Eagle*'s SAR Wessex was on its way. The latter came straight for me and, hoping this one didn't ditch right then, I put the strop around me and was soon safely back on the flight deck looking like a fluorescent Christmas tree festooned with survival aids dangling from their strings. A mere ten minutes had elapsed since the ditching – how time flies when you're enjoying yourself!

But the excitement was only beginning. The ship launched a seaboat with salvage divers to fix a lifting-ring to our Wessex's rotor head so it could be craned aboard. But the seaboat, recently serviced in Devonport dockyard, immediately filled up with water, probably for want of a bung. A hurriedly-launched Gemini inflatable rescued the divers who proceeded with their appointed task, and within forty-five minutes of the ditching the helicopter, divers and seaboat crew were all safely back aboard. The seaboat sank, the coxswain saluting as it went down.

And the cause of all this? A 'manufacturer's defect' had caused a fuel pipe flange to open under pressure, and our engine bay had been slowly filling up with fuel. The engine quit because the tank was empty; and just as well; the spilled fuel was heating up, and a few minutes later '065' would have exploded.

Wessex Mk.I aircrew ditched on average every 500 flying hours. With the exception of the RAF cadet, all our crew had clocked up over 500 hours when

'Mother' in attendance. BCC/MOD via Greener

our turn came to fall in the water. Incidentally, the figure was the same for contemporary American helicopter crews in Vietnam, but, unlike us, they were in a war. In that two-year commission 820 Squadron lost three helicopters, all of whose crews got out safely. Unfortunately two Sea Vixens with both crews were lost in the same period.

Many months later I received a very nice SARBE tankard, courtesy of Ever Ready, the manufacturers of this excellent piece of equipment. The rest of the crew – thanks to me, I can't help pointing out – also got tankards, and of course we all became members of the very exclusive 'Goldfish Club', open only to those who survive a ditching or parachuting into the sea.

Lieutenant Commander John Shears,
Air Engineer Officer, 848 Squadron, Singapore 1969

When it was realized that the return of HMS *Albion* to the United Kingdom in 1969 would leave the Royal Marine Commandos without air support, the decision was taken to split her complement of Wessex Mk.5s: half would go home with the ship as the original 848 Squadron, the rest remaining in Singapore as 847.

Albion was to sail for home on Monday 18 March; those home-going aircraft which had been ashore at RNAS Sembawang were ordered to re-embark on the preceding Thursday; but one Wessex, W-Whisky, normally a very willing and reliable workhorse, had a malaise in her Fuel Control Unit (FCU) and her starboard engine would not start.

Wessex FCUs were not the most reliable items known to man. Often a temporary problem could be overcome by use of an aircrew knife, or the wardroom spoon that Wessex 5 engineers at that time always carried with them, but 'Whisky' stubbornly refused to respond. The starboard FCU could not be changed *in situ* and the ship refused to send a replacement engine, saying that Sembawang's Engineering Department ought to be able to transport the aircraft to the dockyard by road, and that this should be done immediately. Accordingly, I handed over the problem to them, and later in the evening their Deputy Air Engineer Officer, David Morgan, kindly drove me back to the ship to see how things were going.

Ominously, on the route that he took we passed no convoy, and there was no activity on the quayside. Saying goodnight, I made my way up the gangway.

The Quartermaster saluted me aboard.

'Don't want to trouble you, Sir, but somebody rang about one of your aircraft being in a *road accident*?'

After a lightning raid on the squadron office for the keys to the squadron Land Rover, I headed back towards Sembawang, soon to be confronted with a monumental traffic jam, a lot of flashing lights and 'Whisky' lying on her side effectively blocking one of the main roads into Singapore city.

The unfortunate Chief Petty Officer in charge of the move put me in the picture. A tractor was towing 'Whisky' in a convoy led by police motorcycle outriders and a Land Rover, a naval Utilicon following, all flashing lights and everything going fine – until a young Royal Marine officer driving back to Sembawang after a night in town came around the corner a little too fast. Miraculously missing policemen, Land Rover and tractor, the Marine's car neatly amputated Whisky's port undercarriage leg, glanced off the Utilicon and plunged into a monsoon drain. No one was hurt, but the Chief was furious and had the Royal Marine arrested and thrown in jail.

Next morning 'Whisky' was back at Sembawang, upright again on a jury undercarriage, but any Wessex engineer will tell you that if either undercarriage attachment point is badly damaged the airframe is a write-off. Somebody pointed out that even Royal Marine officers ought to have Third Party insurance, and for the first time in history HMG filled out a claim for an aircraft involved in a road accident; predictably, the local insurance assessor said the damage could be repaired at a garage just down the road, and that was probably the end of that.

The ship sailed and I heard no more. My next job was Workshops Officer in the Engineering Training School at Lee-on-Solent, and it did nothing for my professional standing when I had to admit that the Wessex carcass that turned up one day with a big W on its side had been one of mine – until she was run over.

CHAPTER FOUR

THE 1970s

Introduction

This decade began on a high note for the Fleet Air Arm with the emergence of *Ark Royal* from long refit with fully-angled deck, long-stroke catapults and up-rated arrester-gear, and the acquisition of two world-class aircraft, the Sea King and Phantom F4-K. But the venerable *Ark*, whose keel was laid down in 1943, was the only carrier capable of operating the F4, of which there was only one front-line Squadron. In 1972 *Eagle* was scrapped, followed by *Albion* in 1973, the latter replaced in the Commando role by the converted *Hermes*. Fast, heavily armed Lynx helicopters began to replace the small ships' comparatively primitive Wasps in 1976. The Naval Air Stations at Brawdy and Lossiemouth were handed over to the RAF.

The VTOL Harrier jet flew aboard Ark Royal in 1971, and two years later orders were placed for a naval version, the Sea Harrier, for which, in circumvention of political aversion to aircraft carriers, a new type of ship was invented – the Through-Deck Cruiser. The first of these, *Invincible*, entered service with her Sea Harriers and Sea Kings in 1979 looking remarkably like an aircraft carrier. By this time thirty ships of nine other navies (fortunately not the Argentine Armada) were flying Harriers.

Ark Royal was scrapped in 1978 and the Navy handed over its Phantoms and Buccaneers to the RAF. Its AEW Gannets became museum-pieces and theme-park curiosities, some of their radars being installed in superannuated Shackletons as a token of the RAF's commitment to its new responsibility for air defence of the Fleet.

The Fleet Air Arm Roll of Honour contains the names of those who lost their lives in flying operations in the 1970s. The numbers are:

Pilots	28
Observers	5
Aircrewmen	4
Others	8

Lieutenant P.G.T. Woodman,
Supply Officer/Flight Deck Officer, HMS *Naiad*, 1968-70

Up to the 1960s the only Supply Officer to be seen in a frigate or destroyer would be the Flotilla Leader's Secretary, who would spend his entire working life below decks. In other small ships Supply Department responsibilities were shared between First Lieutenant and Engineer Officer.

And even when the increase in size and complexity of destroyers and frigates justified a real Supply Officer, known from time immemorial as the 'Pusser', this was rarely a full-time job – until the advent of the Wasp helicopter, the cutting edge of a whole new weapon system for small ships. The Wasp needed a Flight Deck, the Flight Deck needed a Flight Deck Officer, so it fell out quite naturally that small-ship Pussers became small-ship FDOs.

This was indeed a bonus. On top of the opportunity for a junior officer to have his own Department it was a very welcome chance to play a full part in fighting the ship. Up to then 'Action Stations' for a Pusser meant supervising action messing, which the cooks could do better on their own, or sitting in a corner of Damage Control HQ trying to keep out of the way. Now at last we were part of the team, fighting the ship's principal weapon.

Team was the operative word. Wasp 470, piloted by Terry Taylor, was *Naiad's* main armament, and second by second, as FDO, I was making decisions affecting its operation and safety. Day or night in all conditions of wind and deck movement it was my sole judgement whether it was safe to take off, or land, even move the aircraft and start it up, and I had to win the total confidence of the team, pilot and ground crew – the latter a somewhat more iconoclastic breed than the average matelot, I discovered.

Flight Safety became your watchword, the regular 'fod-plod', looking for loose gear and foreign objects that might damage engines or rotors, part of your life. You watched your 'bird' at night for the first sign that the pilot might be concentrating too much on his instruments and drifting towards the sea. My cry of 'Go up, go up, go UP!' over the ether one night in the vicinity of Portland resulted in a dozen helicopters suddenly shooting skyward.

And of course you also had your own department to run. Picture if you will the young Supply Officer in the small hours of the morning struggling to catch up with his departmental paperwork on a small wooden desk in a corner of the lurching hangar, one ear cocked for his 'bird' coming home – and woe betide you if your pilot's special 'night-flying meal' wasn't ready!

Lieutenant Commander Les Wilkinson,
Pilot, Buccaneer S2, 809 Squadron, HMS *Ark Royal*, Mediterranean, 1970

For a period in 1970 *Ark Royal* operated with severe landing-weight restrictions and only one arrester-wire rigged as a result of problems caused by the newly-introduced Phantom F4-K; and since night flying was most affected, my job as Senior Pilot of 809 Squadron flying Buccaneer S2s, namely getting the Squadron fully night-capable, was made no easier. The Squadron was only half worked-up, 'White Watch' needing two sorties each by day, 'Black Watch', the night-qualified crews, one day and one night. As well as this, whenever Phantoms and Buccaneers were relying at night upon a single arrester-wire, it was necessary to have a Buccaneer tanker airborne all the time as a safety precaution in case of trouble.

This tanker stooged around acting as a target for Phantom intercepts until all fixed-wing aircraft were safely aboard for the night, when it had to dump about 12,000lbs of fuel to get down to landing weight. Because of the weight of the refuelling-pod, this left the tanker only about 1500lb, enough fuel for two Carrier Controlled Approaches (CCAs) and, if the single wire went unserviceable, which was not unknown, or the the hook failed to catch it, a climb to 5000ft for the crew to eject.

Plainly tanker crews needed highly reliable night-deck-landing pilots, and there were just three of us at this stage; but the C.O. was out of the ship on a Board of Enquiry, the Air Weapons Instructor had just disqualified himself by missing the solitary wire or 'bolting' on a good night, which left me. Seven nights in a row I lumbered off the waist catapult in the tanker, and it says a lot for my observer David Thompson, who managed the fuel, that all went well except for two minor incidents.

The refuelling hose streamed of its own accord once as we went off the catapult at minimum launch speed, dragging us down within inches of the water with the audio Angle-of-Attack (AoA) playing the lowest note I ever heard. I always did like the Rolls-Royce Spey for power; raw thrust saved us.

Another night I came off CCA at about a mile, looked up for the ship and saw a very unusual arrangement of lights. Somebody on the bridge had assumed the land-on was finished and turned the ship 20° starboard without telling anybody. Luckily LSO Mike Doust was on the ball and gave me a '*HARD LEFT*' and '*HARD RIGHT!*' to get me on to the centreline. Five knots above the stall I was just able to make the turns and get aboard with minimum fuel, rather pleased with myself – until Mike awarded me a yellow stamp on the Deck-Landing Performance Board for my untidy arrival.

When *Ark* went into Malta for self-maintenance and five Buccaneers disembarked to RAF Luqa with the aim of getting White Watch airborne in the dark, as acting C.O. I continued to supervise this. One fine night, however, receiving a rare party invitation from a helicopter pilot, I handed this chore over to the Senior Observer. It was nearly midnight when he appeared at the party with the following tale of woe.

Unforecast fog having suddenly descended upon Luqa, he ordered the three airborne Buccaneers to divert to Sigonella, a NATO military airbase in Sicily about a hundred miles north whose weather was reported as 'CAVOK, GCA up' - i.e. Cloud And Visibility OK, GCA (Ground Controlled Approach) radar available if required. One Buccaneer, mishearing the order, landed at Luqa in the fog.

The other two found Sigonella far from 'CAVOK': their cloudbase was below

300ft, and their GCA was off the air. Having had to use their own onboard TACAN (TACtical Air Navigation) aid to locate the runway, the first Buccaneer to land there was 'a little fast', and the pilot put his hook down early as a precaution.

Like most NATO jet bases Sigonella had RHAG Rotary Hydraulic Arrester Gear designed to prevent aircraft running off the end of the runway. If a pilot thought he wasn't going to be able to stop, he dropped his tailhook and a hydraulically-braked cable stretched across the runway pulled him smoothly to a halt before he ran out of concrete. But sadly the airfield authorities had rigged the cable on the *downwind* (i.e. touchdown) end of Sigonella's runway; the Bucc picked it up at 140 knots going the wrong way and the result was a mess of tangled cables all over the place and a blocked runway. That Bucc and crew were safely down, but the third one now had nowhere to go except Catania, the nearby civil airport. After some radio and language problems the pilot understood he had been cleared to land there, only to be confronted head-on, feet from touchdown, by a DC-8 back-tracking down the runway straight towards him. He said he aged ten years in the next three seconds, but pulled off the overshoot and eventually landed safely.

We got the Sicilian aircraft back to Malta in a day or two and learned never again to use Sigonella as a diversion without sending somebody there to check it out.

Lieutenant Commander Pete Sheppard,
Pilot, Sea Vixen, RNAS Yeovilton, 1970

When Sea Vixen XJ561 emerged from a nine-month rebuild following a landing accident at Yeovilton she needed a full test-flight, and either I was the only pilot available or I got there first. In any case the flight-test observer, a young RAF-exchange navigator, was already strapped in the 'coal hole' when I reached the aircraft to find there was a delay in the paperwork. Unwisely, as it turned out, he elected to remain where he was while I went off for a coffee. I knew his name, but had never met him and didn't even know what he looked like. Take-off delay was about 45 minutes.

Once airborne, he filled in the report sheet as we went through the test schedule and everything went fine until the last item – a check of the maximum speed warning on the Central Warning Panel or CWP: the 'Vmax warning'. The CWP bells and flashers went off OK at 620 knots, but then there was an almighty BANG and both utility hydraulic warnings also lit up. I slowed down and found the aircraft flew normally, but without utility hydraulics I wasn't going to be able to lower the wheels, flaps or hook.

I had no idea what had happened. Cripples at Yeovilton were normally invited to head out into Lyme Bay fifty miles south and eject over the sea, but I had got that T-shirt by recently ejecting from a Hunter, and after some discussion Yeovilton's Command approved a wheels-up landing on a foamed runway.

'...heading for the trees...' BCC/MOD via Sheppard

While they laid the foam I burned off fuel and told my observer, who by now had been strapped in his seat for going on three hours, to stow everything forward on the cockpit floor in case of accident. As it was, when the time came I blew off my canopy and the observer's cockpit hatch and shut down both engines before touchdown, the foam worked like grease and I carried out the smoothest landing of my career. When we came to rest, with plenty of room to spare, I yelled to the observer 'Go NOW!' and in the few seconds it took me to shut down the electrics, undo my straps and stand up, he was off beyond the left wingtip heading for the trees.

A little later I was watching the salvage crane carrying XJ561 back to the repair yard when a rosy-cheeked young man introduced himself.

'Flying Officer xxxxx, Sir. I was your observer.'

I shook his hand and asked him if he had the flight test report.

'Yes, Sir,' he replied, cheeks growing ever rosier, 'but...'

Poor lad. All the talk of ejecting had triggered an irresistible urge to urinate, which he did in his sick-bag, and when I told him to put all his loose stuff down on the floor, that's where the sick-bag went, along with his report sheet, now barely decipherable.

And the bang? The starboard undercarriage door had blown off at 620 knots, tearing out some hydraulic pipes. Apart from that, and a bit of paint off the bottom, the Vixen was fully serviceable and soon needed another test flight.

Captain K.A. Leppard,

Chief Staff Officer (Operations and Training), Far East Fleet, 1970.

'HAVE STRUCK UNDERWATER OBJECT OFF THE SEYCHELLES AND AM SINKING'. This terse signal from the Royal Fleet Auxiliary *Ennerdale*, received at 1631GMT on 1 June 1970 in the operations room of the Far East Fleet Headquarters in Singapore, set the scene for an operation unique in Fleet Air Arm history.

Although RFA *Ennerdale*, a 62,000-ton fleet tanker attached to the Far East Fleet, operating out of the Seychelle Islands with British officers and a Seychellois crew, had been using a route which was in regular use, it transpired later that two uncharted rock pinnacles had opened parallel gashes in the ship's bottom, each about a metre wide, from bows to engine-room. She sank quickly close inshore, taking with her 42,000 tons of fuel oil, her tanks intact. The crew abandoned ship in good order in the ship's boats.

The problem was her cargo: 42,000 tons of heavy oil represented a potential pollution disaster of *Torrey Canyon* or *Exxon Valdez* proportions, which the rapidly expanding Seychelles tourist industry would only escape if the prevailing south-east winds and current carried the spillage well clear of the islands before the onshore monsoons of mid-August.

A Fleet supply ship, RFA *Stromness*, with a Wessex helicopter and two pilots of 847 Squadron, was hurriedly sailed from Singapore, 3000 miles away. Other auxiliaries and warships were diverted to the scene.

Ennerdale's bow was just showing above the water. The consensus view was that it was going to be necessary to blow up the undamaged oil tanks to release the remaining oil as quickly as possible so that it would drift away from the islands. Warships would supply the large amount of explosives required and a team of Fleet divers flew from Singapore to set the charges.

In worsening weather and heavy swell, after several unsuccessful attempts to place explosive charges on the sunken wreck, it became obvious that diving operations were impossibly dangerous. Torpedoing the wreck having been ruled out for technical reasons, the plan finally decided upon was to make up the required demolition charges locally by modifying anti-submarine mortar bombs and submarine torpedoes, and use *Stromness*'s Wessex helicopter to put these in place and fire them.

It was completely successful. Each of twenty undamaged tanks, up to 100 feet below the surface, had to be demolished individually, so while the pilot hovered in the spray the 900lb TNT charges were delicately lowered one at a time alongside the tanks. The fuse was then lit in the helicopter's rear cabin with just enough delay to get clear before the explosion.

After this, aerial surveys showed no further oil seepage from the wreck and the large oil slick dispersing in the wide expanses of the Indian Ocean to the north-west, well clear of the Islands. On 7 August the Commander Far East Fleet signalled the Governor of Seychelles that the operation was complete and that the islands were out of danger.

Lieutenant Mike Sharp,
Pilot, Buccaneer, 809 Squadron, HMS *Ark Royal*, 1970s

It started as a tanker sortie on a dark and stormy night during one of those 'Northern Wedding' exercises. Flying without a diversion, the tanker held on to his fuel until everybody was safely on deck, then dumped down to landing weight, which with the heavy refuelling pod on one wing left not a lot of fuel. I broke out of cloud and was trying to get a line-up on the bunch of tiny lights pitching and rolling a mile ahead when the two big red wave-off lights shone up from the deck and Flyco called: '032 WAVE OFF -WAVE OFF!'

There was some problem on deck, he told us: we could not land on, and they could not launch the deck-alert tanker to top us up. After a short discussion came the order:

'032 – divert. Call Approach Channel 2.'

Flying *without* a nominated diversion, this was *not* supposed to happen!

'Where's the nearest open airfield?' I asked Mike, my observer.

'I don't know.'

'Well where's the nearest country?'

'Norway I think. North-east.'

North-east we climbed, through black cloud, lightning, hail and incredible turbulence. Mike's book listed a Norwegian Air Force base called Lista on the south coast, as 'Open 24 Hours', so we headed that way and called them. Possibly due to the electric storms, there was no reply on any of their published frequencies, but Mike reckoned that using his own radar he could get us close enough to see it, if it was lit up, and in due course we put down on Lista's well-lit runway, aquaplaning and skidding to a stop right at the end. I hadn't dare look at the fuel gauges for the last 100 miles

The Buccaneer had no taxy lights, but we managed to locate a taxyway resembling a minor road through a pine forest. The rain having eased a little and having taken the precaution of folding the wings, I opened the canopy and drove through the woods with Mike standing on the rear seat shining his torch.

At the control tower, a friendly Norwegian officer greeted us.

'What service do you require?'

'The bar!'

'Today is Monday. The bar does not open until Friday.'

'In that case, transport to the nearest pub.'

'That would be Egersund, 35 miles away.'

So after refuelling and bedding down '032', we settled for the canteen where some 'Red Force' USAF Phantom crews – our exercise 'enemies' – gave us Budweiser beer. Ugh.

In the morning, after cold fried eggs, we were arrested and paraded as POWs in front of the 'Red' Air Boss, a USAF colonel with regulation crew-cut, beer gut, baseball cap and big cigar.

'OK guys, where's the carrier?'

'Ah, we were about to ask you that.'

'All-righty. What is its call sign today?'

'Ah, we were hoping you could tell us that too.'

He gave up. It didn't matter. They weren't flying anyway because of the weather. I wanted to get airborne: if we couldn't find the ship we would land at Karup – my sister lived near there, and they had a bar. Our captors kindly released us.

There was solid cloud from 200 to 40,000ft and we were unable to file an 'Instrument Flight Plan' because all our liquid oxygen had leaked away. The fact that Air Traffic Control accepted our flight plan for a 'visual departure, altitude 50ft, destination unknown' suggested the colonel badly wanted to get rid of us, so after take-off we thanked him by 'wiring' the USAF line – ultra-low at 600 knots along their row of *grounded* Phantoms with condensation bursting over our wings and fuselage. Brave stuff.

The weather was better to the south-west and, to cut a long story short, we found 'mother' and were on board in time for a hot egg roll in the 'Greasy Spoon' before briefing for the second launch of the day.

Between tours in 809 Squadron I spent a year with the Standards Flight at Yeovilton flying Hunters. One day I had to pick up one of these from RNAS Lee-on-Solent after a major refit. I went to their servicing office and signed out what looked like a brand new single-seat Hunter GA11.

It didn't look possible to fly Hunters out of Lee-on-Solent. At one end of its extremely short runway was a new housing estate, at the other a main road with traffic lights, a muddy beach, and the Solent, but I knew it had been done many times. And like all naval Hunters this one had an arrester-hook, and Lee's primitive Chain Arrester-gear (CHAG), a single cable across the runway about three-quarters of the way down, attached to heavy chains, would stop me if anything went wrong. Although it meant a slight tail-wind, I was advised it was better to take off pointing towards the sea than the housing estate.

Having worked out my 'Decision Point' – I must have at least 135 knots approaching the CHAG wire, otherwise I would drop the hook and stop – I confidently began what was going to be a 'Short Field Take-off': full throttle on the brakes, half flap at 120 knots, rotate and leap over the fence. But when I found myself with only 115 knots approaching the wire I pulled the throttle back and banged down the switch to lower the hook, expecting to be dragged to a stop surrounded by old anchor chain. When the hook bounced clean over the wire, leaving me much too fast to stop, far too slow to fly and the fence approaching rapidly, there was only one way out – instant ejection. The Martin Baker Mk.2HAN seat worked perfectly and with hardly time to admire the view I was dumped on the runway half-way through the first swing of the parachute.

The aircraft went through the fence and over the road, demolished a few beach huts and came to rest in shallow water with only its shark-like tail fin showing. Mercifully no one was hurt, though a car which ignored the red traffic lights missed disaster by a couple of feet. The driver declared in the local paper that from now on, in the matter of traffic lights, he was a reformed character.

They pulled the Hunter out and found that a tiny sliver of swarf in the gearing of the airspeed indicator had caused it to under-read by 20 knots. The Board of Enquiry was quite friendly.

Lieutenant H.R. James,

Meteorological Officer, HMS *Bulwark*, Home Waters 1970-72

I had wanted to fly when I joined the Navy in 1965, but an ear problem and a shortage of meteorologists led to me joining HMS *Bulwark* in 1970 as her Senior (and only) Meteorological Officer. I had cut my teeth, weather-wise, with the Fleet Air Arm at RNAS Brawdy on the exposed Pembrokeshire coast, done a lot of flying with the Squadrons there and liked the 'can-do' principle and the flexibility of the air world.

In due course HMS *Bulwark*, Captain B.H. Notley, took on board No.41 Commando Royal Marines and 845 Squadron's Wessex 5 helicopters. The ship's task was to get the Royal Marines to their objective, anywhere in the world, and support them there. I and three ratings comprised her Met Department.

For some reason 845 Squadron was very short of flying hours and a lot of new pilots needed deck training, so *en route* to Stockholm and Helsinki for official visits in April it was decided to cram in as much flying as possible on passage through the North Sea, the onus falling upon me to find some decent weather. This was my first experience of forecasting without a second opinion, and the North Sea in April being notoriously prone to sea fog, I could be excused for starting cautiously. But inevitably, after a long period of bright sunshine the flying hierarchy became a little impatient with my repeated warning of 'risk of fog patches' and the time came when, much against my better judgement, I was persuaded into a slightly more positive forecast. A horde of 845's new pilots gleefully got airborne and I went six decks down to attend to my other duty, the Confidential Books.

When a rasping Tannoy summoned *'Met Officer to Flyco!'* thirty minutes later, I sprinted up six ladders to the bridge to be greeted by a frowning heirarchy and a fog so thick you could not see the end of the ship. Eight helicopters were still airborne, some in fog, some above it, and their reports painted a picture of the carrier Met Officer's nightmare – ship in fog, aircraft airborne out of range of land.

Using radar, the ship's Direction Officers had to talk the pilots down one by one to a position a mile astern of the ship, about as close as they could see them on radar, and from there it was 'Mk1 eyeball', pilots groping through the mist following a series of flares dropped in the wake until they could see enough of the ship to land on in the swirling fog. All got aboard safely, some of the younger aircrew visibly shaken by the experience, which to this day, as a professional meteorologist of many years standing, sticks in my memory. It brought home the obvious fact that whatever the pressure, the buck stopped with me.

My name was mud, my credibility nil. But two weeks later...

Bulwark was one of the largest ships ever to visit the Finnish capital and had to negotiate a long narrow channel to reach the inner harbour from the open sea, the passage so tricky it could only be done in minimal wind. Once in, Captain Notley was concerned about getting out and instructed me to warn him if strong winds were likely: he had a deadline for our return to the UK and could afford no delay.

One afternoon a large percentage of the ship's company of 1400 souls was ashore when the Captain's worst fears began to materialize on my synoptic charts, and in some trepidation I took a chart down to his cabin and gave him my opinion – that I expected wind from the east (the worst possible direction) to reach Force 6 to 7 the next day and persist for two or three days.

He was aghast. Did I know what this meant? My opinion, my chart and I were subjected to every form of assault both fair and foul, but this time I stuck to my forecast, in the face of which he had no option but to cancel the remainder of the visit and sail that evening. He had to get out of the inner harbour before my wind arrived.

Hundreds of sailors, marines and officers were rounded up and got back on board, and in spite of the best efforts of the Finnish police, radio and TV, a good few were left behind when *Bulwark* passed uneventfully out through the narrows and anchored off later that evening. The weather was absolutely flat calm. It is probably not necessary to describe my feelings just then.

But next morning it was smiles all round. The gods smiled on me with a Force 6; I was smiling as we weighed anchor and set sail for the UK, leaving a frigate to pick up the stragglers ashore; the Captain's smile, I thought, was a little smug.

Lieutenant Ed Featherstone,
Observer, 824 Squadron Sea King, South West Approaches, 1971

I was enjoying a weekend at home in Cornwall, 18 October 1971, when a crew member of the Norwegian ore-carrier *Anatina* fell asleep with a cigarette in his hand. Within an hour of the telephone ringing I was in the Squadron offices at RNAS Culdrose planning the first of many long-range sea rescues made possible by the remarkable Sea King helicopter. *Anatina* was disabled and drifting in mountainous seas, her after parts ravaged by fire, two men dead, her cargo of titanium ore shifting dangerously. She was in danger of sinking, 200 miles from land.

As observer in the lead Sea King of a pair manned by scratch 824 Squadron crews, my responsibility was not only to find *Anatina* but also to ensure we didn't run out of fuel. After quickly doing the sums based on her reported position, I checked them with the observer of the other aircraft and told my pilot, 824's C.O. Larry Hallett, that despite the storm force winds we could get there and back with 30-45 minutes on-scene. We set off south-west, flying as low as possible to reduce the headwind, and soon I was talking with a Nimrod maritime patrol aircraft already circling the casualty.

The rescue began to look doubtful when the headwind turned out stronger than forecast and the Nimrod reported the casualty considerably further west than we thought, reducing our on-scene time to a quite inadequate 15 minutes. Faced with this problem, we hatched another plan with Culdrose and headed for the Scilly Isles, and minutes after we landed at St. Mary's airport Sea Kings from 706 pilot training squadron arrived with drums of aviation fuel and a portable pump. Soon we were on our way again with enough fuel for an hour on task if we needed it.

Anatina was rolling heavily, her after end blackened and wrecked, the crew sheltering where they could on the exposed deck, and the only suitable area for winching them up was surrounded by tall derricks and masts carving wild arcs through the air with every roll. We would have to hover so high that the ship would be out of sight of the pilots, who would be relying entirely upon me to con them into position while I operated the winch; this was definitely *not* an occasion for me to use my Auxiliary Hover Trim to control the Sea King, as the observer sometimes did in the hover.

We in '50' started by lowering Petty Officer Dossett to organize the survivors, then a stretcher full of blankets, food and drink and survival equipment. Dossett did an outstanding job and I, at the same time as conning the Boss to hold position, was soon winching people up. When a survivor reached the cabin door I manhandled him inside, removed the strop and strapped him into a seat while '50' moved aside to allow '51' to pick up the next man, and so on until we had

'All that remained was to recover one of the bodies...' Featherstone

sixteen between us. The rest of the crew having now decided to try to salvage the ship, all that remained was to recover Petty Officer Dossett and the last of the bodies.

The body came up in the stretcher, wrapped in a blue blanket which blew away as it reached the door, revealing a big man face-down in the stretcher, his body charred and blackened with lumps of flesh peeling from his head. The smell made me gag, so after shoving the stretcher between the rear crew seats I hurried to the door and busied myself with the problem of Dossett, waiting legs abrace on the heaving deck below. With some difficulty I put the strop in his hand and winched him up, mightily relieved to be safely back in the air – except for the smell. I needed the door shut to see the radar displays, but after a few minutes was forced to compromise with a half-open door to get some ventilation.

The trip home took 90 minutes, zipping along at 2000ft with a strong tailwind, and we landed back at Culdrose after five and a half hours airborne. Some later long-range rescues may have been more dramatic, but this was the first, highlighting the inadequacies of the RAF's SAR Whirlwinds and raising public expectations overnight.

For me the smell is the most powerful memory. Even now I occasionally get a sniff of something that takes me instantly back to the *Anatina*.

A five-and-a-half-hour flight would have seemed short a few years later when I was flying Airborne Early Warning (AEW) Shackletons with No.8 Squadron of the RAF: with its four Rolls Royce Griffon engines and Lancaster antecedents, an ex-Gannet AN/APS20F radar in a 'shack' built around the main spar for the

'...Lancaster antecedents...' Featherstone

operators, the 'Old Grey Lady' was the UK's answer to Soviet low-level air attack threat, and she could fly for seventeen hours. The Squadron was based at RAF Lossiemouth and many of the aircrew were RN; I was there because I wanted a change from helicopters.

By any standards the Shack's equipment was primitive: it took up to forty minutes to tune the 25-year-old radar after take-off, a procedure involving the use of a screwdriver; and if it failed to come on line the whole crew was trapped airborne for hours until the aircraft was down to landing weight as dumping fuel to land was prohibited except in emergency. The underslung radar aerial rotated once every six seconds and often had a 'hit rate' of about one in three, making detection and control of high-speed jets problematic at best: it took considerable moral courage to control two fighters head-on at 900 knots when you only caught a fleeting glimpse of them once every twenty seconds or so. Ventilation, sanitation, everything about the Shackleton was primitive. The RAF used 8 Squadron as a repository for officers with a misdemeanour to their name, one of whom provided some light relief one day. Kevin was an ex-Vulcan Air Electronics Officer who made a superb cup of tea and was undoubtedly our best breakfast chef, a valued member of the crew. He was with us when we took off on what was naturally one of my favourite detachments, to RNAS Yeovilton, the aim being to transit west for some work with Benbecula radar in the Outer Hebrides, then down the Irish Sea plotting shipping, and so to Yeovilton. An entrepreneurial Observer at Lossiemouth had seized the opportunity of shipping a pannier of local fish in the bomb-bay for customers at Yeovilton; as it was winter it would stay nicely chilled en route.

Passing the Isle of Man on our way down the Irish Sea, in an aircraft with thousands of gallons of petrol, somebody smelled burning. The No Smoking lights came on. Somebody else smelled burning. The Captain ordered the aircraft ventilated and the small cockpit windows and side lookout bubbles were opened to draw out the fumes. Kevin, who happened to be negotiating the main spar with a full tray of tea, helpfully turned the handle of the overwing escape hatch, which instantly vanished in the slipstream. The ensuing 150-knot tea-laden gale down the fuselage sucked the heavy curtains from around the radar compartment out into the void leaving the operators blinking owl-like in the sudden daylight.

'I thought it opened *inwards*!' Kevin explained.

'Close the hatches!' ordered the Captain.

'I think I felt a thump on the rudder,' reported the co-pilot.

With possible damage to the rudder, the Captain diverted to RAF Valley in Anglesey and was instructed to remain there until Squadron engineers and a new hatch arrived from Lossiemouth.

'What about the fish?' someone asked in the course of a very congenial evening.

'Not my problem,' the captain said decisively.

By a stroke of luck, Valley suffered a hard frost that night, so the fish was safe. Kevin was forgiven, and no doubt still makes excellent tea.

Lieutenant Pete Hardy,
Observer, Sea Vixen, 890 Squadron, RNAS Yeovilton, 1970s

With a pension to protect, I must make it plain that I am only telling this story after twenty-five years on the understanding that the Statute of Limitations applies.

890 Headquarters Squadron at Yeovilton was a cosy little outfit: four Sea Vixens, three pilots, two observers. The flying task amounted to Fleet Support for ships working-up in Lyme Bay to the south, occasional photo-reconnaissance flights, and refresher flying for pilots requiring back-in-the-saddle time. For a young man like me, fresh from a couple of back-to-back front line tours, it was idyllic.

One evening one of our pilots, a General List regular officer on his way to high places and at that time newly married and rightly proud of his very attractive wife, asked me home to supper. He and I were programmed to fly together on a photographic mission first thing in the morning. The evening went on in a most pleasing fashion, a beer or two in the lovely surroundings of his Olde English Manor, an excellent meal and fine wine, but as it got late, heavy rain began beating on the windows and we became aware that the weather was worsening by the minute.

My host and I looked at each other, we looked at the rain streaming down the windows, we looked at the weather map on the back of the *Daily Telegraph*, and having rightly judged that the photographic sortie was off, quite wrongly assumed the weather would preclude any flying at all. The revelry continued, involving I think quite a lot of home-made beer and green chartreuse.

The weather next morning was indeed dreadful. I felt dreadful, and my usually immaculate host and pilot looked ruffled and wan.

'Your phot trip is cancelled,' the Senior Pilot announced when we got to the squadron.

'Sorry to hear that, Sir,' I replied, relief and insincerity oozing from every pore. All I wanted just then was to find somewhere to lie down.

'No matter,' 'Splot' breezed on, 'We've just been thrown a fast ball. They want an aircraft for radar tracking off the Welsh coast –' he checked his watch, '– airborne in one hour!' *The Fall of the House of Usher.*

For a brief delirious moment when the Central Warning Panel 'attention-getters' sounded off on the runway, I thought divine providence was intervening. From my seat in the 'coal-hole' I could only see my pilot's right thigh and half the instrument panel, and tried to draw his attention to the 'attention-getters', but he merely cursed the bells and flashers and yelled above the din, 'Never say die. Here we go. Ger-*onimo!*' and blasted off in a cloud of spray down the runway in the general direction of Ilchester church.

The outline of the sortie was simple: transit to the range area and act as a target for the radar then under development for the Sea Wolf guided-weapon system. This meant flying over the sea in Cardigan Bay at 1000 feet at a speed of something over 600 knots, near the Vixen's maximum speed, using the pressure altimeters because the radio altimeter was unreliable at that height. No real problem.

Except the weather, no better in Cardigan Bay than it was at Yeovilton; and the crew, who, although breathing 100% oxygen, were decidedly below peak efficiency. We made two runs in cloud and heavy turbulence with the pressure altimeter needles bouncing around between 900 and 1100 feet, not bad, we reckoned, thinking we were doing remarkably well – until towards the end of the third high-speed blind run we caught our first fleeting glimpse of the sea.

It was *horribly* close! Something must be *seriously* wrong with *both* our altimeters! My gallant pilot pulled up fast away from the water, and just about then started complaining that the over-wing fuel tanks were not transferring. I had tried to point out to him, before take-off, that these 'pinion' tanks, holding a thousand pounds of fuel each, had not been filled.

Back at Yeovilton – when our hands steadied and our brains began to function – we reflected strenuously on the riddle of two altimeters reading 1000 feet when at a guess the aircraft was no more than 100 feet above the water. Resorting ultimately to the Sea Vixen Operating Data Manual, we found this highlighted in the section on altimeters: **'CAUTION - At high Indicated Airspeeds at low altitude, the pressure altimeters may over-read by 800 feet.'**

So instead of a relatively healthy 900-1100 feet, we had spent half an hour flying at 600 knots, in turbulent cloud, at a true height of between 100 and 300 feet above the water, and that is close.

My six front-line tours in Sea Vixens and Phantom F4s between 1966 and 1975 made up a uniquely rewarding ten years of extremely exciting flying, and it would please me to attribute a lack of serious mishaps, and an equal number of take-offs and landings, to my innate ability, obsessive attention to detail, careful selection of pilots, etc etc ... but it wouldn't be true. Any contemporary naval aviator reading this will experience the warm glow of *schadenfreude* and agree that, in those days, luck was the essential extra.

Lieutenant Adrian Tuite,
Observer, Phantom F4-K, 892 Squadron, HMS *Ark Royal*, West Atlantic, 1972

Briefing for the third trip that day, a four-ship night maritime-attack mission, I was already feeling a bit jaded when the Duty Officer came in with the news that my Phantom was u/s; its weapons (Lepus flares and 2″ rockets) were being transferred to the spare aircraft and we would be launched last. At the appointed time my pilot Jim Bellamy and I found the replacement Phantom parked in Fly Three just aft of the island, tail hanging out over the water, the armourers just finishing their work. The ship was into wind and Gannet, Buccaneer and Phantom engines all around were creating that bedlam of noise, heat, gale and fumes unique to a carrier deck. It was a dark night, 16 February 1972, on the Viecques weapon ranges off Puerto Rico.

We climbed aboard, started up, taxied onto the cat and blasted off into the night. Our mission with the Lepus flares was to illuminate the target, in this case a 'splash' sled towed by an RFA, for the benefit of the other three F4s who all had four pods of rockets. We would go in ahead of them at low level to a predetermined radar range at which I would give the order to 'pickle'; Jim would then press the firing button and hold it down, pull the nose up at a predetermined rate, and the flare would detach automatically when we got to 45° nose-up. It would continue ballistically to a point above and beyond the target where its timer would deploy a parachute and ignite the two-million candle-power flare, by the light of which all four of us would pound the target with our rockets. Such was the theory.

We ran in at 420 knots, 250 feet on the radio altimeter with the plume of the splash-target showing clearly on my radar. At approximately three miles I called 'Pickle!', but almost as soon as the nose began to rise came the familiar clunk of a heavy weapon punching off a wing pylon.

'What the hell was that?' Jim exclaimed, rolling the aircraft smartly on to its back. He must have suspected the truth, for there, keeping perfect station no more than ten yards below the canopy, was a large white Lepus canister. Fascinated, we stared too long. I had started to tell Jim to get away from it when it went off, its two million candle-power searing our dark-adapted retinas. We were totally blinded. Somehow Jim kept us going up away from the sea until we recovered some limited sight at ten thousand feet, still upside down. Sounding less than pleased, Phantom Leader (the Squadron Boss) called off that attack and ordered us to try again with our second Lepus.

Having recovered most of our sight and some composure, we were setting up the second attack when Jim casually enquired: 'Hey Tooty. You did set the *loft switches*, didn't you?'

I groaned aloud. A technical digression: the setting of the Loft Switches determined the nose-angle (e.g. 45°) at which a weapon (e.g. Lepus) detached itself on a loft-bombing manoeuvre. Mounted on the decking behind the observer's ejection-seat headrest, the switches could only be reached with the canopy open and had to be set before flight – by the observer. Hence Jim's pointed question.

Of course I hadn't set them! And it was no excuse that we had been in a rush. It was my job. How could I be so *stupid*? I was going to be a laughing-stock. This story would follow me to the grave! The thought of it drove me to desperation and I embarked on the biggest cover-up since Watergate. I spluttered something incoherent and clicked my mike switch a few times to make Jim think my intercom had failed, then in feverish haste unplugged everything, unstrapped, put the seat safety pins in, removed my helmet, stood on the seat and, by wedging my head sideways between it and the canopy, with the help of a torch and a very long ruler, managed to stretch far enough to click the hateful little knurled knobs around to the right setting. Phew!

Fortunately Jim did nothing violent with the aircraft before I was securely back in my seat and connected up, and after a few more splutters and clicks the intercom was 'restored'. The next Lepus performed perfectly.

Twenty-five years later I thought it safe to tell the story at one of those occasions where tales of derring-do come out. A certain 'Paul' put down his glass and stared at me in astonishment. 'You swine! I loaded that aircraft! We could never work out what went wrong, and guess who got the blame?' Ouch!

22 October 1974, same ship, same squadron, I was in a pair of Phantoms, Black Section, briefed to conduct First Run Attacks on Teulada range in Southern Sardinia with live 1000lb HE bombs, directed by the ship's Carrier-Borne Ground Liaison Officer (CBGLO or 'C-Balls'). Approaching the Initial Point (IP) for the attack, our radio was so bad that pilot Paul Chaplin and I couldn't agree whether C-Balls wanted us to run in for '2 minutes 26 seconds' or '226 seconds'. However, you don't often get to drop 1000lb HEs, and before even the shorter time had elapsed the boy up front called 'Black 1, target visual', pulled up and tipped into his 20° attack dive.

The peninsula looked the right shape, but what about that one to the west – and the one beyond that? And why no calls of 'Visual' and 'Clear in live' from C-Balls on the ground, to say he could see us and we were clear to drop the bomb? A worm was gnawing in my head and at the last moment I shouted 'No Bomb!' and aborted the attack. We headed back to the IP, he up front not best pleased.

At the IP, Black 2 was nowhere to be seen, having presumably departed on his own attack, and although we could not raise C-Balls on the radio we set off to try again, and at the same point, certain

Lt Tuite (left) and 'the boy up front...' Tuite

now that he had the right target, Paul pulled up for the attack. I was still urging caution when our doubts were at last relieved by C-Balls crackling through the ether: 'I see you! Attack looks good, you are cleared in live.' The bomb fell to earth exactly where we intended, and on the pull-out, as I was looking over my right shoulder at the smoke-plume, C-Balls called 'Target, Target!'. Much

jubilation in the cockpit – until I saw another plume of smoke rising some miles to the west and instantly grasped the horrible truth - C-Balls had been talking to the other Phantom.

'Much jubilation...' Sheppard

No one was hurt and only a few windows shattered across the bay from Cape Spartivento. The subsequent Board of Inquiry, finding almost everyone wanting, spread the 'guano' around fairly thinly.

Lieutenant Colin de Mowbray,
Pilot, Wessex I, 848 Squadron, HMS Albion, Far East 1972

When 847 and 848 Squadrons re-amalgamated in Singapore in 1972, and embarked in HMS *Albion* for passage home, for reasons which I needn't go into the old 848 management regarded we 847 pilots with deep suspicion. So it came as a refreshing gesture of impartiality and trust when within a day or two I was programmed to fly the much-sought-after Helicopter Delivery Service. HDS transferred people, mail and stores between ships in company and, on this particular day, involved a trip inshore to RAF Butterworth, near Penang. Virtually a whole day out! As a bonus I had one of our Ops officers, Peter Flutter, as crewman. It all seemed too good to be true, a cruel hoax perhaps?

I carried my gear out to 'E' for Egg among the panic on *Albion*'s flight deck, everyone chasing everyone else as usual, and with great relief climbed up and took my seat in the cockpit away from it all; but to my intense chagrin E-Egg showed no appreciation of the offer of a whole day away from all this madness and flatly refused to start. This sort of thing in the middle of a crowded range of helicopters is really upsetting, so I unceremoniously abandoned her, dodged across the deck and shouldered my way into the line office demanding another aircraft. 'Take Queenie then!' snapped the Chief, in a hurry to get rid of me, and before anyone could stop us Peter and I were out of there and on our way.

Finally airborne in Q-Queenie and clear of the bedlam of the carrier circuit, I switched to a quiet frequency as soon as I could and relaxed, determined to enjoy my day out. What joy! The weather was fine, the sea was fine, the aircraft was fine, everything was fine... until a voice from the back announced diffidently, 'Er Colin, I hate to tell you, but I've just noticed we don't appear to have a *winch*.'

No winch. HDS that day included at least eight mail and bread transfers among the ships, then the trip to Butterworth and more transfers on the way back. *Without a winch?* This was a disaster. And apart from anything else, 847's reputation was at stake: returning lamely to *Albion* would mean considerable loss of face.

'What about the the tip-socks?' Peter offered. 'We could try using them –'

Tip-socks were the heavy fabric covers slipped over the ends of the rotor blades to stop them flapping around on deck; they were big enough to hold a good ration of loaves, and there were four of them, each with a good length of fairly stout rope attached. Worth a try. After a successful experiment with a tug, hovering overhead and lowering down some bread, we carried on around the other ships and found them quite good at catching 'bread from heaven', and sending stuff up in return, until one frigate, whose flight deck was too small for us to land, produced a passenger for Butterworth, all kitted up and ready for winching. Not a tip-sock job this, nor even a two tip-sock job. With great skill I perched one wheel on a corner of the tiny flight deck and persuaded him to climb on to it so that Peter could pull him aboard. He was plainly keen to get off that ship.

In the best traditions of the service we did everything we were asked to do, returning to *Albion* in the evening very pleased with ourselves after a perfectly splendid away-day. Disappointingly, nobody ever thought to ask how we did it.

Lieutenant Commander D.S. Mallock,
Pilot, Sea King Mk.41, RNAS Culdrose, 1974

For Sea King crews at Culdrose on the morning of 16 January 1974 low cloud, poor visibility and winds gusting 100 knots would normally have meant a day of lectures and paperwork. But the Navy's current SAR helicopters being single-engined Whirlwinds, cast-offs from carrier-borne units, when the Danish cargo vessel *Merc Enterprise* radioed that her cargo had shifted and she was being overwhelmed by enormous seas south of Plymouth, the telephones rang in all of Culdrose's Sea King Squadrons: 706, 824 and the Foreign Training Unit. The first two had the HAS Mk.1 which had been in service for some four years, the latter the German Mk.1, a formidable purpose-built SAR version.

Two 706 Sea Kings were first on the scene, quickly followed by me in a German Mk.41 and another Mk.1 from 824 flown by Lieutenant Tony Baker of the Royal Australian Navy. *Merc Enterprise* had capsized and the surviving passengers and crew were in the water in the shallows around the Eddystone Light, where wind-over-tide was raising seas registering 70 feet on our radio altimeter. We in the German Sea King, with our superior communications outfit, took control as 'Scene of Action Commander' in touch with all helicopters, the Coastguard, the Plymouth lifeboat and the Russian trawler *Leningrad* which was to play an important part in proceedings.

Breaking crests and driven spume made it hard to see the people in the water and the size of the seas made it difficult and hazardous for those who went down on the winches to pick up the cold and exhausted survivors. I saw my crewman

The German Mk41: '...a formidable purpose-built SAR version...' Mallock

carried away on a breaking wave until his wire was almost horizontal, then flying forward on the wire from that one to crash into the next curling breaker. It would be invidious to mention names; suffice it to say that without the outstanding bravery of these aircrewmen most of the crew of the *Merc Enterprise* would have been lost. The Captain of the *Leningrad*, unable to turn his vessel more than a few degrees out of the wind and colossal seas, contrived to manoeuvre close to some of the survivors and in an act of pure heroism, largely unacknowledged by the British media, four Russians tied themselves to ropes, plunged into the water and rescued four Danish seamen.

Late in the evening, with seven survivors and five bodies taken to Plymouth by helicopter, four safe aboard the *Leningrad* and three missing, the Mk.1 Sea Kings had to leave. With more fuel in the Mk.41 I was able to accept a request from the Coastguard to locate the Plymouth lifeboat, which had twice been overwhelmed by the seas, righted herself, but lost her radio aerials. We found her gallantly plugging on towards the casualty and were able to use hand signals to send her back to port, standing by while she negotiated the hazardous course reversal before turning for home ourselves.

It was now 1730, dark, and it was going to take an hour against the 60-knot headwind back to Culdrose. Everybody was tired and hungry. I locked in the autopilot at 180 feet and set course.

Approaching the Lizard peninsula, as I started a climb to avoid the low-level turbulence coming off the land, a noise like machine-gun fire and an unhappy rumble from the starboard engine were the first warnings of disaster. Before anybody could react, the engine's computer did sterling work controlling its temperatures and pressures, but a moment later more machine-gun noises were accompanied by a loud bang and sparks and flames from the engine intakes above my head. Then explosions and surges on both engines began shooting out flames and debris ten feet in front. I put out an emergency call and heard Culdrose scramble Tony Baker, whose still warm Sea King had just finished refuelling.

My Mk.41 was now in real trouble. Reducing power seemed to help, but as we approached the invisible Manacles rocks a simultaneous surge caused the computers to put both engines into flight-idle. We took the only option left when there is no power in a helicopter and went into autorotation and, although this stabilized the engines, I upgraded our emergency to 'Mayday' while gingerly pulling power again to get up over the coastal cliffs.

The wise advice of my very experienced co-pilot, Kapitan Leutnant Onno Reiners of the Federal German Navy, had been invaluable all day; as we crossed the coast I asked if he thought we should try and make it all the way to Culdrose, less than ten miles now. He and the rest of the crew opted for landing while we still had some control over the situation. In reality, our options were running out very fast. I told Culdrose we were going down, lowered the wheels, turned on the landing lights and began the descent into the darkness below, at which moment the starboard engine went into terminal surge with even more flames and debris out front. The port engine, unable to cope with the extra load, immediately followed suit, and we were back in full autorotation. The windscreens were opaque with thick white salt so we whipped the side windows open. I saw trees my side, Onno called 'Field left!' and as I turned that way with a bang and a flash we went through the main Lizard power line. I managed to get 25% torque from the port engine, just enough to cushion the landing in a ploughed field on the side of a hill.

We found ourselves perched precariously on a slope with the aircraft threatening to roll over to starboard, the port engine on fire and, worst of all, a broken power line thrashing around like a demented snake spitting arcs of electricity at everything it touched.

There we stayed, trapped, until at about the same time as we killed the engine fire the Electricity Board cut off power to the grid. Now the problem was that every time anyone moved the aircraft tilted to the right; so we all had to move up-slope inside, and then out of the port-side door to safety, gathering in the lee of a hedge. I had left the lights on for Tony Baker to find us; apart from that, all was as black as an undertaker's hat, and very windy. The welcome lights of a helicopter passed upwind, just beneath the low cloud, but then disappeared from view behind our hedge.

Tony saw us, but then his own troubles began. A flash, a bang and both engines in surge at low level over a blacked-out Lizard peninsula; autorotation, wheels down, landing lights on, 'Mayday, Mayday, Mayday....' The first thing he saw was a farmhouse dead ahead. Too low to turn, he got just enough power from the engines to scrape over the roof before expiring altogether. Their field was reasonably flat, but daylight revealed a deep quarry a hundred yards further on.

Thanks to some kind and hospitable farmers, both crews met up at the same pub, and later a very moving reception in the mess at Culdrose rounded off an exciting day.

The cause of all the excitement? Salt. Salt, in amounts far beyond the design expectations of the manufacturers, had destroyed four engines. Salt burning was found right through them as far back as the power turbines; and the internal build-up of salt deposits, which in the wet salt-laden air close to the sea had remained plastic, eventually hardened sufficiently to interfere with the airflow. This caused the stalling and surging, and the spectacular and destructive backfiring.

Avoidable? Yes. In 1974 the merits of an intake shield which had been successfully used for many years by the Americans and Canadians were still being considered by the 'powers that be', so on this day our engine intakes were completely open to the elements. Soon afterwards, RN and FGN Sea Kings were fitted with engine protection shields.

Lieutenant Paul Bennett
Pilot, Phantom F4-J, VF213 Fighter Squadron, United States Navy, 1974

It was the end of my first sea tour on exchange with the U.S. Navy's VF213 aboard the USS *America*: a big Atlantic NATO exercise and my first 'foreign' port of call – Portsmouth, England! The squadron was ready to disembark and return home to NAS Miramar in San Diego, California, the far side of the U.S.

Flying across the States from east to west was an interesting prospect. I did the journey the other way with the ground crew in the back of a C-9 transport. To make it even more interesting the CO, Commander Bill Heisner USN, offered most of the back seats to non-aircrew. I got a Chief Petty Officer in my back seat, and didn't know how lucky I was.

The trip started uneventfully with twelve F4s flying off to NAS Oceana in Virginia, refuelling and on to a USAF base near Memphis in Tennessee for a night-stop. Our troubles started the following morning: our planned mid-point stop, Cannon Air Force Base (AFB) in New Mexico, had not got our flight plan; it was Saturday, and they adamantly refused to break their 'Prior Permission Required' (PPR) rule. The F4-J being a real fuel burner and very range-critical, after much work with slide-rules and calculators the CO devised on a cunning dodge: we would file a flight-plan to Albuquerque about 200 miles further west, nominating Cannon as our 'Alternate Destination', thus obliging them to accept us 'if the need arose'.

Albuquerque was a long way for an F4-J, so the weather was very carefully checked before the C.O. led off with the first flight of four aircraft. I was in the second flight, led by VF213's Executive Officer and Second-in-Command, Commander Frank Mezzardri. One aircraft in each flight carried a proper navigator (RIO or Radio Intercept Officer in US Navy parlance).

US Air Force, Navy and Marine Corps Phantoms had some degree of commonality; for example they were all started by low-pressure air from a ground supply, but our Navy aircraft needed $4^{1}/_{2}$ pounds air pressure, whereas AFB Memphis had only the feeble $3^{1}/_{2}$-pound starters used by USAF aircraft. So we had to coax our engines up to speed by manually 'milking' the fuel while simultaneously exercising all the flying controls to unload the hydraulic pumps, an extremely sweaty procedure in Tennessee heat and humidity. Starting this way also consumed a lot of fuel, but I was a happy lad as I blasted off the runway with my Chief Petty Officer and climbed in sparkling clear air to 35,000ft. The F4 was a delight to fly, and in such perfect weather a slight defect in the DME (Distance Measuring Equipment), a very useful gadget that tells you in miles the precise distance to a ground beacon, seemed unimportant; of its three digital counters, the first, measuring hundreds, was stuck on '1'.

We must have been about half way to Albuquerque when the euphoria was shattered by our Flight RIO, Gerry Arbini, who was monitoring the continuous area weather broadcasts, announcing that our destination was reporting visibility of 500 yards in fog, and our cunningly selected bolthole, Cannon AFB, 400 yards in fog. After some discussion of the worsening weather all around, Frank

Mezzardri decided to divert to Amarillo in Texas, 200 miles closer than Cannon and 400 miles closer than Albuquerque.

The F4-J's ILS (Instrument Landing System) being incompatible with civil equipment, Frank made a very strong point of getting confirmation from the ground controllers that Amarillo was indeed 'MILITARY ILS-EQUIPPED', and 'yes', he was told each time he asked, until we switched to Amarillo's own frequency and asked the same question. They weren't. Furthermore their visibility was also 500 yards and dropping. This news set me scrabbling around the cockpit looking for an alternative way of getting down at Amarillo, because we had used a lot of fuel getting there. Frank, the XO, managed to land, but only because he had been there before and had 'local knowledge'. I tried one approach using on-board aids and saw nothing but the top of the tower. My fuel state was now getting critical.

On the ground Frank found the visibility getting worse by the minute and told the rest of us to divert immediately to Altus Air Force Base. I was in cloud flying on instruments and hadn't the faintest idea where 'Altus' was. As a new boy crossing the States for the first time, I very rapidly became aware of three things: America is a huge country; I was hopelessly lost somewhere in the middle of it, and I had a useless passenger in the back where my RIO should have been.

'Where's Altus?' I bleated over the ether.

'Head east,' came Frank's reply. 'Stand by for a vector.'

I had to change frequency before I got that vital course to steer for Altus, but was already turning east at high G and climbing fast to get to an economical altitude. I had 2500lbs of fuel left (the F4 would burn that much in three minutes in afterburner). I needed to get to high altitude fast to save fuel, and the controller got very agitated as I busted illegally through the 18,000ft ceiling for 'Visual Flight'. I cared not, and soon he had me under radar control heading for Altus. But try as I might I could not find out how far it was: every time I asked I had to change frequency before getting an answer. I was coming close to having to eject.

At this point, my 'useless passenger' in the back informed me he had tuned in to Altus DME! (it turned out he was an ex-Blue Angel crew Chief with more hours in the F4 than me). The DME locked on, but with the first digit stuck I didn't know whether I had 85 or 185 miles to go. I always thought a premeditated ejection must be far worse than the instant-decision variety and I figured if it was 85 miles I might just make it.

And I did – an F4 will glide, after a fashion. Altus is a C5A Galaxy base with a 13,000ft runway, and I landed with just enough fuel to make it to the flight line without the embarrassment of having to be towed in. All the fire engines were called out for my landing, providing a free show for their families day party, so I was a bit of a celebrity.

But nobody else turned up, so, after refuelling and another laborious start, the Chief and I flew on westward alone to Miramar where the Squadron wives had laid on a fantastic welcoming party with flags and bunting and many bottles of excellent Californian champagne. But none of the others showed up there either, so my wife and I soon slipped away.

The following morning I had a call from the CO: would I mind joining him in his house for a chat? There was going to be an enquiry...

This is what happened. On being told go to Altus, Gerry Arbini's pilot decided he did not have enough fuel (he had 300lbs more than me!) and continued making approaches to Amarillo in the fog. At the very last moment before having to eject for lack of fuel he found the runway and made a safe landing.

'Oly' Olsen in the last aircraft started out for Altus and like me had trouble with the radar controller; but unlike me could not bring himself to bust the 18,000ft Visual Flight ceiling. Below this height there was no way he was going to make the distance, so he landed on Highway 83 in Texas, a standard two-lane road with telegraph poles down one side, fortunately dead straight. On his first approach he spotted a car in the distance but couldn't tell whether it was coming or going, so he made a quick circle and landed next time round on the right side of the road, folding his wings as soon as he could. The car came along, slowed down, the driver looked him over and drove on, plainly annoyed at finding a Navy Phantom on the highway. Oly had to walk two miles to the nearest farmhouse to use the phone.

The CO's Division got into Albuquerque before the fog rolled in, the last division arriving after it lifted, and they all waited there while the Boss flew back to Altus to find out what was going on, which was that the USAF had sent a tanker and helicopters to rescue Oly. The road was blocked off, and without regard to the Load Classification Number of the road surface (supposedly critical for jet aircraft with very high tyre pressures) the CO flew the part-fuelled F4 off Highway 83 and back to Altus. On Monday morning when I went in to work all twelve aircraft were present and correct, lined up outside the hangar. The Formal Enquiry awarded Oly an Air Medal, and The Federal Aviation Authority, Air Traffic Control and the Met Office got severe reprimands. In due course, on time and as planned, Frank Mezzardri deservedly got command of VF213 Naval Air Squadron, United States Navy.

Lieutenant R.M. Turner,
Pilot, Wasp Helicopters, Icelandic Waters 1975

For more than six months, from early November 1975, the news was full of reports of the so-called Cod War between Great Britain and Iceland in which at one time or other seventeen Royal Navy frigates and two Royal Fleet Auxiliary tankers were involved. Stories of rammings and warp cuttings were headlined, and the dangers of close-quarters ship-handling and replenishment at sea were much emphasized, but little was reported about the aviation aspect of this long-drawn-out and bitter struggle with the Icelandic Coastguard Service through the North Atlantic winter.

Each British frigate carried its own Wasp helicopter, the RFA tankers a Wessex Mk.3, and whenever weather conditions permitted – the principal limitations being deck movement and the need to avoid icing – the aircraft flew

'...the principle limitation being deck movement...' (Wasp, HMS Naiad, Cod War) FAAOA

reconnaissance and Helicopter Despatch Service (HDS) tasks

In the short gloomy daylight period, flying conditions were far from ideal. Winds up to Hurricane Force 12 were experienced every three weeks, the average wind being Force 6-7, with temperatures of -10° to +5°C. Weather systems moved quickly, so forecasting was difficult; on one occasion in *Naiad* we had a light breeze and +3°C at a time when trawlers fifty miles north were in a Force 11 at -8°C. Patchy fog was a big problem. Flight-deck crews wore yacht-type safety harnesses attached to wire runners to prevent them being blown or washed overboard, or even pitched over the side by a violent movement of the deck. The bridge would often warn the flight deck down aft when a big 'un' was coming, so they could hang on tight. The helicopter's operational day usually ended at dusk, although night sorties were occasionally required to identify radar contacts.

Starting before dawn, the helicopter's task was to locate the Icelandic gunboats which dodged and hid among the islands close to the coast, and get the frigates into position to 'mark' them and stop them getting in among the trawlers. As an example of 'close marking', HMS *Diomede* (Captain Bob McQueen) was at one time chasing the Icelander *Tyr* in and out of the fleet at twenty knots, and was later rammed four times in an afternoon by the *Baldur*, the final collision tearing a twenty-foot hole in her wardroom..

For such close marking games, the helicopter would be recovered and stowed away for safety. Otherwise, once the gunboat picture was established, the helicopter could revert to the HDS role and ferry television crews, newspaper reporters, stores, mail and movies around the force, and got much excellent practice in 'hi-line transfer' lifting baskets of fish from the lurching decks of friendly trawlers.

Although primarily an integral part of the frigates' anti-submarine systems, the versatile helo proved a very useful machine in the Cod War, and a lot of valuable experience was gained all round.

Lieutenant Davidson,

Observer, Sea King, 706 Squadron, RNAS Culdrose, 1978

Bad weather had forced cancellation of 706 Squadron's routine night flying at Culdrose on 1 February 1978 when Lands End Coastguard received a distress call from the Seven Stones lightship near the Isles of Scilly saying her anchors were dragging. Two Sea King crews came to immediate readiness and awaited developments, but at around 2000 the focus of attention switched to the English Channel where the skipper of a German tug, on passage from Rotterdam to Brazil with the oil rig 'Orion' in tow, was calling Brixham Coastguard reporting his line parted and the rig, with thirty-three crewmen aboard, drifting towards Guersney in Force 10 winds. Off-duty 706 aircrew were called in and briefed.

The lightship by then being out of immediate danger, Culdrose's helicopters were offered to the Coastguard, who scrambled Sea Kings 592 and 594 at around 2230 when the Orion was reported nearing Guernsey; I was the observer of 592. It took 50 minutes to fly the 160 miles from Culdrose to Guernsey – a north-westerly tailwind of about 100 knots.

We located the rig without difficulty shortly before midnight, lit up like a Christmas tree and well aground on Guernsey's Grand Rocques. In a superb feat of seamanship in huge seas near the dangerous rocks, the St Peter Port lifeboat had already taken off two men before having to make a break for the open sea.

Flying in fierce turbulence and spray, my pilot Lieutenant Glen Tilsley, assisted by co-pilot John Wingate, inched 592 into a hover close to the rig's towering 278ft legs so that Chief Aircrewman Alf Tupper could lower me on to the rig's helo platform, by now awash in breaking seas.

Clinging on to the sloping platform in dense spray, I coaxed the crewmen forward one by one and double-lifted twelve of them to safety, Chief Tupper working the winch at the same time as keeping a wary eye on the steel legs swaying close to our rotor blades. After twelve times up and down on the wire I was hauled inboard and 592 flew to Guernsey airport with the survivors, 594 taking our place and picking up another load in similar fashion.

We went back alone for the remaining nine men, 594 having suffered a hydraulic failure on the ground, but in the meantime the stranded rig had yawed through nearly 180 degrees and the only way of getting at the survivors was from a crosswind hover over the platform with very little clearance for both main and tail rotors. I was going up the wire with the second man, sixty feet below the aircraft in the rescue strop, the pilot already at the limit of control in the violently gusting crosswind, when the whole rig began to rotate. The pilot then ran out of tail-rotor control and, according to the citation, 'Only excellent crew co-operation saved the situation'. Sufficient to say we got away with it.

After hovering nearby by for a further forty-five minutes in case the rig toppled over, we returned to the airport; further rescue attempts were abandoned for the night at 0240.

'592 went back and plucked the last four to safety...' Lancaster/Daily Express via Davidson

At first light local rescue teams rigged a breeches buoy and lifted three men off this way before the line broke as conditions became even worse. 592 went back and plucked the last four to safety.

The following notices were published in the Defence Supplement to the *London Gazette* on Tuesday 28 November 1978.

Tupper, King, Crudgington, Eagles, Tilsley, Wingate, Davidson, Matthews. BCC/MOD via Davidson

The Queen has been graciously pleased to approve the following awards:
Air Force Cross
Lieutenant Glen James TILSLEY, Royal Navy
Lieutenant Robert George DAVIDSON, Royal Navy
Lieutenant Anthony James EAGLES, Royal Navy★
Lieutenant Paul CRUDGINGTON, Royal Navy★
Queen's Commendation for Valuable Service in the Air
Chief Aircrewman Malcolm John TUPPER
Chief Aircrewman Terence Anthony KING★
★Pilot, Observer and Winchman of Sea King 594

Paul Crudgington and I may have been the first Observers to be awarded AFCs for Gallantry, but there was a very thin line between that and potential court martial if things went wrong. I had to wait another ten years for the latter when I was Captain of HMS *Guernsey* and went aground off Aberdeen on Good Friday, 1987.

Captain Bob McQueen
Pilot, Commanding Officer, RNAS Portland, 1979/80.

'Helicopter flying is great fun, but it's no substitute for aviation.' I probably shared the sentiments of most Fleet Air Arm fixed-wing pilots when in 1979 I was appointed in command of HMS *Osprey*, the Navy's large busy air station at Portland, flying nothing but helicopters.

The Old Man's Chopper Course at Culdrose gave me a handful of hours flying Hillers and Whirlwinds, not much for the Captain of a rotary-wing station; I therefore arranged a full 23-hour conversion on the Wessex 5 at Yeovilton, but nevertheless arrived at my new command with less than 50 hours helicopter experience. I was keen to learn though, and in an uncharacteristic flash of brilliance briefed the CO of 772 Squadron, Paul Barton, as follows: 'I want to fly with your Squadron, but I am an inexperienced helicopter pilot. You are to treat me like any other junior pilot when authorizing me to fly, and if I have an accident the first thing I, as your Captain, will examine is whether you exercised proper supervision over me as a junior pilot.'

Early in my tenure I had to visit RAF Valley in Anglesey, naturally by helicopter, but when the day came the weather was so bad I thought we would have to cancel the trip. My Commander (Air), John Neville-Rolfe, seeing an opportunity to further my education, decided otherwise. We flew in cloud up to the Bristol Channel, letting down to a landfall exactly where Leading Aircrewman Casey (sadly killed in the Falklands War) said we were and squeezed between cliffs and cloudbase into RAF St Athan in South Wales for a 'hot refuel', using one engine as an Auxiliary Power Unit. From there we coast-hopped round Wales and arrived at Valley exactly on time - mission accomplished! I was learning, especially about the extraordinary Dead-Reckoning navigation abilities of the Aircrewman in the back, who of course could only see out sideways.

As time went on I was spared none of the indignities which all aircrew had to undergo, tests and checks and drills and dunkings, and was thus as well qualified as anyone else; but every now and again, if the weather was a bit doubtful, just as I was about to take off, Paul Barton or his Senior Pilot would sidle into the left-hand seat beside me with a casual 'Just thought you would like a bit of company, Sir..' They were usually right.

Dummy-deck training on a lighter in Portland harbour was generally held to be pretty boring stuff, except when I was demonstrating 'ground resonance' for the benefit of flight-deck crews under training. Ground resonance can shake a helicopter to pieces in seconds, with great risk to life and limb for anyone nearby, if a helicopter's wheels pick up the vibration from the rotor and transmit it to the airframe. This usually happens when there is not enough weight on the wheels, as when I was trying to 'kiss' them gently onto the deck, the hallmark of a good *fixed-wing* landing and a habit I found hard to shake off. I never quite reached the point where the aircraft thrashed itself to pieces, but I understand my expertise in demonstrating this condition, and recovering from it, was acknowledged by the *cognoscenti* as a true art form.

Towards the end of my time in command, when with a full load of ten passengers I badly messed up the awkward approach to HMS *Vernon*'s landing area down at Portsmouth, I had cause to be thankful for that inspired cautionary briefing I gave at the outset of my short and undistinguised career as a helicopter pilot. A calm 'I have control, Sir!' from 772 Squadron's new Senior Pilot who was 'keeping me company' that day, just before the situation got completely out of hand, preserved my clean record: for two and a half years Portland's 'junior boy' had been supervised perfectly without incident.

Looking back on it, I sometimes think I should have recommended them all for medals, but I am sure they would say they were only looking out for themselves.

CHAPTER FIVE

THE 1980S

Introduction

In 1980 Through-Deck Cruiser *Invincible* replaced the 'ugly and unsuccessful' Helicopter Cruisers *Tiger* and *Blake*. *Hermes* was made Harrier-capable and next year she and *Invincible* were fitted with the ingenious 'ski-jump' to augment the Sea Harrier's take-off performance. In retrospect it seems unintelligent of the Argentines to have waited until 2 April 1982 to invade the Falkland Islands, for by then the only ships capable of deploying air power to oppose them were fully worked-up and ready. Within three days of the invasion *Invincible* and *Hermes*, with twenty Sea Harriers between them, were on their way south.

To quote John Winton on the Falklands War, 'Despite the years of peace, exercises and soft living, shortcomings in diplomacy, Airborne Early Warning and ship design, all the Royal Navy's aircraft performed superbly. Air superiority (without which opposed landings are impossible) was established against odds of 6-1. The RAF was fortunate they were not called to provide the Fleet's air cover 8000 miles from the UK with no airfields. What would they have done?'

Naval helicopters – Sea King Mk.2, 4 and 5, Wessex 3 and 5, Lynx Mk.2 and Wasp, flying at more than three times peacetime operating rates from the two carriers, nine frigates, two Assault Ships, four Fleet Auxiliaries and improvised shore-bases, lifted troops, stores, weapons and ammunition and, vital but largely unsung, for twenty-four hours a day maintained the anti-submarine screen around the many ships of the Falklands Task Force. Lynxes engaged surface targets with brand new Sea Skua missiles, scoring eight hits with eight firings, destroying one Argentine ship and seriously damaging two others; others carried out reconnaissance and acted as decoy for Exocet missiles. Wasps did all they could, including shoreline reconnaissance.

Twenty-eight Sea Harriers of three Squadrons maintained 95% availability and flew 99% of all planned missions. Three weeks after the first landing, their Air Force effectively neutralized as a fighting force – seventy-two aircraft shot down plus fourteen 'probables', thirty-three destroyed on the ground – the isolated and demoralized Argentine invaders threw in the towel. Fleet Air Arm aircraft accounted for twenty of the air kills, plus three 'probables'; ship-launched missiles killed twenty-one, plus two 'probable', shore missiles twenty-four plus eight, and most of the rest fell to naval guns.

Ironically, the Royal Air Force's participation could only emphasize this vindication of maritime air power: their ground-attack Harriers operated from naval flat-top ships and their helicopters came by sea with naval escort and operated from land secured and protected by naval air power.

179

In 1943 Admiral Keyes wrote that 'Many thousands of seamen perished, millions of tons of shipping were lost, scores of men-of-war destroyed or damaged because when war came [the RN] had no Naval Air Service commensurate with the Navy's needs.' *Plus ça change.* 'The absence of AEW,' remarks the official report on the Falklands War, 'was a severe handicap.' Far beyond the range of the RAF's moribund AEW Shackletons, the effectiveness of the Navy's flat-tops was much reduced by having to keep out of range of the Argentine Navy's aggressive low-level Super Etendards against which, with no AEW, there was no defence. Good ships and many lives were lost as a result.

Within eleven weeks of the conflict, in another ironic twist, the Navy had resurrected its own AEW by fitting 'Searchwater' downward-looking radars, designed for the RAF Nimrod maritime patrol aircraft, to a Squadron of its own Sea Kings.

In the Falklands War, which reinstated the aircraft carrier in UK defence terminology, the Fleet Air Arm lost six Sea Harriers, five Sea Kings, nine Wessex and three Lynx. Five pilots, one observer, three aircrewmen and nine other Fleet Air Arm personnel lost their lives.

The Fleet Air Arm Roll of Honour contains the names of all those who lost their lives in flying operations during the 1980s. The figures are:

Pilots	25
Observers	10
Aircrewmen	6
Others	1

Lieutenant M. Tidd,
Pilot, Wessex Mk.5, 845 Squadron 'C' Flight,
RFA *Tidespring*, South Georgia, 1982

South Georgia, a crescent-shaped island 105 miles long and 18 miles wide, rises sheer out of the sea to a height of between 7500ft and 9500ft along its spine. Over half its land mass is permanently covered by glaciers. It lies in the South Atlantic on the edge of Antarctica and bears the full brunt of the wild weather that sweeps around Cape Horn. Having been the first piece of British territory captured by the Argentines, it was planned to be the first to be recaptured, for reasons partly political but also to provide a cross-decking point for civilian ships acting as troop transports.

Lieutenant Michael Tidd, Royal Navy. Tidd

The South Georgia Task Group consisted of HMS *Antrim* carrying 'D' Squadron SAS, HMS *Plymouth* with further SBS elements, and RFA *Tidespring*, a Fleet Tanker with 'M' Company of 42 Commando Royal Marines embarked. The senior aviator was *Antrim*'s Flight Commander, Lieutenant Commander Ian Stanley, who had a Wessex Mk.3, while I was Flight Commander of 845 Squadron 'C' Flight in *Tidespring* with two Wessex Mk.5s. Much of this story turns on the difference between the Mk.3 and Mk.5 Wessex: *Antrim*'s Mk.3 had radar and a fairly sophisticated Automatic Flight Control System (AFCS); my Mk.5s, 'YA' (Yankee Alpha) and 'YF' (Yankee Foxtrot) were basic battlefield utility helicopters with no such refinements. Both types were fairly long in the tooth by now, but the Mk.5 was still a rugged,

SAS Operation – Fortuna Glacier. Tidd

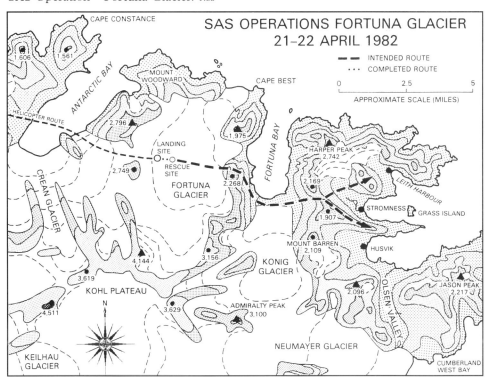

manoeuvrable and reliable airframe, much loved by all who flew her.

HMS *Endurance* joined the Group on the way south and we received detailed briefings from Tony Ellerbeck, her Flight Commander, on the terrain and weather conditions in South Georgia. Having trained in Northern Norway, we were used to Arctic conditions, but in terms of violence and unpredictability the weather Tony described sounded ominous. Nevertheless in our innocence I think we equated the conditions he described with the *worst* of the weather we had met in the Arctic. As will be seen, this was equating a tabby to a tiger, and we got sorely bitten.

The first phase of the plan called for a detailed reconnaissance of the Argentine garrison, our mission being to insert Captain John Hamilton's SAS patrol 2500ft up on the Fortuna Glacier, from where they were to make their way along the spine of the island to a point from which they could observe the Argentine base at Leith. And it is a measure of our totally unrealistic concept of the conditions that we first planned to do this at *night*! My Wessex 5s were fitted with formation lights and we hatched a plan to do a night join-up with *Antrim*'s Mk.3, which would lead us in using its radar. Fortunately for us all, as events will show, the join-up proved far too difficult, and after one abortive and frightening attempt on 15 April we decided that discretion was the better part of valour and opted for a daylight 'insertion'.

Off the north-west tip of South Georgia on the morning of the 21st, after Ian Stanley had carried out an initial reconnaissance in the Mk.3, we embarked the troops and set off through thick snow showers towards the coast. As normal in Commando operations, my two Mk.5s were flying with a single pilot and aircrewman, myself in Yankee Alpha with Tug Wilson, and 'Pullthrough' Pulford, our RAF exchange pilot, in Yankee Foxtrot with Jan Lomas.

Landfall at Cape Constance, black cliffs rising 1000ft vertically from the sea in driving snow, was awe-inspiring, as was the brute force of the turbulence. Skirting the landward end of Cape Constance into Antarctic Bay, where the Fortuna Glacier disgorges into the sea, I was using full power one moment just to maintain height, then full autorotation (no power at all) the next and still going up.

By the time we got to the glacier it was shrouded in impenetrable snow and, after orbiting in Antarctic Bay for some time, Ian Stanley made the decision to return to the ships to refuel and we made our way back through heavy snowstorms. *Tidespring*'s deck could only take one aircraft at a time; I landed first and left Pullthrough hovering off the port quarter with his aircraft building up an impressive accumulation of snow and ice until mine was folded and pushed into the hangar to let him on.

At 1145 we tried again, this time making better progress up on to the upper slopes of the glacier, though it was still very murky and there was severe turbulence, with the wind whipping up deep streams of driven snow. To add to our 'deep joy and happiness', we found that the surface of the glacier was heavily crevassed which meant that we would have to be extremely careful about where we put down. Ian Stanley took us near the top of the glacier and turned into wind to make his approach, using the Mk.3's doppler and Automatic FCS to let himself down onto the surface. When I tried to do the same and realized how few visual references were going to be available for the landing – the flying snow here was 200 feet deep – I had to overshoot and discuss the problem with Tug in the back.

This was going to be a challenge to say the least. We decided that I would orientate myself as best I could, by using distant references, and let Tug talk me down gradually to the surface, which is what we did. Apart from the visibility problems, the updraught was so strong I was forced to go into virtual full autorotation to get the aircraft to descend. The crevassing turned out to be even worse than we thought and we eventually touched down with a yawning crack in the ice about ten feet away on our starboard side. I gave the order to start off-loading the troops. With the wheels on the ice I had 60 knots of airspeed on the clock, and even with the collective lever fully down we were sliding sideways. I found the only way I could prevent us sliding into the crevasse was to tilt the rotor into wind and 'fly' the aircraft on the ground as the troops jumped out. When the last one was clear we bounded into the air and scuttled off down the glacier and thankfully back out into Antarctic Bay.

Back on board *Tidespring*, Pullthrough and I agreed we had never seen conditions like these before: 'Thank Christ we'll never have to do that again!' How wrong you can be!

We were ordered to keep one aircraft on standby for Casevac (Casualty Evacuation), but as night came on the barometer dropped 30 Millibars in an hour and the wind rose to peak at over 80 knots. This happened so quickly we

Barograph trace. BCC/MOD via Ward

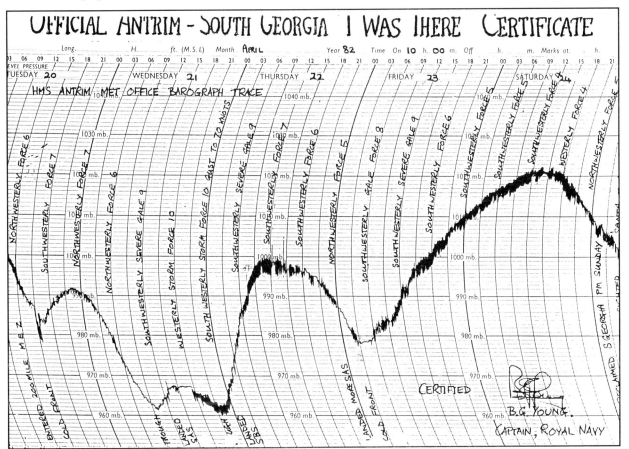

were unable to get the rotors of the deck alert aircraft folded in time, and the tipsocks, which were meant to anchor the tips of the blades to prevent them thrashing up and down in the wind, started tearing themselves apart. We anchored the blades as best we could with heavy manila mooring line, wedged ourselves in our bunks and tried to get some rest. As a glance at the barograph trace will show, this was not easy. By morning the wind had eased to a mere full gale, and despite my doubts the exposed aircraft was still there on deck, and all in one piece.

But up on the Fortuna glacier things were not looking so good. Overnight up there the wind had reached over 100 knots, destroying the SAS's tents, and they were now dangerously cold, wet and starting to become hypothermic. At 1000, suffering from frostbite and exposure, they called for urgent evacuation.

At 1030 we launched between snowstorms, with me flying Yankee Foxtrot and Ian Georgesson in Yankee Alpha, and headed for the shore. Ian Stanley from *Antrim* was ahead of us in his Mk.3 and the weather over the glacier looked so bad he ordered us to land on the low ground at Possession Bay while he went ahead for a closer look. Unable to find a break in the weather, he ordered a return to the ships to refuel and wait.

Back in the bay an hour or so later we found a break in the cloud and set off up the glacier. I was acutely aware that we were going to be very short of escape options up there. In peacetime no sensible pilot would allow himself to be sucked into a position like this: there was only one way in and one way out, with mountains on either side; if we got caught in the air by the weather we couldn't climb because of the icing we were already experiencing, and might be unable to land because of whiteout, and our Wessex 5's had neither the radar, doppler or Automatic Flight Control System essential for safe flight in such conditions. However, this was not peacetime; this was war, and if we didn't go men would die.

Approaching the top of the glacier, we quickly spotted the SAS's smoke grenades. They were huddled in the lee of some rocks in an area relatively free of crevasses only a few hundred yards from where we dropped them. The grenades stained the snow around them, making it easier to see the ground for landing, and we set down uneventfully, facing our escape route down the glacier, which at this point was a fairly shallow ice slope leading down to a ridge about a mile away, on the other side of which the ice dropped away steeply. As soon as we had our quota of half a dozen soldiers aboard Tug shut the door and broke out some hot soup, while I radioed Ian Stanley for permission to depart. I could see a fresh belt of cloud and snow brewing up near our escape route.

When he said Go! I needed no second bidding, lifted off and headed down the valley at about 60 knots and 100ft, which should have given me the option of landing again if conditions got too bad. But it all happened too quickly. Half a mile down the glacier the wind suddenly shifted and without warning I was enveloped in thick driving snow. *Whiteout!* The affect of whiteout is difficult to describe. Thick flying snow over white featureless ground deprives you of all visual references and leaves you totally disorientated. Bad enough on skis. Airborne in a helicopter over a glacier with 'cumulo-granite' mountains all around, unable to climb, and a fissured glacier underneath, very bad news indeed. My only option was to try to put the aircraft down on the ground – if I could see where it was.

I called down to Tug to let him know that we had a problem and, making an instant arbitrary decision that probably saved our lives, banked left. I had seen a small clump of rocks on that side a few seconds earlier. Tug threw open the cabin door and leaned out to look for the surface as I continued turning and searching for a landing reference. What neither of us could see was that we were in a dip in the ice-field. I glanced in at the radio altimeter half-way round the turn and saw the needle winding down at an alarming rate. It was telling me we were about to crash. I had no idea where the ground was coming from but pulled in power and flared the nose up to cushion the impact. The aircraft hit tail first, left wing low, doing about 30 knots, sheering the port undercarriage leg off and crashing down and grinding along on its left side. Held by my straps, I experienced a feeling of intense frustration as the left-hand side of *my cockpit* filled up with debris and snow, and I thought, 'Mrs Tidd isn't going to like being a widow!'

But Yankee Foxtrot ground to a halt and I was still alive. The inertia switches in the nose had crash-stopped the engines, and apart from the wind and the futile squeak of my windscreen wiper all was suddenly quiet. I reached down beside me to turn off the fuel cocks and electrics only to find that the whole lot was buried under snow and broken glass. To my huge relief Tug called through from the cabin that everyone seemed to be in one piece, so I hauled open the starboard cockpit door, climbed up on to the side of the fuselage and helped Tug get the cabin door open.

The blizzard cleared as quickly as it came, allowing the other two helos to land nearby. I staggered across to Ian Stanley's Mk.3 and plugged myself into the intercom lead that Fitz, his aircrewman, handed out to me. 'You've left your windscreen wiper on!' was Ian's greeting, to which I replied with some feeling, 'If you're so damn clever you can go and turn it off!' The three aircrewmen made short work of dividing up the survivors between the two remaining helos while Jock Georgesson started jettisoning fuel to bring his Mk.5's weight down so he could lift the extra load. The press of bodies in the back of the Mk.3 forced me to unplug from the intercom and, lost in my own thoughts, I don't remember

'You must be the SAS...' 'YF's broken tail on right. Tidd

much about the flight back to *Antrim*.

I climbed out, gave Ian Stanley a thumbs up by way of thanks and made my way into *Antrim's* unfamiliar hangar where First Aid parties were busy laying out stretchers and making up saline drips, obviously expecting casualties. I took my bonedome off and grabbed hold of Chief Heritier, Ian Stanley's Senior Maintenance Rating.

'Relax, Chief,' I told him. 'Our only casualty was a cut cheek!'

He looked at me for a moment and then took me by the arm: 'The other Wessex 5 crashed into a cliff on the way out. We don't know yet if there are any survivors.'

The shock hit me like a blow in the stomach. Tug, Jock Georgesson and Jan Lomas were good friends of mine. The news left me feeling physically sick.

I heard the Mk.3 lift off again and then, in something of a daze, was taken up to the bridge. Considering that Brian Young, *Antrim's* Captain and the Task Group Commander, had just seen his whole operation come off the rails and blow up in his face, he was very sympathetic. Ian Stanley must have told him about conditions on the glacier the day before. He listened understandingly as I told him how we had been overwhelmed, and the speed with which it all happened, and told me not to blame myself. I was led away to the wardroom for a hot drink while we waited for news.

I don't think I registered much more until, to my indescribable relief, the Ops Room broadcast that Ian Stanley had made contact with the Yankee Alpha's crew, and they had all survived! It was some time before he managed to find a hole in the weather to get in and pick them up, and the story of that remarkable piece of flying is best left to him. Suffice to say he and his crew managed to pack sixteen armed men into an aircraft that normally feels cramped with four people in it, and made it back to the ship for an overweight landing on a heaving deck. This feat, and others, earned him a well-deserved DSO.

When Jock Georgesson had dried off he filled me in on what had happened. They had started off down the glacier through a break in the weather with the Mk.3 in the lead, and like me, within half a mile they were in whiteout. Ian Stanley in the Mk.3 was able to cope with this, his automatic height-hold allowing him to maintain height over the surface, and initially Jock was able to formate on him, which would have been all right if the surface had been flat. When the terrain fell away on the far side of a substantial ridge of ice, the Mk3's height-hold automatically put it into a descent. Struggling to follow the other helicopter down through the blinding snow, Jock suddenly noticed his radio altimeter winding down, like mine, at an alarming rate, indicating the ground was coming up to meet him.

He pulled in power to cushion the landing and probably would have got away with it without the 50-knot side-wind. Yankee Alpha touched down hard and rolled over. What Stewart Cooper, Ian Stanley's co-pilot, had mistaken for the aircraft running headlong into a cliff was the explosion of snow thrown up by the thrashing blades.

Miraculously, again no one was hurt – with the exception of the sergeant who already had a cut on his cheek from the cabin-mounted machine gun in my aircraft, and now had a matching cut a little further down his cheek from the same weapon in Jock's! Georgesson and his crewmen soon had the troops mustered out on the ice, got a photo of the crew sitting on the wreckage, inflated the life-raft and got them all in out of the weather. For the next few hours, until Ian Stanley managed to get back and rescue them, they played cards.

The loss of two-thirds of the Task Group's air-lift assets was a major blow to the operational plan, but as it turned out, not a fatal one. HMS *Brilliant*, a Type 22 frigate with two Lynx helicopters, was diverted from the main Falklands Task Force to reinforce the South Georgia Task Group.

After another four days and several more trials and tribulations which are a tale in their own right, *Antrim's* Wessex 3, one of the Fleet Air Arm's oldest helicopters and affectionately known as 'Humphrey', attacked and damaged the Argentine Guppy class submarine *Santa Fe* with Mk.11 depth charges, probably the oldest airborne weapon in the Navy's inventory. Tony Ellerbeck in his Wasp then scored several hits on the submarine with AS12 missiles (the first action firing of guided missiles by the Royal Navy), forcing her to limp back into Grytviken where she was beached in sinking condition.

Tidespring and the main body of troops were over 100 miles away at this point, but the moment was too good to waste. An assault group was hastily formed out of the SAS, *Antrim's* Royal Marines and the military Headquarters Staff and flown ashore by 'Humphrey' and the two Lynxes. Georgesson and I, being temporarily unemployed, took over the Military Operations Room. *Antrim* and *Plymouth* steamed in at high speed to provide Naval Gunfire Support. I stepped out on to the upper deck for a moment on the way in and will never forget the sight of the long grey hulls with Battle Ensigns flying, plunging through heavy seas with the barrels of their 4.5″ guns lifting and training towards the shore, a sight probably not seen since the Second World War. The big Battle Ensigns were good psychology, but turned out to be incompatible with modern warship design as they insisted on wrapping themselves around the radar antennae.

The ships laid down an impressive barrage of high explosive around the Argentine positions, the aim being to keep their heads down and demoralize them rather than do any physical damage, as we needed the buildings intact. Duly impressed, the invaders soon surrendered and by early evening the Task Group Commander was able to send the historic signal: ' Be pleased to inform Her Majesty that the White Ensign flies alongside the Union Flag at Grytviken, South Georgia. God save the Queen'.

Despite some setbacks, the first phase of the operation to recover the Falkland Islands was successfully completed.

Throughout the Falklands campaign the weather was to inflict far greater aircraft casualties than the enemy. At this point the score was: South Georgia-2, 845 Squadron 'C' Flight-0.

And we had only just begun!

The two Mk.5 carcasses are still there. They come up to the surface every year in the spring melt. Several years after the war, Tony Ellerbeck, who was awarded the DSC and after whom a mountain in South Georgia is now named, brought me the panel clock and collective lever from the wreck of 'Yankee Foxtrot'.

Lieutenant Commander David Morgan DSC,
Pilot, Sea Harrier, HMS *Hermes*, 1 May 1982

Grey fingers of dawn probed the eastern sky as twelve fighter pilots, weighed down with survival kit and maps, fanned out across *Hermes*'s gently heaving deck towards their Sea Harriers. I had done this many times before, but not with the awkward bulk of a loaded pistol, and never with so many live weapons on my aircraft. *Hermes* herself had never, in twenty-three years in commission, been to war. We were all new to this.

In four weeks and eight thousand miles from Portsmouth to the Falklands, the mood aboard the Flagship had noticeably changed as it became plain the Argentines were not going to be frightened into giving up their illegal occupation of these far-flung islands. We in the Sea Harrier Force had always assumed we would be called upon to show our mettle, an occasion I imagine every fighter pilot anticipates with a mixture of eagerness and foreboding, and entered into a daily round of planning and practice to hone our already considerable skills to a razor's edge before closing with the enemy. Day after day we practised ship attacks and Air Combat, dropped or fired every weapon in the armoury and planned assiduously for every conceivable contingency. By the third week in April, when it became clear we were going to have to fight, we were confident, despite the enemy's ten-to-one advantage in the air, that we would give a good account of ourselves.

This morning, 1 May, planning and practice were finished. After the mission briefing which had included last-minute escape and evasion instructions, and the issue of a 9mm Browning automatic with two loaded magazines – more of a psychological prop than any practical use, even for a passably good shot like myself – and a few half-hearted jokes, each pilot took refuge in his private thoughts. Some left letters to wives or girlfriends. It was a relief at last to be able to immerse oneself in the well-practised and comforting routine of preparing to fly.

I was largely responsible for planning this first assault on Stanley Airfield and was very aware that the odds were against us all returning safely. My part in the plan, the integrity of which depended upon each pilot carrying out his individual role as perfectly as possible, ran through my mind while I checked over my aircraft. I double-checked all the weapons, and then the Head-Up-Display (HUD) aiming data, adding two little marks of my own on the sight glass in case of a display failure. These marks coincided with the weapon aiming point, one as seen from my normal sitting position, and a further one to be used when crouching down behind the gunsight camera, which is where I expected to be in the final stages of the attack.

At 1040Z the Flight Deck broadcast boomed: 'STAND CLEAR OF JETPIPES AND INTAKES. START THE SEA HARRIERS!' When I held up five fingers to my plane captain to confirm the ejection seat safety pins were all out and stowed, he signalled me to start. Engines whined into life all around me, and after a few minutes twelve flashing anti-collision lights signalled twelve fighters ready to go. There was time for a quick glance at the en-route map while *Hermes* turned into the westerly wind and chocks and lashings were removed leaving us free to fly.

As the hands on my watch moved oh so sluggishly to 1050, I entered Ship's Heading on the Inertial Nav and rechecked Flaps down, Armament Master switch LIVE, Nozzle Stop 35°, Trim 3° nose-down, Ejection Seat LIVE, etc etc.

On the second at 1050 Flyco's traffic-light turned green and Tony Hodgson, the Flight Deck Officer, dropped his green flag to launch the Squadron Boss, Lieutenant Commander Andy Auld, just ahead, me taxying forward to the take-off point through his jetwash as his aeroplane threw itself off the end of the ski-jump. Down on deck Tony braced against the buffeting jetblast and showed me the green flag and I gave a final nod and slammed the throttle fully forward. In one second my locked wheels were dragging; in two seconds ten tons of engine thrust were accelerating the jet at a terrific rate towards the ramp, and when the bow flashed away underneath I rotated the nozzles and leapt into the air seventy knots below conventional stalling speed, acclerating like a rocket. Seconds later I was wheels-up in a tight left turn to join the Boss with the others streaming off the deck behind.

In loose transit formation a hundred feet above the sea, everybody scouring the sky for enemy aircraft, we headed west for ten minutes then wheeled south for our planned landfall on the north-east point of East Falkland, Macbride Head. I spotted a couple of dark shapes closing rapidly from the east hugging the water and yelled 'BREAK PORT! BOGIES LEFT TEN O'CLOCK LOW!' and nine jets pulled into a screaming left turn before I realized the 'bogies' were our three spare aircraft en route to hit Goose Green. Fred Frederiksen obligingly hopped his formation over ours and we got back on heading with pulses racing and caught our first sight of the islands - a dark scar of land between the restless sea and layers of cloud stacked up over the higher ground to the south.

It looked so like Scotland it was quite difficult to believe this was not just another exercise, the daily round of the peacetime fighter-pilot, but a real errand of destruction and death. We swept down the coast towards our Initial Point near Volunteer Beach. I was struck by the complete absence of trees, the beauty of white sandy beaches, and the one lone cow that paused in mid-chew to look up as we swept by on our deadly mission.

In three sections we left Berkeley Sound with ninety seconds to run: four aircraft were pulling up off Volunteer Point to toss 1000-lb bombs on to the anti-aircraft defences; three were setting up an attack line from the north-west; Andy Auld and I headed for the east side of the pair of 900 ft mountains to the north of Stanley.

In a state of intense concentration, my eyes flicking between engine instruments and weapon display and the inhospitable rock-strewn tussock grass whipping past 50ft below, I urged my machine at 500mph towards the craggy outline of Mount Low.

Tucked behind and slightly left of my leader I rounded the east face of the mountain and saw the target. At first it was hard to take in the sight that greeted me in the thin grey dawn light. The entire peninsula on which Stanley airfield was built seemed to be alive with explosions. Shell-bursts carpeted the sky over the runway up to a height of 1000ft, so thick it seemed impossible for anything to fly through unscathed. Missiles from the airfield and town area streaked across my path. Long white missile-trails chased the previous attackers out to the south-east. Guns started sending feelers of tracer in my direction, the scarlet shells curving lazily without conveying much feeling of danger until they began bouncing off the grey sea all around me and my brain froze in horror for a fraction of a second. Somebody was trying to kill me! Then the years of training took over and I took evasive action and flew even lower, accelerating to nearly 600mph and hauling hard left and then right to pass between the Tussock Islands and Kelly Rocks, looking up at their 30ft sand dunes. Gunsight film of the run-in registered my height between five and fifteen feet.

Argentine soldiers were firing down at me from the sand dunes on the north edge of the airfield, their bullets kicking up the water all around. I dropped the trigger on the front of the stick and squeezed hard, expecting the roar of 30mm cannon and eruptions of flame and smoke among the enemy. Nothing! In the heat of the moment I had forgotten the Gun Master Switch.

Crossing the beach I yanked back on the stick hoping to flatten the defenders of the dunes with my jetwash, levelling at 150ft, the minimum fusing height for my cluster bombs. The airport buildings were billowing smoke, broken aircraft lolled at drunken angles on the hard-standing and the fuel dump to my right was a storm of orange flame under a pall of oily black smoke. Huge lumps of debris were still falling out of the sky from the explosions of the thousand-pounders. I lined up my bombsight on a small civilian Islander aircraft which seemed undamaged, raised the safety catch and mashed the release button to despatch my three bomb canisters. Each of these ejected 147 bomblets which fell to earth like a cloud of death the size of a football pitch, every bomblet capable of killing a tank or fragmenting into a vicious anti-personnel weapon.

After the first two thumped off the wing and centreline pylons a third of a second apart, there was a huge explosion and the aircraft started vibrating like a road drill on heat. It was so bad I couldn't read any of the instruments to check for damage, but we seemed to be still flying, so as soon as the last bomb canister cleared the wing I dived for the cover of the smoke beside the Control Tower. I have a clear recollection of entering the cloud of thick black smoke *below* the level of the Tower windows★. Inside the smoke I pulled into a maximum rate turn to the east to clear high ground and run down the beach to safety, but as soon as I punched out into the clear again a strident high-pitched warning blast from my Radar Warning Receiver told me an anti-aircraft gun radar had locked-on. To get the radar at right-angles to my flight path I racked the aircraft into a bone-crushing $6^{1}/_{2}$g break left and flicked the airbrake to dump a bundle of radar-blinding chaff - a last-minute Heath Robinson wire and string device 'invented' on the way down south. The little strips of silver foil did their job, the radar broke lock and I was able to haul my vibrating Sea Harrier back onto an easterly heading to run out to sea and safety.

Clearing the target area I switched channels and checked in on the new frequency. Because of the known strength of the ground defences I expected we would probably lose two or three aircraft on this raid, so it was with a tremendous surge of elation that I heard everybody else had checked in. I slowed down and climbed gently up to 10,000ft. At the lower speed the vibration eased so that I could check out the aircraft systems, and the only thing wrong, in itself of no consequence to the operation of the aeroplane, but indicating damage to the tail, was the tiny gauge which showed the position of the rudder trim.

Circling back overhead *Hermes* at 5000ft, Flight Lieutenant Ted Hall came alongside and inspected my aircraft. 'Ah yes,' he said at length, like a doctor finishing his examination, 'you've got a bloody great hole in the tail.' All the normal aerodynamic control surfaces appeared to be working correctly, but the possibility of damage to the reaction controls, the 'puffer jets' essential for hovering, meant I would have to do a rolling landing. Since this entails flying the aircraft on to the deck with a fair amount of forward speed and a distinct danger of running over the side into the sea, it is not what is known as a 'Cleared Manoeuvre', i.e. it is not normally permitted. But it was my safest option and I had enough fuel to overshoot and try again if I didn't like the first approach.

Wheels and flaps down, I set myself up for a straight-in approach about a mile astern of the ship. At half a mile I could see there were too many people on the flight deck, made a short call and was relieved to see them getting off the deck fast: I didn't know what was going to happen and didn't want anybody else to get hurt if I lost control. To give a steady rate of descent at 50 knots and compensate for the rise and fall of the carrier's deck in the long ocean swell needed constant adjustments of power and nozzle angle all the way down, but I managed to achieve a good firm touchdown about 50ft up the deck, braked cautiously to a halt and found myself following the Marshaller's signals to park at the base of the ski-jump.

Not until I opened the canopy to admit a biting 30-knot gale of wind was I aware how profusely I was sweating. I found it unusually difficult to undo my straps and all the various connections to the ejection seat. A crowd had gathered down on the windswept slippery deck, staring at my tail. I gave a thumbs-up to Bernard Hesketh of the BBC, climbed carefully down and walked a little unsteadily round the back to inspect the damage. A 20mm shell had entered the left side of the fin at a narrow angle from ahead and exploded, causing considerable damage to the right side of the fin and tailplane. I reflected that the shell, one of the forty rounds per second aimed at me from this particular gun, must have passed very close indeed to my head.

Thus ended our first sortie of the war. We had flown twelve Sea Harriers against two heavily defended airfields, delivered a total of thirty-six bombs, destroyed a large number of enemy aircraft, fuel storage sites and buildings, and escaped almost unscathed. Euphoria replaced the shaded concern of the pre-dawn briefing. The first operational sortie, the most important in any pilot's life, was over. Life would never be the same again.

That evening the BBC's Brian Hanrahan ended his report of the raid with the words which became famous: 'I cannot say how many aircraft took part in the raid, but I counted them all out, and I counted them all back'.

*Returning to Stanley after the war, I found that the Control-Tower windows were less than twenty feet above the ground.

[*The Falklands Campaign* (HMSO Cmnd.8758) relates of the twelve Sea Harriers involved in this attack: '... one hour after their return the same aircraft were airborne for air defence patrols.']

Lieutenant Commander 'Sharkey' Ward DFC AFC
C.O. 801 Squadron, Sea Harriers, HMS *Invincible*, Falklands, 1982

[Authorized extract from *Sea Harrier over the Falklands* by Commander 'Sharkey' Ward, DSC, AFC, Royal Navy, (Leo Cooper, 1992)]

There were two ways to approach the CAP stations, transiting north or south of the missile zone, and on this first mission we had been given the southerly CAP station. The early morning clag had abated a little, but there were still extensive layers of medium to low cloud partially covering the islands, especially to the north of Falkland Sound. Three of us descended in battle formation past Darwin and took up the CAP station, with Alasdair sticking to Steve's wing. In the morning sun the Sound was a beautiful sight with an amazing mixture of startlingly clear blues, greens and shades of turquoise. Banks of yellowish kelp seaweed took their form from the currents and the colour of the water, in sharp contrast to the muddy browns and greens of the surrounding landscape.

It was initially a quiet mission with no trade until we had commenced our climb-out after 45 minutes at low level. As we were passing about 10,000 feet the *Antrim* controller came on the air. 'I have two slow-moving contacts over the land to the south of you. Possibly helicopters or ground-attack aircraft. Do you wish to investigate?'

As soon as the controller said the word 'south', I rolled hard to starboard and down. Steve Thomas and Alasdair followed suit.

'Affirmative. Now in descent heading 160°. Do you still hold the contacts?'

'Affirmative. Ten miles. Very low.'

Steve spotted them first. It was a good sighting against the indistinct colours of the gently undulating terrain. 'Got them, Sharkey! Looks like two Pucaras on the deck. About 15 degrees right of the nose.'

'Not visual. You attack first.' Then, as I spoke, I saw one of the Pucaras. Steve was closing in on the aircraft from its high right, 4 o'clock. I decided to attack the same aircraft from astern as I couldn't see the second target. 'Got one visual now. Same one you are going for. I'll attack from his 6.'

My Numbers Two and Three opened fire in unison against the target, their cannon shells ripping up the ground beyond the Pucara. I had a little more time for tracking and closed in astern of the enemy aircraft, which was hugging the ground and weaving gently; with any more bank its wing tip would have been in the dirt. I had a lot of overtake, centred the Pucara at the end of my hotline gunsight in the HUD [Head-Up Display], and squeezed the trigger. The aircraft gave its familiar shudder as the 30-mm cannon shells left the two barrels. They were on target.

The Pucara's right engine burst into flames and then the shells impacted the left aileron, nearly sawing off the wing tip as they did so. I was very close and pulled off my target.

Meanwhile, Steve had reversed to the left of the Pucara and was turning in for a second shot from a beam position. I had throttled back, jinked hard right and left, and prepared for a second stern shot. As the ground to the right of the enemy took the full weight of Steve and Alasdair's cannon fire, I dropped half flap. I wanted to get as low as possible behind the Pucara and dropping flap brought my nose and gun axis down relative to the wing-line. Aiming... hotline on... firing! The left engine of the Pucara now erupted into flame and part of the rear cockpit canopy shattered. My radio altimeter read-out in the HUD told me I was firing from as low as 10 and not higher than 60 feet above the ground.

I pulled off a second time, fully expecting the pilot to have ejected. Must be a very brave bloke in there because he was still trying to evade the fighters. Steve's section attacked again from the right, but it just wasn't his day – the ground erupted in pain once more. I was amazed that the Pucara was still flying as I started my third and final run. Sight on – and this time you're going down. Pieces of fuselage caught fire. I ceased firing at the last minute and as I raised my nose off the target, the pilot ejected. The aircraft had ploughed into the soft earth in a gentle skid by the time the pilot's feet hit the ground. He had only one swing in his parachute.

Later, I was to find out that the pilot's name was Major Tomba. He managed to hoof it back to his base at Goose Green after his ejection; before the war was over the man's bravery was to prove useful to both sides.

Our division of three SHARs [Sea Harriers] then resumed the climb and return to the ship. Needless to say, we were pretty short of fuel.

Everyone was keen to hear the gory details when I got to the crewroom.

Steve and I flew the next mission as a pair. There was no trade for us under the now clear blue skies, but we could see that to the south of the Sound HMS *Ardent* had seen more than enough action for the day. She was limping northwards and smoke was definitely coming from more places than her funnel. We were to see more of her on our third and final sortie of the day.

For this final 'hop' we were given a station to the west of San Carlos over the land. We descended from the north-east and set up a low-level race-track patrol in a wide shallow valley. As always, we flew in battle formation – side by side and about half a mile apart. When we turned at the end of the race-track pattern, we always turned towards each other in order to ensure that no enemy fighter could approach our partner's 6 o'clock undetected. I had just flown through Steve in the middle of a turn at the southerly end of the race-track when I spotted two triangular shapes approaching down the far side of the valley under the hills from the west. They were moving fast and were definitely Mirages, probably Daggers. I levelled out of the turn and pointed directly at them, increasing power to full throttle as I did so.

'Two Mirages! Head-on to me now, Steve. 1 mile.'

'Passing between them now!' I was lower than the leader and higher than the Number Two as they flashed past each side of my cockpit. They were only about 50 yards apart and at about 100 feet above the deck. As I passed them I pulled hard to the right, slightly nose-high, expecting them still to try to make it through to their target by going left and resuming their track. I craned my neck over my right shoulder, but they didn't appear. Instead I could see Steve chasing across the skyline towards the west. My heart suddenly leapt. They were going to stay and fight! Must have turned the other way.

They had turned the other way, but not to fight. They were running for home and hadn't seen Steve at all because their turn placed him squarely in their 6 o'clock. Steve's first missile streaked from under the Sea Harrier's wing. It curved over the tail of the Mirage leaving its characteristic white smoke trail and impacted the spine of the jet behind the cockpit. The pilot must have seen it coming because he had already jettisoned the canopy before the missile arrived; when it did, he ejected. The back half of the delta-winged fighter-bomber disappeared in a great gout of flame before the jet exploded.

I checked Steve's tail was clear, but he was far too busy to think of checking my own 6 o'clock. Otherwise he would have seen the third Mirage closing fast on my tail.

Steve was concentrating on tracking the second jet in his sights and he released his second Sidewinder. The missile had a long chase after its target, which was accelerating hard in full burner towards the sanctuary of the west. At missile burn-out the Mirage started to pull up for some clouds. The lethal dot of white continued to track the fighter-bomber as the jet entered cloud. I clearly saw the missile proximity-fuse under the wing. It was an amazing spectacle.

Adrenalin running high, I glanced round to check the sky about me. Flashing underneath me and just to my right was the beautiful green and brown camouflage of the third Dagger. I broke right and down towards the aircraft's tail, acquired the jet exhaust with the Sidewinder and released the missile. It reached its target in very quick time and the Dagger disappeared in a ball of flame. Out of the flame ball exploded the broken pieces of the jet, some of which cartwheeled along the ground before coming to rest, no longer recognizable as parts of an aircraft.

Later I was to discover that the third Mirage Dagger had entered the fight from the north and found me in his sights. As he turned towards the west and home he had been firing his guns at me in the turn, but had missed. It was the closest shave that I was to experience.

'and released the missile.' BCC/MOD via Ward

We were euphorically excited as we found each other visually and joined up as a pair to continue our CAP duties. We had moved a few miles west during the short engagement and now steadied on east for some seconds to regain the correct patrol position. As I was looking towards San Carlos, about 10 miles distant behind the hills, I noticed three seagulls in the sunlight ahead. Were they seagulls?

I called *Brilliant*. 'Do you have any friendlies close to you?'

'Wait!' It was a sharper than usual reply.

A second or two later, *Brilliant* was back on the air. 'Sorry, we've just been strafed by a Mirage. Hit in the Ops Room. Man opposite me is hurt and I think I'm hit in the arm. No, no friendlies close to us.'

Full power again. 'Steve, those aren't seagulls ahead, they're Skyhawks!' What had looked like white birds were actually attack aircraft that had paused to choose a target. As I spoke the three 'seagulls' stopped orbiting, headed towards the south and descended behind the line of hills. And from my morning flight I knew where they were going.

'They're going for *Ardent*.' I headed flat-out to the south-east, passing over the settlement of Port Howard at over 600 knots at 100 feet.

In quick time I cleared the line of hills to my left and was suddenly over the water of the Sound. Ahead and to the left were the Skyhawks. To the right was the stricken *Ardent,* billowing smoke like a beacon as she attempted to make her way to San Carlos. I wasn't going to get there in time but I knew that Red Section from *Hermes* should be on CAP on the other side of the water. 'Red Section! Three Skyhawks, north to south towards *Ardent*! I'm out of range to the west!'

Red Section got the message and appeared as if by magic from above the other bank of the Sound. I saw the smoke of a Sidewinder and the trailing A-4 exploded. The middle aircraft then blew up (a guns kill, so I heard later) and the third jet delivered its bombs into *Ardent* before seeming to clip the mast with its fuselage.

I looked around to see where my Number Two had got to.

'Steve, where are you?' He should have been in battle formation on the beam. No reply. My heart missed several beats. There was only one answer: he must have gone down!

I called *Brilliant*. 'Believe I've lost my Number Two to ground fire. Retracing my track back to the CAP position to made a visual search.' I didn't feel good. My visual search resulted in nothing. But I did hear the tell-tale sound of a pilot's SARBE rescue beacon. Maybe that was Steve? '*Brilliant*, I can't locate my Number Two but have picked up a SARBE signal. Could be him or one of the Mirage pilots. Can you send a helicopter to have a look please? I'm very short of fuel and must recover to Mother immediately.'

I felt infinitely depressed as I climbed to high level. Losing Steve was a real shock to my system. At 80 miles to run, I called the ship.

'Be advised I am very short of fuel. I believe my Number Two has been lost over West Falkland. Commencing cruise descent.'

'Roger, Leader. Copy you are short of fuel. Your Number Two is about to land on. He's been hit but he's OK. Over.'

'Roger, Mother. That is good news. Out.'

Invincible could be clearly seen at 60 miles. She was arrowing her way through the water towards me like a speedboat, leaving a great foaming wake. Good for JJ [Captain J.J.Black MBE] – doesn't want to lose a Sea Jet just for a few pounds of fuel. My spirits had suddenly soared and it felt great to be alive.

I throttled back and didn't need to touch the power again until I was approaching the decel to the hover. On landing with 200 pounds of fuel remaining, I couldn't help thinking what a remarkable little jet the Sea Harrier was. The fuel was right on the button. I had calculated 200 pounds at land-on before leaving San Carlos.

On board, I heard from Steve that he had been hit in the avionics bay by 20-mm machine-gun fire from Port Howard. He had lost his radio, couldn't communicate with me, and thought he might just as well go home. I was too pleased to see him to be angry.

'What was I supposed to think, then?'

'Oh, you were hightailing it after those Skyhawks, Boss. You can look after yourself and as I didn't have any missiles left I thought the best thing was to get the aircraft back and get it fixed.'

'Steve, that is definitely worth a beer!'

'Generation gap?' 'Sharkey' Ward with 'Hoagy' Carmichael, Sea Fury pilot who shot down a Chinese MiG-15 in the Korean War. Ward

Lieutenant Commander Rupert Nichol

Instructor Officer, Press Liaison Officer and Official War Diarist,
HMS *Hermes*, South Atlantic, 1982

Extracts from 'Letters from a Task Force':-

April 12th. 'My job is both fascinating and privileged, as my action station is on the bridge next to the Captain, observing all the flying, and the movements of the other ships of the fleet, while I record everything that takes place in the War Diary. In addition, I run the ship's television studio (an important morale factor) and our two reporters, Brian Hanrahan and Michael Nicholson (of BBC and ITV respectively) actually work for me, producing filmed reports of each day's activities on board: I am the programme controller and these eminent journalists are my reporters!'

April 17th. 'Standing on the bridge, I watch plumes of spray break over the bows and spatter against the bridge windows, 100 feet above the sea. Our enormous deck rises and falls with the swell, and I watch the frigates and destroyers around us bucket and plunge through these heavy seas. Apart from the rolling motion, one is insulated from the world in *Hermes*. Working down below, you would never know the time or the temperature; daylight is a surprise when I come from the wardroom or classroom to the bridge, but now in my cabin on the waterline, I hear the perpetual rush of water against the ship's side.'

May 2nd. 'Dawn Action Stations sees me on watch on the bridge, ready with the Ship's Diary to write the 'Captain's Memoirs' (as he refers to our work on the narrative). There is enormous tension and concern as the first Harriers line up with their bombs beneath them and roar down the deck to an uncertain jump into the air. Today has broken unbelievably fine and clear, and the ships around us are brilliantly lit by the sunrise against blue water, with a background of impressive autumnal cloud effects. Suddenly, a hold-up: one of the aircraft is unable to take off. He is quickly wheeled out of line while the others continue their leaps into the sky. Nothing is seriously wrong, though – at the end of the sequence he backs down the deck to follow them up in his turn. This was one of our RAF pilots, Flight Lieutenant Bertie Penfold, and his problem was only that, with a heavier bomb-load than the other three, he needed a longer take-off run than they. He went on to score the best 'hits' of the morning.'

15th May. 'Last night after we had finished transmitting I flew back to *Hermes* in [fleet tanker] *Olmeda*'s own helicopter. Flying from the tiny platform is always exciting as it is so small and so close to the funnel as you take off or come in to land. The platform was built for the smaller Wessex, and the Sea King's blades seem to skim the very edge of the superstructure.

'When the helicopter returns in the dark from an anti-submarine patrol all you see from the deck are four small lights, two fixed reds and a floating red and green. However close the helicopter comes, however loudly the blades thunder and the engines roar, nothing except these lights can be seen in the inky blackness. The unseen noise grows huger and huger, but never resolves itself into a shape. It is quite extraordinary to fly in this way.'

May 25th. 'We are in the middle of an air battle...a Mirage has just been shot down by one of our ships. How long can their aircraft keep on coming at us like this?...They are really heroes, these Argentinian pilots, and we have seriously underestimated their pertinacity. My objectivity is slipping, though. ...I am actually glad to hear that the Etendards may have been destroyed, and so cannot hit us with Exocet. I hope it is true. <u>Still</u> we wait for their carrier, the *Veinticinco de Mayo...*

'The final part of my job here is educational. I spent my off-duty time yesterday - D-Day - in rounding up my candidates for City and Guilds Examinations. I have various subjects to administer in the near future, including Law and English Literature at A-Level next month; but the immediate papers due, which have just arrived in the mail, are 'Agriculture, Phase II: Grassland, Forage and Feed Cereal Crops'. The students are prepared, and I cannot deny them their chance to sit their exams.'

May 27th. 'We seem to have recovered from the shock of the loss of the *Atlantic Conveyor* much more quickly than that of *Sheffield*. So many ships are sinking now, we must be becoming inured. It was eerie to watch her burning, though, and to see the sickening glow of explosions lighting the cloud base at night. It was a miracle that so many men escaped safely, thanks to the heroism of the helicopter pilots.

'Meanwhile, here on board *Hermes*, steward service continues in the wardroom mess, with kipper pâté and jellied eggs as hors d'oeuvres at dinner, and beautifully made savouries to end the meal (cheese éclairs tonight, anchovies last night) eaten by men wearing boiler suits and flying overalls, or, in my case, a blue shirt and anti-flash gear, with life-jacket and survival suit strapped round my waist. Other ships leave their hatches open for greater comfort and convenience, but the meals they serve are thick stews six-hourly in action messes; I think I prefer the *Hermes* approach ...

'Sleeping accommodation remains something of a trial: I am still bedding down on top of a classroom table, but I find it quite comfortable. Not all ships have placed their below-waterline cabins out of bounds, as *Hermes* has - but I sleep much easier on the island! Some displaced traditionalists have resorted to hammocks, in preference to camp beds in corridors, and these make a pleasant sight swinging gently above the wider passageways. *Hermes* is old enough to have been fitted with deckhead ringbolts for slinging hammocks.

'I have just been 'lurked' by the Supply Officer to do an audit over the next few days, so I shall have to do less writing for a while.'

Surgeon Captain Rick Jolly OBE
PMO, Royal Marines Field Hospital, Ajax Bay, Falklands 1982

An hour before dawn I got up and stepped outside. The boys were tucking into breakfast, whispering to each other over their baked beans and sliced compo. At first light the galley burners would be doused and Red Beach stand-to positions manned. Yesterday's devastating attack by the *Fuerza Aerea Argentina* on the *Sir Galahad* and *Sir Tristram* might be a prelude to much worse: the clear pre-dawn sky promised more fast jet activity.

While none of us at Ajax Bay had actually *seen* a Sea Harrier, their mounting tally against the Mirage and A-4 Skyhawks made encouraging reading at our regular evening briefings. We had been forced to put our trust in the 'Sea-Jets', and the surrounding Rapier SAM posts, rather than the Red Crosses on the roof. The two unexploded 400Kg bombs lodged in the back of our refrigeration plant 'hospital' were a constant reminder of our luck, so far.

For now, my priority was to move the eighty burnt and helpless young men in our overcrowded 'wards', and seventy-odd more in the ships lying out in San Carlos Water, to Her Majesty's Hospital Ship *Uganda*. But how? *Uganda* had no casevac assets of her own, and no military communications fit; she might not even know about yesterday's events at Fitzroy Cove, or out in Falkland Sound where HMS *Plymouth* had been worked over by a gaggle of Mirages.

The final push on Stanley was imminent and every airframe that could engage rotors was booked for restocking the front line with combat supplies, so the prospects for my bid concerning one hundred and fifty-six mostly stretcher-borne casualties for immediate evacuation were rather poor. Some ignoramus of a staff officer had even sent me a signal requesting 24 hours' notice of my casevac requirements! I thought about a landing craft, but one had been sunk yesterday and those assets were now limited, as well as offering a long and bumpy ride.

I went inside and looked again at the ghostly Flamazine-covered faces of the young Welsh Guardsmen. Hair and eyebrows had been singed short, or replaced by reddened skin and oozing crust. Inside the plastic bags which kept the dirt out but allowed some movement, their damaged swollen fingers looked like tinned sausasges. As our eyes met, some of the cracked and blistered lips parted in a vain attempt to smile. They were all so young – and **brave**. Somehow, I had to get them out of danger, before the next Air Raid Warning Red, away to the cool comfort and devoted nursing of the Hospital Ship.

My worst fears were soon confirmed. No helicopters were available for Casevac: we would simply have to manage on our own until the situation improved. A Medical Services Officer came from HQ to apologize and explain. His attitude changed completely when he saw the ghastly reality that lay behind the paper casualty statistics, and he left promising to find some helicopters from somewhere.

Then a familiar sound penetrated the primitive gloom of the hospital – our faithful, but occasional, Casevac Wessex 5! Grabbing my helmet I ran outside again and plugged into the intercom to explain the problem. Two tired faces stared back at me as pilot and aircrewman absorbed the details, then they were gone. They climbed to the top of the dark ridge of the Sussex mountains behind us, circled a couple of times and came straight back with a firm thumbs-up!

Uganda was in Falkland Sound, but with no military radios because of her Red Cross status. I scribbled a note to her Medical Officer in Charge as the first load came out – Guardsman Simon Weston on a stretcher with an escorting (Welsh) medical officer, and two walking wounded wrapped in blankets.

Three down, 162 to go. Would the Skyhawks come back? The Wessex returned; we reloaded it – and found a Sea King waiting behind it. Then another, and another. Anti-submarine Sea Kings, Commando Sea Kings – the morning passed in a blur, interrupted by several air raid warnings which the helicopters simply ignored. Each time, I was hearing the same message, some from distantly remembered faces from Culdrose days: 'Hello Sir, we hear you've got a problem. We can take a load for you, before we go for fuel or – ' this or that.

By midday the job was done. Ajax Bay was empty of suffering, the stretchers cleaned and stacked, ready-use stores replenished, intravenous fluid bags run-through and hung up ready for the next group of casualties. Our young Wessex pilot and his crewman dropped in for lunch and ate a precious egg, awarded only to our friends.

The Staff Officer from HQ came back, apologized for failing to get any helicopters and enquired about our evacuation plans; he was a decent chap and wore a green beret, like me, so I replied as politely as possible. We had moved the lot, I told him, and without a single formal Casevac request, thanks to the flexibility, dedication and total commitment of a group of Royal Navy helicopter crews. The PMO of Ajax Bay tried not to show his feelings, but he was a very proud, as well as grateful man.

In the hour of his greatest need, the young men of his Fleet Air Arm family had not let him down.

Commander H.S. Clark DSC,
Pilot, C.O. 825 Squadron, Sea Kings, Falklands 1982

In March 1982, taking command of 706 Sea King training squadron at a small ceremony at RNAS Culdrose, I made some pompous comment to the assembled troops about 'all belonging to a Service where we could be asked to lay down our lives for our country'. I recall some funny looks from some of the Senior Rates. 'Who *is* this guy?'

Well. On 2 April Argentina invaded the Falklands; on the 5th *Hermes* and *Invincible* sailed with the Task Force. Left behind like many others, on Saturday 1 May I was digging my garden when the phone rang: 'Form a new utility helicopter Squadron!' it said. 'And by the way, you sail in a week.'

Having earmarked ten 706 Sea Kings, thirty aircrew and a hundred maintainers, including the sceptical Senior Rates, and culled military equipment from all over the UK, on Monday 3 May, my 35th birthday, I started to put together a heavy-lift transport Squadron to operate ashore with the Royal Marines and Army in the Falklands. Not for the first time a team of sailors were to become 'soldiers', living, working, eating, sleeping, and even fighting alongside the Army. The logistic support was fantastic, and on 7 May I commissioned 825 Naval Air Squadron, motto '*Nihil obstat*'.

The first wave of thirty ground crew were to sail on 8 May in RFA *Engadine*, the Squadron Command Team on 10 May in RMS *Queen Elizabeth II*, the

'*QE II* went straight to South Georgia...' Clark

remainder on the 14th in SS *Atlantic Causeway*, sister-ship of the ill-fated *Atlantic Conveyor*. On 8 May my wife and I were privileged to dance the ancient Furry Dance through the streets of Helston; on the 10th, in the Southampton Water, I inaugurated *QE II's* new flight-deck with its first deck-landing. The paint was still wet.

Atlantic Causeway made a record passage and disembarked aircraft to San Carlos fourteen days out of Southampton. *QE II* went straight to South Georgia and there, in an amazing logistic exercise using 'STUFT' [Ships Taken Up From Trade] trawlers and our two Sea Kings, the whole of 5 Brigade transhipped into *Canberra* and the ferry *Norland*. Thirty-six hours later on a cold and cheerless dawn we flew ashore and reassembled the Squadron on a field at San Carlos Settlement next to Blue Beach 2, a wet and windy place of tents, slit-trenches and constant Air Raid Warnings.

With the Antarctic winter approaching, at 51° South the Falklands had about the same ten hours of useful daylight as Birmingham at 51° North, and, the war being fought in GMT, sunrise was about 1000 on our watches. The day started

'...never failed to start...' Clark

two hours before dawn, out of bed, tooth wash, clear up bedding, square away tents, check your rifle and pistol, 'Compo' breakfast, crew brief and load up; all aircrew carried basic kit and bedding in case of 'unscheduled landing'. For safety reasons, because we had no night-flying aids, and to rest the aircrew, it was decided we should not fly at night; but from dawn to dusk everybody flew.

What did we do? Everything. Briefings in the Command Tent (my bedroom) were delightfuly vague: on HF radio the Commodore Amphibious Warfare aboard HMS *Fearless* might instruct me to send, for example, four Sea Kings to Goose Green to support 5 Brigade; three to Estancia House to support 3 Commando Brigade; one to move Rapier units at Teal Inlet, and another to be the San Carlos Anchorage ferry. After briefing we would set off with our packs to the gullies a mile or so from camp where the aircraft were dispersed against air attack. So far as I remember, none of them ever failed to start, even in the worst weather - thank you, Westlands, Rolls Royce and 825 maintainers!

Most of the work was exhilarating 'nap of the earth' flying, 15-50 feet above the ground at maximum speed following the natural contours for protection from fighters and ground fire, 'lorrying' stores, ammunition, guns, vehicles and people forward to the front line: Paras, Royal Marines, Special Forces, Chaplains, Doctors, Islanders, Prisoners of War and rice for Gurkhas. Almost every shell used in the bombardments was carried by helicopter and every gun was put in position by a Sea King. A crew would normally stay with an aircraft all day, often logging over ten hours flying, hot-refuelling with engines running at the various fuel dumps and ships, pilots taking turns to stretch their legs.

'Thank you...825 maintainers.' <small>Clark</small>

Snacks were eaten on the move, and if we were lucky there would be a hot drink on board some ship. Occasionally, near the front line, moving troops forward or supplying the guns, we came under fire and suffered a few minor bullet and shrapnel holes in the aircraft. Somebody managed to capture some Argentines; I am not sure who was the more surprised.

One bright sunny afternoon I took a survey party to Fitzroy to assess a possible Harrier operating site. We shut the aircraft down on the village green overlooking Pleasant Harbour. Two ships lay at anchor in the cove about five hundred yards apart, RFAs *Sir Galahad* and *Sir Tristram*. *Sir Tristram* appeared to have stopped unloading, but there was plenty of activity round *Sir Galahad*. I told the other two members of my crew to find some tea. It was just after lunch, a quiet peaceful scene, and we were going to be there about an hour. There was a fresh breeze and visibility was exceptional.

I made my way to 5 Brigade headquarters, a barn overlooking the harbour, to get a briefing on the tactical position, and was sitting on a crate doing just that when a sudden whistle of jets and the crump of bombs sent everyone diving to the ground. The surprise was complete. The barn and my Sea King seemed obvious targets so I ran and hid under a bulldozer while a second attack went through, after which the enemy Skyhawks disappeared at low level to the South leaving smoke pouring from *Sir Galahad*. *Sir Tristram* appeared undamaged. A couple of helicopters were approaching fast from the East.

It took us just under five minutes to get to *Sir Galahad* - the only time I ever

'...a fresh breeze, and visibility was exceptional.' Clark

used the 'Emergency Start' switch to wind up a Sea King - by which time three other Sea Kings and a Wessex were starting work. It was evident the ship was badly hit, crew and soldiers assembling on the fo'c'sle or abandoning her by boat and life-raft. Her forward end was clear of smoke and exploding ammunition, but down aft a number of men were trapped and prevented from moving forward by the intense heat. Some got away in life-rafts, others jumped and clung to flotsam and, with no time to collect life-jackets or survival suits, were soon in a bad way with burn shock and hypothermia in the cold water.

There were enough helicopters moving survivors from the small foredeck, so I decided to concentrate on the people down aft, and in the water around the stern. I don't remember how many we picked up: we just continued until the area was clear. This bit of flying looked spectacular on film, but even close into the stern I had the waterline and the ship's name for hover reference, so it was not too difficult; and although it got a bit smoky in the cockpit with the recirculating downwash, I was more worried about the danger of exploding ammunition and, indeed, of the whole ship blowing up. The alarming thumps and bangs coming from deep in the bowels of the vessel were causing a certain tightening of one's fundamental muscles. It was going to take too long to lift the survivors out of their life rafts, so to get them clear of the ship we blew the rafts away towards the shore with rotor downwash, winching out the seriously burned or injured and leaving the remainder to be towed ashore by boat.

Once the ship was clear of survivors, the rest of the day was spent moving the injured from the first aid post at Fitzroy back to the field hospital at Ajax Bay. This took about thirty minutes' flying time and was a terrible journey for the injured. The smell of burnt flesh which permeated everything will remain with me always. There is little you can do to ease suffering in the back of a helicopter.

Fortunately, that was not a typical day. As usual, however, we were home just before dark, landing in the field to unload and refuel before taking the aircraft out to the dispersed sites where the ground crews took over while we walked back to camp calling the password to successive cordons of sentries. The second hot meal of the day followed, more 'Compo' with an occasional fresh vegetable. As we came to know the manager of the local settlement we enjoyed the odd

204

bullock, sheep or Upland Goose, a stringy local bird; once we discovered the trick of walking the animals close to the galley before dispatching them, butchery was no problem.

Settling down for the night, there was usually a small medicinal whisky or can of beer to be had. Sometimes we got BBC World Service on the HF receiver, then sleep - for half an hour if you were lucky, until with whistles blowing and shouts of 'Air Raid Warning Red - Stand To!' you would be out of bed, grabbing your weapon and into the trench an hour before 'Air Raid Warning Yellow' and back to bed. And so on.

At the time of the *Sir Galahad* tragedy the principal fighting units had moved forward and 825 aircrew were fortunate to become the guests of the settlement

Author with Squadron runabout. Clark

manager and his family. For me, Pat and Isobel Short and their children were what this war was all about: any doubts I may have had about the whole affair were dispelled when I saw what liberation from invasion meant to people such as these.

After the cease-fire 825 reverted to 'Islands Taxi Service', based at San Carlos, moving anything and everything as before, only in a more ordered fashion, until mid-July when, with thick snow on the ground, it was time to go home. Soon all ten Sea Kings, plus the Squadron 'runabout', a captured Argentine UH1-H 'Huey', and the ground crew, were heading north on board our old friend *Atlantic Causeway*.

This left the aircrew standing on the field at San Carlos, trying to hitch a lift to Stanley in one of the newly arrived RAF Chinooks. Eventually one turned up and in we piled, only to find its Captain complaining firstly about bad weather on the hills, and then something called 'Crew Duty Time Limitations.' A tense situation developed and I think I recall some loosening of Navy sidearms, but eventually, after some forceful nautical briefing, like 'We're on a bloody ISLAND, chum! - try flying around the coast till you come to Port Stanley!', we got there, and so by Hercules to Ascension Island and VC10 to RAF Brize Norton and an amazing welcome.

Everybody was back in the UK before the first of August and after some leave and cleaning up the aircraft I disbanded 825 Naval Air Squadron on 17 September 1982; job done, no losses, no casualties. At the disbanding dinner my Senior Maintenance Rating and a couple of the Watch Chiefs buttonholed me in the early hours of the morning: 'You know that speech when you took over, Boss? We thought you must be a bit of a prat, all that stuff about dying for your country - but you know, you could have been right!'

I was privileged to lead a fine team of men, and when I had the honour to go to Buckingham Palace with my family, it was as their representative. My only regret was that they could not all have been there to share my award.

Lieutenant J.T. Betteridge,
Pilot, Wasp, HMS *Lowestoft*, Atlantic, 1985

On 14 March 1985 I was Flight Commander in HMS *Lowestoft*, deployed in the Atlantic with *Invincible* and other ships of the 7th Frigate Squadron for a large Anti-Submarine Warfare exercise. *Lowestoft*, the only Type 12 frigate in the group, was equipped with 'Towed-Array' – a string of listening devices about a mile long towed behind the ship to detect quiet submarines – and a Wasp helicopter.

The day dawned with ships spread across the ocean about 60 miles apart to make best use of the Towed-Array, and my first task with the only Wasp in the group was to take Captain (F) and his Staff Officer Operations from *Cleopatra* to *Phoebe*, returning in the afternoon. The morning pick-up and 40-minute transit went without a hitch and on *Phoebe*'s flight deck I shut down, refuelled and went below leaving my Wasp, XS 538, lashed down on deck. So far, so good.

Circumstances began to conspire in the middle of lunch when another visitor arrived in a Wessex whose pilot, understandably in view of the amount of ship motion, asked to use the flight deck rather than the fo'c'sle for his winch transfer.

My Wasp having no gust lock to protect its tail-rotor from his downwash, I offered to take off and stay out of the way until the Wessex had finished. It was a simple matter to get my cab flashed up and clear the deck – or would have been, had this been my own ship: *Lowestoft* had a swivel attachment to secure the Wasp to the deck while allowing it to rotate into wind for take-off. *Phoebe* was a Lynx ship with a harpoon grid – a development of the swivel idea; the Lynx fires a harpoon down into a grid on the deck and this both holds it down and acts as a swivel. I couldn't use this, but the bridge promised me a good 'red' wind (from the port side), and without my two passengers I would have a good power margin for take-off. No problem at all.

The start was uneventful and I ran through the pre-take-off checks as the ship started turning into wind. Because of the Towed-Array this was going to take some time, and while I waited news came that my passengers were ready to go and were making their way aft. Again no problem. That just put me back up to my originally planned take-off weight.

The passengers climbed aboard, shut the rear doors and strapped in – I was flying without front doors to save weight. The ground crew started removing the lashings holding us to the deck. Out of the corner of my eye I was aware that both the starboard lashings had gone and one of the port ones had been removed when an unusually large wave rolled *Phoebe* heavily to starboard; the Wasp's front wheels lost their grip on the stainless steel harpoon grid and began to slide, my artificial horizon tilted towards 25° of heel, and it very rapidly became clear that full negative pitch and all the will-power I could muster was not going to stop the slide. We were about to roll off the deck into the nets, or on to the ground crew.

This was no time for finesse. With the collective control up in my left armpit I hauled the Wasp off the reeling deck at about 25° of bank, fifteen feet out over the sea to starboard. But going downwind with no speed, despite my best efforts at 'cushion-creep transition', we were never going to fly. After about two hundred yards with the overtorque warning bells ringing incessantly in my ears, we hit the sea.

I had managed to turn a little and was not far out of wind on impact. The flotation bags inflated and the aircraft remained level. The cockpit filled ankle-deep in water. Both passengers were still strapped in with their doors closed. Instinctively hanging on to the controls, I discovered I still had plenty of power, and that paddling the rudder pedals produced heartening amounts of yaw, indicating the tail rotor was OK; this encouraged me to continue pulling power until we eventually unstuck from the top of a large wave. With water streaming out of the cockpit, flotation bags flapping in the breeze, we were back on the flight deck after an absence of less than two minutes, shaken – and quite stirred.

Neither passenger could remember how to open or jettison his door, so it was lucky we did not sink immediately, like most ditched Wasps. But notwithstanding the experience, a few years later when Captain (F) was Flag Officer Sea Training and I was a Lynx Flight Commander in *Sheffield*, he made a point of asking for me to fly him whenever possible – a brave and touching tribute!

Incidentally, I flew XS 538 three more times, ferrying from ship to ship to get a replacement, and apart from the electrics and avionics, she was mechanically sound until consigned to the Air Engineering School for 'damage-repair instruction'. Her successor XS 527 is in the Fleet Air Arm Museum at RNAS Yeovilton.

Lieutenant Commander M.R. Thompson,
Pilot, 826 Squadron. Sea King, RFA *Olna*
Lieutenant Commander J.J. White,
Pilot, Wasp Flight, HMS *Endurance*
Leading Aircrewman J.J. Doyle
Antarctic *1985*

On 5 March 1985 Royal Fleet Auxiliary tanker *Olna*, with two Sea Kings of 826 Squadron, was despatched to join HMS *Endurance* to attempt the rescue of the leader of a Joint Service Expedition to Brabant Island, a remote and desolate place on the edge of Antarctica. Lieutenant Commander Waghorn had broken a leg and was lying in considerable pain 3,500 feet up a snow-covered glacier. 800 miles from civilization, their only shelter a flimsy tent, he and his companion were being battered by blizzards in temperatures down to -30°C. Rescue attempts by aircraft from the British Antarctic Survey team, and a group of Chilean scientists, had failed in atrocious weather.

Olna rendezvoused with *Endurance* off Brabant on 7 March for the start of what turned out to be a marathon 36-hour rescue operation.

Throughout that first day and the early part of the next, despite wind and sea state that frequently put the flight deck well out of normal limits for operating aircraft, *Olna*'s Sea Kings flew more than 14 hours trying to reach the casualty, only to be frustrated again and again by low cloud, severe turbulence, gale-force winds and 'white-out' conditions. The disorientating mixture of vast featureless glaciated valleys, blinding snow, turbulence and vicious downdraughts was totally alien to naval anti-submarine aviators. The survivors were surrounded by mountains, the one escape route for helicopters constantly threatened by shifting cloud and fogbanks.

On the afternoon of the 8th a break in the weather allowed *Endurance*'s Wasp, flown by Lieutenant Commander White, to make an attempt to find the campsite, and by hugging the mountainside he was able to spot the two men through a chink in the dense low cloud. They were on a jagged rock face between two large crevasses at the head of a glacier.

Unable to lift them both out with the Wasp, White radioed for the Sea Kings

– only to be told that at that moment they were grounded in thick fog on *Olna's* flight deck; so he flew closer to the survivors' tent to assess the possibility of rescuing one at a time. Then came the message that, despite the fog, the Sea Kings would be on the scene in ten minutes, and with very little fuel remaining, cloud intermittently obscuring the campsite and a thick bank of fog advancing rapidly towards it, White remained on station until the big helicopters could take over.

Keeping low enough to see the ground, the Sea Kings crept up the glacier and came to a hover about a hundred yards from the camp. White then departed with barely enough fuel to reach *Endurance*.

Cautiously inching over the ground in clouds of mist and driven snow, the Sea Kings plucked the two men from their icy ledge minutes before it disappeared in fog and, carefully retracing their route back to the ship, landed on a violently pitching deck in fog and wind conditions beyond anything they had ever experienced, before or since.

The three named aircrew received The Prince Philip Helicopter Rescue Award from the The Guild of Air Pilots and Navigators.

Lieutenant D.E. Sealy,
Pilot, Sea King, 771 SAR Squadron, RNAS Culdrose, 1988

At an early hour on 20 August 1988 I was rudely awakened by the SAR Captain's overnight companion, the 'Bat Phone': when I picked it up, some Titled Fellow on the other end insisted I should activate 'Operation Boomerang', *instantly*!

Boomerang? Boomerang? A slow recollection crawled into my sleepy brain. A few days ago the Senior Pilot had mentioned 'Operation Boomerang'. 'If anything should crop up,' he said, 'the instructions are in my desk.'

I hit the floor running, hit the SAR klaxon, hit the front of the Senior Pilot's desk to get the jammed drawer open and entered the crewroom brandishing a large brown envelope enblazoned OPERATION BOOMERANG in very big letters.

'Isn't that something to do with Maggie?' asked somebody, and a couple of minutes later we knew that we were indeed required to pick up the Prime Mininster from her secluded holiday retreat on the north Cornish coast.

But then what? Titled Fellow had given no indication as to when, why and, most importantly, whither we were to take the Great Lady. Consulted urgently by phone, he casually instructed us to drop her at Wellington Barracks, London, as soon as possible. But Wellington Barracks was not in our 'List of Approved Landing Sites' and nobody knew where it was, exactly. Our observer thought it might be near the Mall.

My co-pilot and I flashed up the duty Sea King, a standard-fit SAR machine with only rudimentary canvas seating in the back, whilst our enterprising observer called the guardroom at Wellington Barracks and asked the duty soldier to explain how to get there; when this turned out to be less than straightforward, in desperation he suggested the man imagine himself standing in the middle of the Mall looking at Buckingham Palace and say which side of the road the Barracks was on.

The man came back. 'Actually, Sir, you can't see Buck House from the Barracks, because of all the trees.'

Thirty minutes after the Bat-phone rang we were clattering across the glorious Cornish landscape towards a grid reference near Newquay. A dozen police cars marked the spot, and we were soon on our way to London with the Prime Minister and her husband seated cosily behind what we affectionately called the broom cupboard, a compartment full of vertical control-runs. Intended only for uncomplaining survivors, these must be the least comfortable and most claustrophobic of all aircraft passenger seats, no view whatsoever, worse even than a holiday jet.

I now had time to consider our final destination which, as well as offering a superb sightseeing opportunity for my co-pilot, Lieutenant Nelson of the US Coastguard on exchange posting, was likely to prove somewhat challenging. If it all looked horribly wrong, I decided, we could always drop our passengers at Battersea Heliport. The American, amazed at the Prime Minister flying in a non-VIP aircraft, wondered if he could ask 'Maggie' for her autograph.

We were intending to follow the published helicopter route 'H10' along the Thames. However, our special IFF transponder code told every radar controller along the way that we were carrying the Prime Minister and, approaching the city, all they said was, ' Go wherever you have to, other traffic will be kept clear.' This was something different: usually a deviation of 25 yards off the London Helo Routes prompts a reprimand from Control, particularly in the vicinity of Buckingham Palace.

On arrival, I circled the Palace to get the general lie of the land, flew up the Mall low level a couple of times from Admiralty Arch, into the hover in the middle of the Mall alongside the parade ground, slid over the 100 foot trees – which did indeed block the view of the Palace – and slotted into a gap the size of a letter-box in front of the barracks. The place was full of large black cars and men in suits, and as soon as the main wheels were on the deck a car creamed up, we bade a cheerful farewell to our exalted passengers and were waved back into the air.

Now for some breakfast at RAF Lyneham, I was thinking, and then a leisurely stooge back down to Cornwall, when an urgent radio message cut in: 'Check your aircraft for left luggage,' – and there, under the troop seat behind the broom cupboard, lay the famous *handbag*!

To my intense relief we did not have to go back to the Mall in the middle of the morning rush-hour. Titled Fellow ordered the handbag to be delivered back to the police at Newquay, who would take it back to London.

On a more serious note, on returning to the Squadron we found out the reason for the Prime Minister's precipitate return to the City. Sadly, it was to do with yet another IRA bombing in Northern Ireland.

OberLeutnant zur See Udo Heeren,
Federal German Navy, Pilot, Chipmunk and Bulldog, 1989-91.

Arriving at the Naval Air Survival School at Seafield Park near Gosport in the South of England to commence my flying training with the Royal Navy in June 1989, I was quickly convinced that Britons are very different from the rest of the world. You only needed to meet 'Gordon' to know this.

He told us we would start the next day with a little morning run, so I put on my smart jogging stuff and came downstairs early, all ready to go. I was a little surprised how scruffy the rest of the course looked when they turned up, old shorts and tee-shirts and shoes you wouldn't give to charity; and my second surprise was, it's not just a morning run. Gordon has prepared some logs for us to take along, some which needed six people to carry them, and other smaller ones to be passed from hand to hand as we went along. We started running. It was not the way I used to run. There were frequent stops which gave the opportunity to exchange logs and rest the legs by doing push-ups, and when Gordon thought I was beginning to look hot he plunged into the sea and led us half-way to France. No time to take off the smart jogging kit. After this we did some push-ups in the mud, so now I knew why everybody wore scruffy clothes.

When the serious survival bit of the course started, I lost 14kg in 8 days. The course took me to my limits and then further. I learned a lot about myself. I got so hungry I couldn't wait to get my hands on one of the rabbits and slaughter it the way Gordon showed us. I still remember one of Gordon's sayings: 'Move, or I'll rip your head off and s——t in your neck-hole.' The thing was, we weren't sure if he would do it or not. The survival phase ended with a long interrogation phase, about which all I am allowed to say is my Name, Rank and Serial Number.

Next we went to Roborough near Plymouth for the three-week flying-grading course which we had to pass before going any further. I wondered on the first trip what I should do if the instructor, who looked older than my grandpa and seemed to have difficulties climbing into the cockpit, gets a heart attack? And I was not encouraged when I pulled, perhaps a little too hard in my enthusiasm, on the ring to fire the starter-cartridge of the fifty-year-old Chipmunk. It came off in my hand. But my worries were not necessary. Once in the cockpit the old man in the back became part of the machine, getting off, spinning around, pulling Gs till I hardly knew what was happening, and him behind me talking away all the time as calmly as if he was just having tea. But I got on all right, and after a few days and a lot of very bouncy landings, suddenly landings were not a problem any more, and although we weren't expected to go solo my instructor Mr. Sinclair (who I learned had been in action in the Pacific in World War Two) sent me off on my own for one circuit. It was very different without him in the back, and the other thing I missed was the bang on the back of the head whenever I forgot something. I never did get full flap down for the landing, but nobody said anything.

After grading we moved to RAF Topcliffe in Yorkshire for basic training on

Bulldogs, and here I nearly killed myself. It was a really nice day with some little fluffy clouds around. I was flying solo, and I wanted to do some aerobatics. Everybody in the crewroom had been talking about something called a Cuban Eight, or Lazy Eight, which was two loops joined together, but although I had asked, so far my instructor had not done this fantastic manoeuvre with me. Well, I thought, here I was in sole charge of one of Her Majesty's aircraft, I could do single loops so why not two joined together? This was my chance. Nobody was watching. I started climbing. When I got to the aerobatic safety height that I had calculated in accordance with the rules, I decided to add another couple of thousand feet - just in case.

I had a good look around, put the nose down at full throttle to get the speed up and pulled up into the first loop. So far OK. But when I tried rolling over to get into the second loop something went wrong and the needle on the airspeed indicator was suddenly moving towards the limiting speed so fast that it would be through the red line if I didn't do something fast. I pulled harshly on the stick trying to slow down and get level again. This made the G build up very quickly, and when my vision contracted to a grey tunnel and my head started buzzing I thought 'This is it!'. By reflex action I released the pull on the stick, vision returned, and something like normal brain function. I got level and started climbing away from the ground. I had lost 4000 feet of my height, and the G-meter needle was stuck on the edge of the red sector at 6.5G. If I had started at the normal 'safe height for aerobatics' I would probably be dead. Even so, could it be the end of my flying career? I told no one, except asking the ground-crew to look carefully at the aircraft when I signed it in, hoping it wasn't bent. Again, nobody said anything, and a few days later my instructor showed me the Cuban-Eight and I realized where I had gone wrong.

I valued my life a lot more after that experience, and on through my helicopter training in Gazelles and Lynxs I only ever flew manoeuvres I had been taught.

The main things I remember about my time with the Royal Navy are the friendly people, fair instructors, and the way things seemed to be run by common sense, instead of thousands of regulations. And those *parties*!

CHAPTER SIX
THE 1990s

Introduction

Iraqi naval power was swiftly neutralized by missile-armed Lynx helicopters operating from HMS *Cardiff* and *Gloucester* in the opening stages of the 1991 Gulf War, and Fleet Air Arm Sea Kings in heavy-lift configuration deployed ashore in support of British ground forces. After that War carrier-borne Sea Harriers maintained UN patrols over southern Iraq until, in 1999, they were rapidly switched to the NATO operation in Kosovo.

Agreeably surprised by this flexibility of sea-borne air power, the government sanctioned two 50,000-tonne carriers to be in service by 2012, post-Cold War Strategic Defence Reviews having already embraced the philosphy of Joint Operations involving the formation of a 'Joint Helicopter Command' and 'Joint Force 2000', the latter combining RN and RAF Harriers, all carrier-capable.

Carriers *Invincible*, *Illustrious* and *Ark Royal* have been joined by *Ocean*, and new amphibious ships *Albion* and *Bulwark* are building to replace *Fearless* and *Intrepid*. The powerful Merlin helicopter is entering service. And there has been a rapid and successful assimilation of women, in small numbers so far, into the fighting arm.

Thus, despite the closure of Naval Air Stations at Portland and Lee-on-Solent, leaving only Culdrose, Yeovilton and Prestwick in commission, at the end of the millennium the signs are positive for British Naval Aviation. And although very big changes are afoot, particularly the shift from single-service to joint operations, the requirement for aircraft to be embarked whenever a ship of frigate size or above leaves harbour will continue to demand the unique blend of seamanship and airmanship which the Fleet Air Arm brings to its daily task.

The Fleet Air Arm Roll of Honour contains the names of all those who lost their lives in flying operations in the 1990's. The figures are:

Pilot	**1**
Aircrewman	**1**

Lieutenant Commander Mark Salter,
C.O. 845 Squadron, Sea King Mk4, Iraq, Turkey, Bangladesh, 1991

A classic 'pier-head jump' – three weeks' notice to assume command of 845 Squadron of Sea King HC4s in October 1990 – was for me the start of the 1991 Gulf War.

While our sister Squadron, 846, headed for the Gulf in RFA *Argus*, my first job was to reduce 845 to six Sea Kings in which, while the airframes were painted desert pink and fitted with many long-awaited enhancements like GPS (Global Positioning System) navigation equipment, radar warning receivers and anti-jam radios, the aircrew started a hefty training programme covering desert flying techniques and Nuclear Biological and Chemical (NBC) equipment. In mid-December came the order to embark aircraft, vehicles and stores in the container ship MV *Atlantic Conveyor* (successor to the *Conveyor* sunk in the Falklands) for shipment to Al Jubayl in Saudi Arabia. When this was done I sent the Squadron home for Christmas.

A Kuwaiti 747 flew us out on 5 January to Al Jubayl where we set up home in an oil workers' compound, with a car park in the King Abdul Aziz Naval Base designated as the Helicopter Operating Base, thereafter known as NAS 'Flip-Flop'. *Atlantic Conveyor* arrived on the 7th and two days later twelve aircraft, mine and 848's, were flying from the car park, preparing to move into the desert. Early plans were for both Squadrons to operate in support of the British 1st Armoured Division who were with the US Marine Corps on the eastern flank.

As from nowhere, more 'enhancements' arrived: Night Vision Goggles (NVG), infra-red formation-lights, chaff and flare dispensers, armoured seats and body-armour, and the vital Mode 4 IFF (Identification Friend or Foe) to enable us to work with the Americans. Nobody objected to the heavy training programme imposed by this plethora of new equipment: the Sea King was beginning to look very impressive.

Air-raid warnings heralded the start of the air war at 0300 on the night of 16 January and continued while SCUD and Chemical/Biological attacks remained a threat. On the 20th, now part of a Helicopter Force including RAF Pumas and Chinooks, we moved 150 miles inland to a tented encampment, and in temperatures of -10°C at night and barely 5°C by day, and rain, dug in and created NAS 'Strawberry Fields'. With 848 Squadron we were to provide casualty evacuation (Casevac) for 1st Armoured and some nearby US units whose helicopter support was limited, and for this the Sea King crews were augmented by an RAF aeromedical assistant who was to prove invaluable.

A sandstorm soon grounded everything for twelve hours. A Patriot missile engaging a Scud exploded three hundred feet above Strawberry Fields in a shower of wreckage and burning rocket fuel, fortunately causing no casualties or serious damage. The tempo increased throughout February, helicopter HQ moving forward to within 30 miles of the Iraqi border.

When the ground war started on the 24th the speed of advance took everybody by surprise and very soon the distances involved in Casevac work became too much for the RAF's short-legged Pumas. In a four-hour mission in appalling weather on the night of the 25th, a Sea King captained by Australian exchange pilot Lieutenant Commander Nelson brought British and Iraqi casualties out of the battle zone, flying at fifty feet altitude all the way and rarely able to see the ground. Nelson was awarded the Air Force Cross. Casualties being generally light, Sea Kings also evacuated prisoners and their guards, a task that went on after hostilities ceased.

I flew the surrender papers into Kuwait and soon the Squadron re-located there; my abiding memory of the following days is of the total wanton destruction wrought by the Iraqis, predominantly on the oilfields: whole areas of Kuwait were inaccessible to helicopters as oily smoke turned day into night, visibility no more than twenty yards, everything covered in a thin film of crude oil. The night sky was lit up on all sides by burning wells.

As well as many long Casevac sorties – the field hospitals were in Saudi Arabia and casualties continued to arise throughout the battlefield area, one of our own Royal Marine aircrewmen being seriously injured in a road accident – and battlefield tours for the generals, our task extended to searching for minefields and ammunition dumps left all over Kuwait by the invaders.

By 31 March we were back at Al Jubayl preparing aircraft and equipment for shipment home. Half left on 4 April. The remainder, led by my Senior Pilot, returned to Kuwait to work with the British Battle Group, setting up a base near Doha which became known as NAS 'Alamo'. Meanwhile, back at Yeovilton another operation was developing to provide assistance to displaced Kurds in northern Iraq and I was recalled after two days' leave for 'Operation Haven'. Three aircraft deployed to Incerlik in northern Turkey on 21 April, but the aircrew soon returned when it became apparent that numbers there were in excess of requirements.

With the Kuwait task likewise beginning to wane, two aircraft left Alamo for Al Jubayl and home, the third being ordered on 8 May to embark in RFA *Fort Grange* in company with an 846 Sea King for cyclone relief in Bangladesh – 'Operation Manna' – which called for some very demanding flying

In the Bay of Bengal, the aircrew faced increasingly difficult flying conditions as the monsoon closed in, violent rainstorms, rising seas and sudden wind changes. 845's Sea King was flying between storm clouds when it was struck by lightning: it needed two new rotor blades and an engine had to be replaced; tail-rotor malfunction eventually made it totally unflyable. (Desert operations had taken a considerable toll, as we discovered when we got the aircraft home: all four of 845's Sea Kings unloaded at Southampton on return from Turkey on 11 June were unflyable.) The crew of another Sea King forced down in the sea near the ship escaped without injury, but attempts to recover the aircraft had to be abandoned in appalling weather. *Fort Grange* crews shared 846's aircraft to lift 400 tons of much-needed aid into the Cox's Bazar area of Bangladesh until the relief effort wound down and *Fort Grange* was released on 3 June to return to UK. The Bangladeshi Prime Minister, Mrs. Zia, sent a message of thanks to the ship praising the skill and courage of the Royal Naval aircrew.

All back under one roof at the end of June after a momentous period in its history – one war and two disaster-relief operations in six months over desert, mountain and sea and half of the northern hemisphere, saving many lives – the Squadron was rewarded with the Fleet Air Arm's most prestigious award, the Boyd Trophy.

Lieutenant Commander Mike Mason, Observer
Commanding Officer, 814 Squadron, Sea Kings, HMS *Invincible*, 1992

It would be hard to imagine a scene farther removed from the day-to-day work of an anti-submarine squadron, but 17 June 1992 provided the most rewarding day's flying I can remember. It started in Mombasa, where HMS *Invincible* and RFA *Fort Austin* arrived after five weeks at sea as part of Exercise ORIENT 92 and were asked to provide airlift helicopters for the Kenyan Wildlife Service.

The task was to put a radio transmitter on the summit of a large granite outcrop known as Ithumba Hill, deep inside Tsavo National Park, to improve communications in the war against increasingly well-equipped big-game poachers. It would take two Sea Kings. *Fort Austin*'s Mk.4C, an 845 Squadron commando version, was a natural first choice; the other would be a Mk.6 anti-submarine version from my Squadron – an excellent opportunity for the C.O. to 'lead from the front', I thought.

A ground reconnaissance team drove a 4-wheel-drive vehicle 200 miles on dirt roads through 'lion country' to Uthumba, marked out a landing site and came back with photographs and details of the local conditions and the loads, and armed with this information *Invincible*'s Mobile Air Operations Team (MAOT) set out overland next day.

On June 17 Lieutenant Commander John Middleton and I lifted off from our respective ships in Mombasa harbour at 0600, just as the sun was rising. The transit north was spectacular, sleepy suburbs soon giving way to the vast and dramatic African landscape, small settlements and wildlife stirring into activity as we roared overhead. Our own morning weariness evaporated as the trip turned into an exciting aerial safari with numerous sightings of elephant, giraffe, buffalo, antelopes and earthbound safari parties.

At 0745, after landing in a maelstrom of red African dirt at Ithumba, we tested the refuelling facility set up by the MAOT, two 3000lb portable fuel containers. If this didn't work, the helicopters would have to go home. It did, so we immediately flew a handling team up to the drop-zone and started load-lifting. It was going to be a race against the heat of the day, for the hotter it got the less we could lift.

The summit posed two problems: there wasn't enough room for a Sea King to land, and there was too much risk of engine damage from flying debris to hover and use the winch. Mission impossible? No. Commando pilots like John, 'junglies' as they are known, revel in this sort of thing: he showed us how to put the main wheels down on a small area of exposed clean granite, hang the tail out over the precipice, and, conned by the aircrewman in the back, hold the Sea King steady while freight was off-loaded and people jumped in and out. Novel flying indeed for an anti-sub chopper crew, and as it got hotter and thermal winds built up, more and more exciting: on our third transfer a fierce gust knocked us sideways and a Kenyan who was half-way in only just managed to hang on.

To keep our engines out of the red dust down at the base camp we used very long lifting strops, the ground parties struggling in the choking downwash. Snakes and scorpions abounded in both areas. Many of the African helpers had never even heard of a helicopter, let alone seen one before, and ran away every time we came to pick up a load.

Nevertheless by 1100 the job was done. The journey back was no less breathtaking than the flight up, but in contrast to the smooth dawn air we now had the violent turbulence and thunderstorms of the African noon heat. Also we took a different route, following a river, with much nervous talk of crocodiles in case we should ditch. Weary and dusty, we landed-on at 1245.

Not a typical day in the life of an 814 Squadron helicopter, but a rare and rewarding challenge to the versatility of the Sea Kings and crews. And it was a tremendous pleasure to be able to help the Kenyans in their fight against those who stalk the bush with assault rifles and slaughter the magnificent animals that we were privileged to see. It's good to feel you've made a difference.

Lieutenant Commander J.C. Snowball,
Pilot, Sea King, 845 Squadron, Bosnia 1994.

When a garbled 'help' message, received on an Army radio from a team of mine-disposal experts, reached 845 Squadron's Casualty Evacuation (Casevac) alert station at Gornji Vakuf at 1820 on the evening of 7 December 1994 the Alert Sea King scrambled and picked up an Explosive Ordnance Disposal (EOD) and medical team from Bugojno and flew them in the dark to a position near the incident in the Dreznica valley. With the EODs and medics safely on the ground, the Sea King began a search along the Land Rover's route, an area notorious for mines, to locate the casualty and to provide a communications link. Weather conditions were good, but towards midnight low cloud and shallow valley fog were expected to reduce light levels below the minimum for the crew's Night Vision Goggles (NVG).

The road the Land Rover was supposed to have followed was a narrow woodland track with a rapidly steepening gradient. The search was hampered by fading light and the nature of the ground, a steep-sided valley with mountains rising 7000ft to the north and 5000ft west and south. Nothing being found at the reported position, the Sea King searched further up the track towards the head of the valley.

Flares and torches were seen, but when these were found to be Bosnian fighters in their outposts on the Confrontation Line, and the EOD team, making slow progress up the track on foot, reported troop movements and weapons being cocked in the darkness around them, the Sea King pilot made a rapid 180-degree turn and headed back down the track. Viewing the scene from a different angle, the aircrewman spotted the vague shape of a damaged Land Rover and some people, but landing was impossible owing to the gradient of the track and the risk of detonating more mines. The EOD and medical teams then asked to be picked up and dropped nearer the accident, but approaching them the helicopter ran into fog and the pilot, unable to see the ground, pulled up into an emergency climb through 300ft of cloud into clear air on top and had to fly five miles west to find a hole in the cloud to let down to refuel. After another attempt to reach the rescue teams failed, conditions by this time being unsafe, he landed at Jablinica, where thirty minutes later the casualties were brought in by road.

A few stars could be seen through shallow valley-fog when the Sea King lifted off from Jablinica for the nearest field hospital at Bugojno, ten miles north of Gornji Vakuf. Again, the weather en route looked good, but the fog was spreading and thickening all around and on approaching Bugojno it became obvious that a landing would be impossible: hospital and town were buried in fog, which was beginning to roll down the valley towards Gornji Vakuf, whence the pilot made a speedy return, calling ahead for ambulances. Minutes after landing, the entire valley was completely fogbound.

A week later the same aircraft was tasked to pick up a party of VVIPs from Mount Igman and fly them to Split. The landing-site had been used the day before by a French Puma.

On approach, bursts of gunfire were heard and bullets struck the aircraft, one in through through the cargo door and out through the roof. The pilot rapidly cleared the area, checked out the aircraft and set course for the nearest secure landing site at Kiseljak, some fifteen minutes' flying time away; although there was a strong smell of fuel the flight was uneventful. At Kiseljac somebody said the Sea King looked like a tea-bag; the Battle Damage Repair team, airlifted in, borrowed a crane and worked through the freezing night to get it fit for 'one flight only' back to Split. Another 845 Sea King was shot at in the vicinity of Kiseljak shortly after this, but was not hit.

Lieutenant Commander Snowball sums up: 'Even after two years' experience in the theatre, you never knew, on your approach to the next hill or ridge – is this the day *Bosnia Bites Back?*

Index